S0-AEQ-609

MAKE THE RIGHT CALL

The Official Playing Rules
of the NFL

Paul Tagliabue, Commissioner

**Edited by Jerry Seeman,
NFL Director of Officiating**

Triumph Books
CHICAGO

Copyright © 1993 by the National Football League. All rights reserved.

Produced by the Creative Services Division, National Football League Properties, Inc.

This book is available in quantity at special discounts for your group or organization. For further information, contact:
Triumph Books
644 South Clark Street, Suite 2000
Chicago, Illinois 60605
(312) 939-3330
FAX (312) 663-3557

PRINTED IN THE UNITED STATES OF AMERICA

Order of the Rules

Plan of the Playing Field

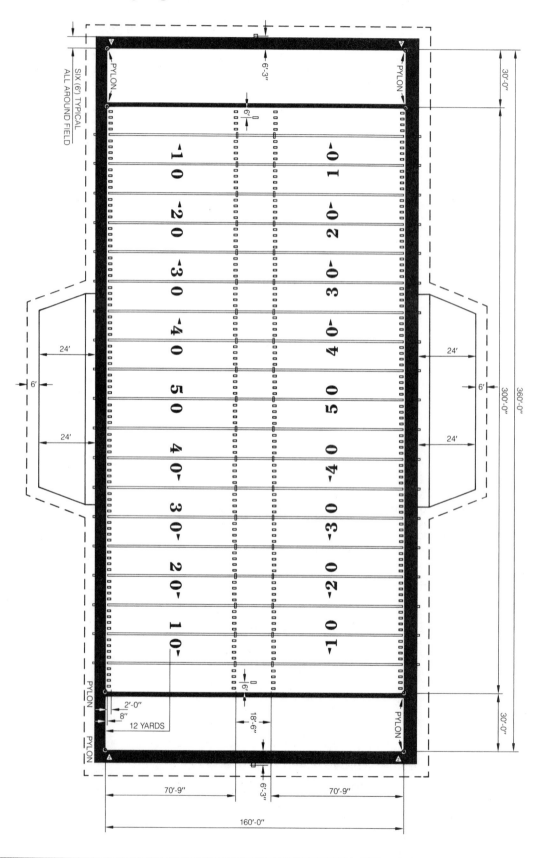

Field Markings

1. The playing field will be rimmed by a solid white border a minimum of six feet wide along the end lines and sidelines. An additional broken limit line six feet farther outside this border is to encompass the playing field in the non-bench areas, and such broken line will be continued at an angle from each 32-yard line and pass behind the bench areas (all benches a minimum 30 feet back from the sidelines). In addition, within each bench area, a yellow line six feet behind the solid white border will delineate a special area for coaches, behind which all players, except one player charting the game, must remain. If a club's solid white border is a minimum of 12 feet wide, there is no requirement that the broken restraining line also be added in the non-bench areas. However, the appropriate yellow line described above must be clearly marked within the bench areas.
2. All lines are to be 4 inches wide, with the exception of the goal line and yellow line, which are to be 8 inches wide. Tolerance of line widths is plus one-fourth inch.
3. All line work is to be laid out to dimensions shown on the plan with a tolerance of plus one-fourth inch. All lines are straight.
4. All boundary lines, goal lines, and marked yard lines are to be continuous lines.
5. The four intersections of goal lines and sidelines must be marked at inside corners of the end zone and the goal line by pylons mounted on flexible shafts. Pylons must be placed at inside edges of white lines and should not touch the surface of the actual playing field itself.
6. All lines are to be marked with a material that is not injurious to eyes or skin.
7. No benches or rigid fixtures should be nearer than 10 yards from the sidelines. If space permits, they may be further back.
8. Player benches can be situated anywhere between respective 35-yard lines. Where possible, a continuation of the dotted yellow line is to extend from the 30-yard lines to a point six feet behind the player benches thereby enclosing this area.
9. A white arrow is to be placed on the ground adjacent to the top portion of each number (with the exception of the 50) with the point formed by the two longer sides pointing toward the goal line. The two longer sides measure 36 inches each, while the crossfield side measures 18 inches. The 18-inch crossfield side is to start 15 inches below the top, and 6 inches from the goalward edge of each outer number (except the 50).
10. The location of the inbounds lines is 70'9" for professional football, 53'4" for college football. On fields used primarily by the NFL, the professional inbounds lines should be 4 inches wide by 2 feet long. Alternate college lines, if they are to be included, should be 4 inches wide by 1 foot long.
11. Care must be exercised in any end zone marking, decoration, or club identification at the 50 yard line, that said marks or decorations do not in any way cause confusion as to delineation of goal lines, sidelines, and end lines. Such markings or decorations must be approved by the Commissioner.

Inbound Yard Markers

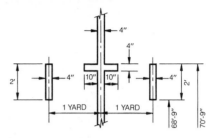

Dimensions for Numerals on the Playing Field

Dimensions for the Directional Arrows

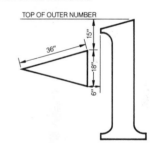

Rule 1   Field

Section 1   Dimensions

Playing Lines

The game shall be played upon a rectangular field, 360 feet in length and 160 feet in width. The lines at each end of the field are termed End Lines. Those on each side are termed Sidelines. Goal Lines shall be established in the field 10 yards from and parallel to each end line. The area bounded by goal lines and sidelines is known as the Field of Play. The areas bounded by goal lines, end lines, and sidelines are known as the End Zones.

Field of Play

The areas bounded by goal lines and lines parallel to, and 70'9" inbounds, from each sideline, are known as the Side Zones. The lines parallel to sidelines are termed Inbound Lines. The end lines and the sidelines are also termed Boundary Lines.

The playing field will be rimmed by a solid white border a minimum of six feet wide along the end lines and sidelines. An additional broken limit line six feet further outside this border is to encompass the playing field in the non-bench areas, and such broken line will be continued at an angle from each 32-yard line and pass behind the bench areas (all benches a minimum 30 feet back from the sidelines). In addition, within each bench area, a yellow line six feet behind the solid white border will delineate a special area for coaches, behind which all players, except one player charting the game, must remain. If a club's solid white border is a minimum of 12 feet wide, there is no requirement that the broken restraining line also be added in the non-bench areas. However, the appropriate yellow line described above must be clearly marked within the bench areas.

Section 2   Markings

Line Markings

At intervals of five yards, yard lines (3-41-2, p. 14) parallel to the goal lines shall be marked in the field of play. *These lines are to stop eight inches short of the six-foot solid border.* The four-inch wide yard lines are to be extended four inches beyond the white six-foot border along the sidelines. Each of these lines shall be intersected at right angles by short lines 70 feet, nine inches long (23 yards, one foot, nine inches) in from each side to indicate inbounds lines.

Inbound Lines

In line with the Inbound Lines there shall be marks at one yard intervals between each distance of five yards for the full length of the field. These lines are to begin eight inches from the six-foot solid border and are to measure two feet in length.

Bottoms of numbers indicating yard lines in multiples of 10 must be placed beginning 12 yards in from each sideline. These are to be two yards in length.

Two yards from the middle of each goal line and parallel to it, there shall be marked in the Field of Play, lines one yard in length.

All boundary lines, goal lines, and marked lines are to be continuous lines. These, and any other specified markings, must be in white and there shall be no exceptions without authorization of the Commissioner. Field numerals must also be white.

Care must be exercised in any end zone marking or decoration or club identification at the 50 yard line that said marking or decorations do not in any way cause confusion as to delineation of goal lines, sidelines, and end lines. Such markings or decorations must be approved by the Commissioner.

The four intersections of goal lines and sidelines must be marked, at inside corners, by pylons mounted on flexible shafts. In addition, two such pylons shall be placed on each end line (four in all).

SUPPLEMENTAL NOTES

Goal Line

All measurements are to be made from the inside edges of the line marking the boundary lines. Each goal line marking is to be in its end zone so that the edge of the line toward the field of play (actual goal line) is 30 feet from the inside edge of the end line. Each goal line is to be eight inches wide.

All lines are to be marked with a material that is not injurious to eyes or skin. It is desirable that the yard line markers be flexible in order to prevent injury. No benches or rigid fixtures should be nearer than five yards from sidelines.

In league parks where ground rules are necessary, because of fixed conditions that cannot be changed, they will be made by the Commissioner. Otherwise they will be made by mutual agreement of the two coaches. If they cannot agree, the Referee is the final authority after consulting his crew.

Section 3   Goal

Crossbar

In the plane of each end line there shall be a centrally placed horizontal Crossbar 18 feet 6 inches in length whose top face is 10 feet above the ground. The goal is the **vertical plane** extending indefinitely above the crossbar and between the lines indicated by the outer edges of the goal posts.

Goal
Posts

All goal posts will be the single-standard type, offset from the end line and bright gold in color. The uprights will extend 30 feet above the crossbar and will be no less than 3 inches and no more than 4 inches in diameter. A ribbon 4 inches by 42 inches is to be attached to the top of each post.

Note: Goal posts must be padded in a manner prescribed by the league.

Section 4   Players' Benches

Players'
Benches

At the option of the home team, both the players' benches may be located on the same side of the field. In such a case, the end of each bench shall start at the 45-yard line and continue towards the adjacent goal line.

Note: When both benches are so located, chain crew and linesmen are to operate during entire game on opposite side to benches. See 15-4-1, p. 101.

Section 5   Chain Crew and Ball Boys

Chain Crew
and Ball
Boys

Members of the chain crew and the ball boys must be uniformly identifiable as specified by the Commissioner. White shirts are to be worn by members of the chain crew.

Section 6   Sideline Markers

Sideline
Markers

The home club must provide and use the standard set of sideline markers that have been approved by the Commissioner.

Rule 2 Ball

Ball Dimensions

The Ball must be a "Wilson," hand selected, bearing the signature of the Commissioner of the league, Paul Tagliabue.

The ball shall be made up of an inflated (12½ to 13½ pounds) rubber bladder enclosed in a pebble grained, leather case (natural tan color) without corrugations of any kind. It shall have the form of a prolate spheroid and the size and weight shall be: long axis, 11 to 11¼ inches; long circumference, 28 to 28½ inches; short circumference, 21 to 21¼ inches; weight, 14 to 15 ounces.

The Referee shall be the sole judge as to whether all balls offered for play comply with these specifications.

Ball Supply

The home club shall have 24 balls available for testing with a pressure gauge by the Referee one hour prior to the starting time of the game to meet with league requirements.

A pump is to be furnished by the home club, and balls shall remain with and be returned to the ball attendant prior to the start of the game by the Referee.

In the event a home team ball does not conform to specifications, or its supply is exhausted, the Referee shall secure a proper ball from visitors and, failing that, use the best available ball. Any such circumstances must be reported to the Commissioner.

In case of rain or a wet, muddy, or slippery field, a playable ball shall be used at the request of the offensive team's center. The Game Clock shall not stop for such action (unless undue delay occurs).

Note: It is the responsibility of the home team to furnish playable balls at all times by attendants from either side of the playing field.

Rule 3   Definitions

Section 1   Approved Ruling (A.R.)

Approved Ruling

An Approved Ruling (A.R.) is an official decision on a given statement of facts and serves to illustrate the intent, application, or amplification of a rule. Supplemental notes are often used for the same purpose (3-32, p. 13).

Technical Terms

Technical Terms are such terms that have a fixed and exact meaning throughout the code. Due to their alphabetical arrangement in Rule Three, certain ones are used prior to being defined. In such cases they are accented only the first time they are used.

Section 2   Ball in Play, Dead Ball

Ball in Play

Article 1   The Ball is in Play (or Live Ball) when it is:

(a) legally free kicked (6-1-1 and 2, p. 30), or

(b) snapped (7-3-1, p. 39).

It continues in play until the down ends (3-7-1, p. 6; 7-4-1, p. 41).

Dead Ball

Article 2   A Dead Ball is one that is not in play. The time period during which the ball is dead is Between Downs. This includes the interval during all time outs (including intermission) and from the time the ball becomes dead until it is not in play.

Loose Ball

Article 3   A Loose Ball is a live ball that is not in player **possession,** i.e., any **kick, pass** or **fumble.** A loose ball that has not yet struck ground is In Flight. A loose ball (either during or after flight) is considered in **possession** of team **(offense)** whose **player kicked, passed,** or **fumbled.** It ends when a player secures possession or when **down ends** if that is before such possession.

Fumble

Article 4   A Fumble is any act, other than a pass or legal kick, which results in loss of player possession. The term Fumble always implies possession.

Note: If a player pretends to fumble and causes the ball to go forward, it is a forward pass and may be illegal (8-1-1-pen. a, c, p. 45).

> **A.R. 3.1**   While runner A1 is in possession, defensive player B1 grabs the ball away from him.
> **Ruling:** Fumble.

> **A.R. 3.2**   While runner A1 is in possession, defensive player B1 bats or kicks the ball away from him.
> **Ruling:** A foul during a fumble. A kick or an illegal bat is a foul (2-1-5, 6, p. 77).

Muff

Article 5   A Muff is the **touching** of the ball by a player in an unsuccessful attempt to obtain **possession** of a loose ball.

*Note: Any ball intentionally **muffed** forward is a **bat** and may be a **foul.** (3-2-5-g, p. 5; 12-1-6, p. 77; 10-1-4-S.N. 3, p. 66).*

Touching the Ball

Touching the Ball refers to any contact. Ordinarily there is no distinction between a player touching the ball with his hands or any part of his body being touched by it except as specifically provided for (9-10-Exc., p. 61, 3-14-3-Note, p. 9).

Note: The result of the touching is sometimes influenced by the intent or the location.

Touching Free Kick

(a) See 6-2-1 and 4, pp. 31-32, for touching a free kick.

Intent or Location of Touching

(b) See 6-3-1-Exc., p. 33, for touching a free kick before it goes **out of bounds** between the goal lines.

Ineligible Player Touching a Pass

(c) See 8-1-5, p. 47, for **ineligible offensive player** touching a forward pass **on, behind,** or **beyond** the line.

Pushed Into a Kick

(d) See 9-1-7, p. 60, for touching a kick on or behind the line, and also 9-1-10, p. 61, for being pushed into a kick by an opponent.

Touching Kick Attempt During Field Goal	(e) See 11-5-1-b, p. 72, for touching a kick during an attempted **field goal.**
Simultaneous Touching	(f) Simultaneous touching by two opponents of a fumble, pass, or kick is treated under their respective sections.
Bat or Punch	(g) A Bat or Punch is the intentional striking of the ball with hand, fist, elbow or forearm. See 12-1-5, p. 77.

Player
Possession

Article 6 A player inbounds other than an eligible receiver is in possession when he has held the ball firmly in his grasp long enough to have established control. In order for an eligible receiver of a forward pass to be in possession, he must control the ball throughout the act of clearly touching both feet, or any other part of his body other than his hand(s), to the ground inbounds. If the Player is hit causing the ball to come loose simultaneously while clearly touching inbounds both feet or any other part of the body except the hand(s), there is no possession. If, when the ball comes loose, there is any question whether the above acts are simultaneous, the ruling shall be no possession. This definition would apply whether on the field of play or in the end zone. The terms Catch, Intercept, Recover, Advance, and Fumble denote player possession (as distinguished from touching or muffing).

Catch

(a) A *Catch* is made when a player inbounds secures possession of a pass, kick or fumble in flight. See 3-20, p. 10, 8-1-6-S.N.5, p. 47.

Interception

(b) An *Interception* is made when a pass or fumble is caught by an opponent of the passer or fumbler.

Recover

(c) The term *Recover* indicates securing possession of a loose ball after it has touched the ground by either the offense or defense.

Note: Recover as used in an Approved Ruling (3-1, p. 4) does not imply advance unless so stated.

A.R. 3.3 Third-and-10 on B40. Runner A1 fumbles the ball at the B36 near the sideline and defensive player B1 tries to recover the ball, but he can't grab it to hold it. The ball rolls out of bounds on the B35.
Ruling: A's ball fourth-and-six on B36. (7-5-6-(a), p. 44).

A.R. 3.4 A forward pass is intercepted by defensive B1. B1 runs 10 yards, is tackled, fumbles, and passing team player A1 recovers.
Ruling: It is a legal interception, a fumble, and recovery. The ball belongs to the passing team with first down (7-1-1-b, p. 35).

Team
Possession

Article 7 A team is in possession when a player of that team is in possession of a live ball and also while the ball is loose following such player possession (3-2-6, p. 5).

Note: For brevity, terms such as kick, pass, fumble, etc., are used to denote the ball during the time it is affected by the act. Hence, reference is made to a player touching, catching, or recovering a "kick."

Section 3 Blocking

Blocking

(1) During a legal block, contact can be made with the head, shoulders, hands and/or outer surface of the forearm, or any other part of the body.

(2) Hands (open or closed) can be thrust forward to initially contact an opponent on or outside the opponent's frame, but the blocker must work to bring his hands on or inside the frame.

Note: Pass blocking: Hand(s) thrust forward that slip outside the body of the defender will be legal if blocker worked to bring them back inside. Hand(s) or arm(s) that encircle a defender — i.e., hook an opponent — are to be considered illegal and officials are to call a foul for holding. Blocker cannot use his hands or arms to push from behind, hang onto, or encircle an opponent in a manner that restricts his movement as the play develops.

(3) Hands cannot be thrust forward *above* the frame to contact an opponent on the neck, face or head.

Note: The frame is defined as the part of the opponent's body below the neck that is presented to the blocker.

(4) As the play develops, a blocker is permitted to work for and maintain position on an opponent as long as he does not push from behind or clip (outside legal clip zone). A blocker lined up more than two yards outside the tackle is subject, also, to the crackback rule *and cannot move into the clip zone and push or clip from behind.* (See 12-2-10, p. 80).

(5) By use of up and down action of the arm(s), the blocker is permitted to ward off the opponent's attempt to grasp his jersey or arms.

Section 4 Chucking

Chucking

Chucking is a means of warding off an opponent who is in front of a defender by contacting him with a quick extension of arm or arms followed by the return of arm(s) to a flexed position, thereby breaking the original contact. See 12-1-4-Exc. 1, p. 76.

Section 5 Clipping

Clipping

Clipping is throwing the body across the back of the leg of an opponent or charging or falling into the back of an opponent below the waist after approaching him from behind, provided the opponent is not a *runner* or it is not *close line play.*

Note: See Supplemental Notes under 12-2-9, p. 80, for additional interpretations or restrictions concerning clipping.

A.R. 3.5 Runner A1 advances 10 yards and is hit from behind by defensive player B1, who throws his body across the back of A1's leg.
Ruling: Legal and not a clip, because A1 was a runner. If A1 was not a runner, it would have been a clip.

Section 6 Disqualified Player

Disqualified Player

A Disqualified Player is one who is banished from further participation in the game and must return to his dressing room within a reasonable period of time for any of the following:

(a) flagrant striking, kneeling, or kicking an opponent (12-2-1, p. 77);

(b) flagrant roughing of a kicker, passer, or any other opponent (12-2-6, p. 78, and 12-2-11, p. 80);

(c) a palpably unfair act (12-3-3, p. 83);

(d) flagrant unsportsmanlike conduct by players or non-players (Rule 13, p. 85); or

(e) repeat violation of a suspended player (Rule 5-3-pen. c, p. 29A).

Note: Disqualified player is not to reappear in his team uniform nor return to any area other than to which spectators have access.

Section 7 Down

Down

Article 1 A Down (or Play) is a period of action that starts when the ball is put in play (3-2-1, p. 4) and ends when ball is next dead (7-4-1, p. 41).

Scrimmage Down

A down that starts with a snap is known as a Scrimmage Down (3-29, p. 13).

6

Free Kick Down A down that starts with a free kick is known as a Free Kick Down (6-1-1 and 2, p. 30).

Series of Downs **Article 2** A Series of Downs is the four consecutive charged scrimmage downs allotted to the offensive team during which it must advance the ball to a yard line called the necessary line in order to retain possession (7-1-1, p. 35).

Necessary Line The Necessary Line is always 10 yards in advance of the spot of the snap (which starts the series) except when a goal line is less than 10 yards from this spot. In that case the necessary line is the goal line.

Charged Down When the offensive team has been constantly in possession during a scrimmage down, the down is counted as one of a series except as provided for a foul (14-8, p. 97), and is known as a Charged Down.

First Down The initial down in each series is known as the First Down and if it is a charged down, subsequent charged downs are numbered consecutively until a new series is declared for either team (7-1-1 and 2, p. 35).

Section 8   Drop Kick

Drop Kick A Drop Kick is a kick by a kicker who drops the ball and kicks it as or immediately after it touches the ground.

Section 9   Fair Catch

Fair Catch A Fair Catch is an unhindered catch by any player of the receivers of a free kick or of a scrimmage kick except one that has not crossed the line of scrimmage (3-17-3, p. 10), provided he has legally signalled his intention of attempting such a catch (10-1-1, p. 65).

Mark of the Catch **Article 1** The Mark of the Catch is the spot from either:

(a) where the ball is actually caught by a receiver after a fair catch signal, legal or illegal (10-1-2, p. 65); or

(b) the spot of ball after a penalty for fair catch interference (10-1-4, p. 66).

Section 10   Field Goal

Field Goal A Field Goal is made by kicking the ball from the field of play through the plane of the opponents' goal by a drop kick or a placekick either:

(a) From behind the line on a play from scrimmage; or

(b) During a fair catch kick. See 11-5-3, p. 73 and 3-9, p. 7.

Section 11   Foul and Spot of Enforcement

Foul **Article 1** A Foul is any infraction of a playing rule. Spot of Enforcement (or Basic Spot) is the *spot* at which a *penalty* is *enforced*. Four such spots are commonly used. They are:

Spots of Enforcement (a) Spot of Foul — The spot where a foul was committed or is so considered by rule (14-1-1, p. 87).

(b) Previous Spot — The identical spot where the ball was last put in play.

(c) Spot of Snap, backward pass, or fumble — The spot where the foul occurred or the spot where the penalty is to be enforced.

(d) Succeeding Spot — The spot where the ball would next be put in play if no distance penalty were to be enforced.

Enforcement After Touchdown **Exception:** If a foul occurs after a touchdown and before the whistle for a try, the succeeding spot is the spot of the next kickoff.

Notes: A penalty is never enforced from the spot of a legal kick from scrimmage (9-1-17, p. 63).

An enforcement includes a declination (14-6, p. 96). See 14-1-5, p. 87, for definition of basic spot and 3 and 1 rule.

Article 2   Types of Fouls

Continuing
Action Foul

(a) A Continuing Action Foul (or a subsequent foul) is spiking the ball, or a *personal* foul (12-2, p. 77) that occurs during the continuing (subsequent) action immediately after a down ends (14-5, p. 95). See 14-1-7 to 10, pp. 88-89.

Note: A continuing action foul may occur with the game clock either running or stopped, and is always enforced from the succeeding spot.

Multiple Foul

(b) A Multiple Foul is two or more fouls by the same team during the same down, unless they are part of a double foul (14-4, p. 94).

Double Foul

(c) A Double Foul is a foul by each team during the same down and includes any multiple foul by either team (14-3, p. 92).

Foul
Between
Downs

(d) A Foul Between Downs is one that occurs after a down has definitely ended and before the next snap or free kick (3-1-2, p. 4).

A.R. 3.6   A's ball second-and-5 on A25. Runner A1 runs out of bounds on the A45, after which offensive A2 clips on the A30.
Ruling: A's ball first-and-25 on A30. A continuing action foul. See 14-1-7, p. 88. It happened after the down ended and was a personal foul. See A.R. 14.55, p. 95.

A.R. 3.7   Defensive B1 holds an offensive player on the line of scrimmage. Defensive B2 was offside.
Ruling: A multiple foul because it was two fouls by the same team during the same down. See 14-4, p. 94.

A.R. 3.8   The offensive team is offside. The defensive team interferes with an eligible receiver downfield. The pass falls incomplete.
Ruling: A double foul because each team committed a foul during the same down. See 14-3, p. 92.

A.R. 3.9   The offensive team clips after Runner A1 scored.
Ruling: A foul between downs because the down ended when the score was made. Penalize on subsequent kickoff. See 14-1-7, p. 88 and 14-5, p. 95.

Section 12   Free Kick

Free Kick

Article 1   A Free Kick is one that puts the ball in play to start a free kick down (3-2-1, p. 4, 6-1-1, p. 30): It includes:

(a) kickoff;

(b) safety kick; 6-1-2-a, p. 30

(c) fair catch kick (6-1-3-3, p. 30), (3-9, p. 7).

Free Kick
Lines

Article 2   The Free Kick Line for the offensive team is a yard line through the most forward point from which the ball is to be kicked (6-1-4, p. 30).

The Free Kick Line for the defensive team is a yard line 10 yards in advance of the offensive team's free kick line (6-1-4, p. 30).

Section 13   Huddle

Huddle

A Huddle is the action of two or more players of the offensive team who, instead of assuming their normal position for the snap, form a group for getting the signal for the next play or for any other reason (7-2-5, p. 38).

Section 14   In Touch and Impetus

In Touch

Article 1   A Ball is In Touch when:

(a) after it has come from the field of play, it touches a goal line (plane) while in player possession; or

(b) while it is loose, it touches anything on or behind a goal line.

Note: If a player while standing on or behind his goal line touches a ball that has come from the field of play and the official is in doubt as to whether the ball actually touched the goal line (plane), he shall rule that the ball was in touch.

Ball Dead in Touch

Article 2 A Ball Dead in Touch is one dead on or behind a goal line and it is either a *touchdown,* a *safety,* a *touchback,* a *field goal,* or the termination of a *try* (11, p. 69), or a loss of down at previous spot (8-1-5, p. 47).

Note: Sometimes a safety, touchdown, or try-for-point (unsuccessful) is awarded because of a foul. In such cases they are penalties. Also note exceptions 8-4-2-Exc. 3, and 8-4-2-S.N., p. 55.

Impetus

Article 3 Impetus is the action of a player that gives momentum to the ball and sends it in touch.

The Impetus is attributed to the offense except when the ball is sent in touch through a new momentum when the *defense* muffs or *bats:*

(a) a kick or fumble;

(b) a backward pass after it has struck ground; or

(c) when the defense illegally kicks any ball (12-2-17, p. 83).

Note: If a player is pushed or blocked into any kick or fumble or into a backward pass after it has struck ground, and if such pushing or blocking is the primary factor that sends such a loose ball in touch, the impetus is by the pusher or blocker, and the pushed (blocked) player will not be considered to have touched the ball. See 9-1-10, p. 61.

Section 15 Kicker

Kicker

A Kicker is the player of the offensive team who legally punts, placekicks, or dropkicks the ball. The offensive team is known as the Kickers during a kick.

A Receiver is any defensive player during a kick. The defensive team is known as the Receivers during a kick.

Section 16 Kickoff

Kickoff

A Kickoff is a free kick used to put the ball in play:

(a) At start of the first and third periods;

(b) After each Try-for-Point; and

(c) After a successful field goal (6-1-1-c, p. 30).

Note: Onside kick (see 6-3-1, Note, p. 33).

Onside Kick

If a kicker obviously attempts to kick a ball short and it goes less than 20 yards, it is defined as an onside kick (this also applies to a safety kick).

Section 17 Line of Scrimmage

Scrimmage Line

Article 1 The Line of Scrimmage for each team is a yard line (plane) passing through the end of the ball nearest a team's own goal line. The term *scrimmage line,* or *line,* implies a play from scrimmage.

Player on Line

Article 2 A Player of Team A is On His Line when:

(a) He has both hands on the ground, or both feet or a hand and the opposite foot on or not more than one foot behind his line, or his head if he takes a position with neither hand touching the ground; or he has a hand on or not more than one foot behind his line, if such hand is touching the ground, while

(b) His shoulders face Team B's goal line and he stands, crouches, or kneels with both feet at a distance not more than one foot behind his line. Interlocking legs are permissible.

A.R. 3.10 Offensive A1 assumes a three-point stance with his shoulders facing defensive B's goal line. One hand is on the ground and it is on or not more than one foot behind his line. Neither of his feet or the other hand is within one foot of his line.
Ruling: A1 is legally on his line.

Ball Crosses Line

Article 3   The ball has crossed the scrimmage line *(crosses line)* when, during a play from scrimmage, it has been passed or legally kicked by a Team A player, through the plane of their line and has then touched the ground or any one *behind* Team B's line.

Note: At the snap the scrimmage lines are definitely fixed. After the snap the lines are no longer definite and the Official may construe the line of scrimmage as an indefinite area in the immediate vicinity of the two lines.

Section 18   Neutral Zone, Start of Neutral Zone, and Encroaching

Neutral Zone

The Neutral Zone is the space the length of the ball between the offense's and the defense's scrimmage lines (planes). It **starts** when the ball is ready for play.

Encroaching

A player is Encroaching (7-2-2, p. 36) on the neutral zone when any part of his body is in it and contact occurs prior to the snap. The official must blow his whistle immediately.

Exception: The **snapper** is not considered in the neutral zone if no part of his body is beyond Team B's line at the snap (7-2-2, p. 36).

Note: The Field Judge is responsible for the 40/25-second count with the start of the neutral zone (4-3-9, p. 21, and 4-3-10, p. 22).

Section 19   Offside

Offside

A player is Offside when any part of his body or his person is beyond his scrimmage or free kick line when the ball is put in play.

Exceptions: The *snapper* may be beyond his line provided he is not beyond the defensive line *(3-18-Exc., p. 10)*.

The *holder* of a *placekick* for a free kick may be beyond it *(6-1-5-b, p. 31)*.

The *kicker* may be beyond the line but his kicking foot may not be *(6-1-5-b, p. 31)*.

Section 20   Out of Bounds and Inbounds Spot

Player or Official Out of Bounds

Article 1   A player or an Official is Out of Bounds when he touches:

(a) A boundary line; or

(b) Anything other than a player on or outside a boundary line.

Ball Out of Bounds

Article 2   The Ball is Out of Bounds when:

(a) the runner is out of bounds;

(b) while in player possession it touches a boundary line or anything other than a player on or outside such line; or

(c) a loose ball touches a boundary line or anything on or outside such line.

Inbounds Spot

Article 3   The Inbounds Spot is a spot 70' 9" in from the sideline on the yard line passing through the spot where the ball or a runner is out of bounds between the goal lines.

Under certain conditions, the ball is dead in a side zone or has been placed there as the result of a penalty. See 7-3-7, p. 41 and 7-5-1 to 6, pp. 43-44.

Note: Ordinarily the out of bounds spot is the spot where the ball crossed a sideline. However, if a ball, while still within a boundary line, is declared out of bounds because of touching anything that is out of bounds, the out of bounds spot is on the yard line through the spot of the ball at the instant of such touching.

A.R. 3.11   Runner A1, with his feet inbounds, touches an official who is touching a sideline.
Ruling: Out of bounds.

A.R. 3.12   Runner A1, with his feet inbounds, touches any player who is touching a sideline.
Ruling: Inbounds.

A.R. 3.13   Runner A1 fumbles and the loose ball touches a defensive player B1 who is standing on sideline, and then ball rebounds into the field of play where B1 falls on it.
Ruling: Dead ball and out of bounds as soon as the loose ball touches the player on sideline. Offensive team's ball at inbounds spot.

A.R. 3.14   Runner A1 touches the shaft of the defensive team's goal line marker with any part of his body.
Ruling: Dead in touch. Position of ball determines. If, at instant of touching, any part of the ball is on or behind defensive goal line, it is a touchdown (11-2, p. 69). If, at the instant of touching, any part of the ball is one foot from the goal line, it is Runner A1's ball on the defensive one-foot line.

Section 21   Pass and Passer

Pass and Passer

Article 1   A Pass is the movement of the ball due to handing, throwing, shoving (shovel pass), or pushing (push pass) by a runner (3-27-1, p. 12). Such a movement is a pass, even though the ball does not leave his hand or hands, provided a teammate takes it (hand to hand pass).

Note: The term is also used to designate the action of a player who causes a pass as in, "He will pass the ball."

Forward Pass

Article 2   A Forward Pass (8-1-1, p. 45) is a pass that:

(a) moves forward (to a point nearer the opponent's goal line) after leaving the passer's hands and before touching another player; or

(b) is handed (regardless of the direction of movement of the ball) to a player who is in advance of a teammate from whose hands he takes or receives it.

Exception: When the ball is handed forward to an eligible pass receiver (8-1-2, p. 46) who is behind his line, it is not a forward pass. If the receiver muffs, it is treated as a fumble.

Note: A fumble or muff going forward is disregarded as to its direction, unless the act is ruled intentional. In such cases, the fumble is a forward pass (8-1-1, p. 45) and the muff is a bat (12-1-6, p. 77).

A.R. 3.15   A pass legally handed forward to an eligible pass receiver is followed by a forward pass in flight from behind the line.
Ruling: A legal pass because the first handoff is not considered a forward pass (see Exception above).

A.R. 3.16   A pass is legally handed forward to an eligible pass receiver, who muffs the ball and it is recovered by the defensive team.
Ruling: Not an incomplete pass. It is treated as a fumble and the defensive team keeps the ball.

Passer, Passing Team

Article 3   A player who makes a legal forward pass is known as the Passer until the pass ends. The teammates of any player who passes forward (legally or illegally) are known collectively as the Passing Team or Passers.

Backward Pass

Article 4   A Backward Pass (8-4-1, p. 54) is any pass that is not a forward pass.

SUPPLEMENTAL NOTES

Forward, Beyond, In Advance

(1) Forward, Beyond, or In Advance Of are terms that designate a point nearer the goal line of the defense unless the defense is specifically named. Converse terms are Backward or Behind.

(2) A pass parallel to a yard line or an offensive player moving parallel to it at the *snap* is considered backward.

(3) If a pass is batted, muffed, punched, or kicked in any direction, it does not change its original designation. However, such an act may change the impetus (3-14-3, p. 9) if sent in touch or may be a foul (12-1-1-6, 7, p. 77).

A.R. 3.17 The ball, moving backwards in the hands of an offensive player A1, is possessed by offensive player A2 who is in advance of A1.
Ruling: A forward pass unless A2 is behind his line and is eligible to receive a forward pass.

A.R. 3.18 The ball moving forward in the hands of offensive player A1, is possessed by A2 who is behind A1.
Ruling: A backward pass.

Section 22   Piling On

Piling On

Piling On is causing the body to fall upon any prostrate player (other than the runner), or upon a runner after the ball is dead (12-2-7, p. 79).

Section 23   Placekick

Placekick

A Placekick is a kick made by a kicker while the ball is in a fixed position on the ground except as provided for a permissible manufactured tee at kickoff (6-1-5, p. 31). The ball may be held in position by a teammate. See 11-5-4, p. 73.

Section 24   Pocket Area

Pocket Area

The Pocket Area applies from a point two yards outside of either offensive tackle and includes the tight end *if* he stays on or drops off the line of scrimmage to pass protect. Pocket extends longitudinally behind the line back to the offensive team's own end line.

Section 25   Post-Possession

Post-Possession Foul

A foul by the receiving team that occurs after a ball is legally kicked from scrimmage prior to possession changing. The ball must cross the line of scrimmage and the receiving team must retain the kicked ball. See 9-1-17-Exc. 2, p. 63.

Section 26   Punt

Punt

A Punt is a kick made by a kicker who drops ball and kicks it while it is in flight (9-1-1, p. 59).

Section 27   Runner and Running Play

Runner

Article 1 The Runner is the offensive player who is in possession of a live ball (3-2-1, p. 4), i.e., holding the ball or carrying it in any direction.

Running Play

Article 2 A Running Play is a play during which there is a runner and which is not followed by a kick or forward pass from behind the scrimmage line. There may be more than one such play during the same down (14-1-12, p. 90).

SUPPLEMENTAL NOTES

(1) The exception to a running play is significant only when a foul occurs while there is a runner prior to a kick or pass from behind the line (8-3-2, p. 53, 9-1-17, p. 63, and 14-1-12, p. 90).

(2) The statement, a player may advance, means that he may become a runner, make a legal kick (9-1-1, p. 59), make a backward pass (8-4-1, p. 54) or during a play from scrimmage, an offensive player may forward pass (8-1-1, p. 45) from behind his scrimmage line, provided it is the first such pass during the down and the ball had not previously been beyond the line of scrimmage.

A.R. 3.19 Receiving team player player B1 catches a kickoff, advances, and fumbles. Kicking team player A2 recovers and advances.
Ruling: While runners B1 and A2 were in possession, there were two running plays during the same down.

Section 28   Safety

Safety

A Safety is the situation in which the ball is dead on or behind a team's own goal line provided:

(a) the impetus (3-14-3, p. 9) came from a player of that team;

(b) it is not a touchdown (11-2, p. 69); or

(c) it is not a pass violation by Team A behind its own goal line (8-1-1-Pen. A, p. 45).

Section 29   Scrimmage, Play From Scrimmage

Scrimmage Down

A Scrimmage Down is one that starts with a snap (3-31, p. 13). From Scrimmage refers to any action from the start of the snap until the down ends or if Team A loses possession and Team B secures possession. Any subsequent action during the down, after a change of team possession, is **Not From Scrimmage.**

Scrimmage Line

Notes: The term scrimmage line *or* line *implies a play by A from scrimmage. Line is used extensively for brevity and is not to be confused with side, end, or yard line. Line is also used for free kick line. For given reasons, action during a free kick down (6-1, p. 30), is sometimes referred to as a play* Not From Scrimmage.

Section 30   Shift

Shift

A Shift is the action of two or more offensive players who (prior to a snap), after having assumed a set position, simultaneously change the position of their feet by pivoting to or assuming a new set position with either one foot or both feet (7-2-5, p. 38).

Section 31   Snap and the Snapper

Snap and the Snapper

A Snap is a backward pass that puts the ball in play to start a scrimmage down. The Snapper is the offensive player who attempts a snap. See 7-3-3, p. 39, for conditions pertaining to a legal snap.

Section 32   Supplemental Notes (S.N.)

Supplemental Notes

Supplemental Notes (S.N.) are descriptive paragraphs used to amplify a given rule, which would otherwise be too cumbersome or involved in its scope or wording.

An Approved Ruling (A.R.) is often used for the same purpose (3-1, p. 4). Additional Approved Rulings are also found in *The Official Casebook of the National Football League.*

A Note or Notes are usually more specific and apply to a particular situation. They are also used to indicate pertinent references to other rules.

Section 33   Suspended Player

Suspended Player

A Suspended Player is one who must be withdrawn, for at least one down, for correction of illegal equipment (5-3, p. 27).

Section 34   Tackling

Tackling

Tackling is the use of hands or arms by a defensive player in his attempt to hold a runner or throw him to the ground (12-1-4, p. 75).

Section 35   Team A and B, Offense and Defense

Offense and Defense

Article 1   Whenever a team is in possession (3-2-7, p. 5), it is the Offense and, at such time, its opponent is the Defense.

Team A and Team B

Article 2   The team that puts the ball in play is Team A, and its opponent is Team B. For brevity, a player of Team A is referred to as A1 and his teammates as A2, A3, etc. Opponents are B1, B2, etc.

Note: A team becomes Team A when it has been designated to put ball in play and it remains Team A until a down ends, even though there might be one or more changes of possession during the down. This is in contrast with the terms Offense *and* Defense. *Team A is always the offense when a down starts, but becomes the defense if and when B secures possession during the down, and vice versa for each change of possession.*

Section 36   Time Out or Time In

Time Out

Article 1   A Time Out is an interval during which the Game Clock is stopped (4-3-1, p. 16) and includes the intermissions (4-1-1 to 6, p. 15).

Note: The term Time Out *(general) is not to be confused with a charged team time out, which is specific. (4-3-3, p. 17).*

Time In

Article 2   Time In is the converse (4-3-2, p. 17) and is also used to indicate when the clock operator is to start his clock.

Section 37   Touchback

Touchback

A Touchback is the situation in which a ball is dead on or behind a team's own goal line, provided the impetus came from an opponent and provided it is not a touchdown (11-6, p. 74).

Note: See 8-1-1 to 5, pp. 45-47 for exceptions to touchback, when impetus by an opponent is an incomplete pass.

Section 38   Touchdown

Touchdown

A Touchdown is the situation in which any part of the ball, legally in possession of a player inbounds, is on, above, or behind the opponent's goal line (plane), provided it is not a touchback (11-2, p. 69).

Section 39   Tripping

Tripping

Tripping is the use of the leg or foot in obstructing any opponent (including a runner) below the knee (12-1-3, p. 75).

Section 40   Try-for-Point, or Try

Try-For-Point
or Try

A Try-For-Point, or Try, is an opportunity given a team that has just scored a touchdown to score an additional point during one scrimmage down (11-3, p. 69).

Section 41   Yard Line, Own Goal

Own Goal

Article 1   A team's Own Goal during any given periods is the one it is guarding. The adjacent goal line is known as its (own) goal line.

Yard Line

Article 2   A Yard Line is any line and its vertical plane parallel to the end line. The Yard Lines (marked or unmarked) in the field of play are named by number in yards from a team's goal line to the center of the field.

Note: The yard line 19 yards from team A's goal line is called A's 19-yard line. The yard line 51 yards from A's goal line is called B's 49-yard line. (For brevity, these are referred to as A's 19 and B's 49.)

Rule 4   Game Timing

Section 1   Length of the Game

Length of Game and Intermissions

Article 1   The length of the game is 60 minutes, divided into four periods of 15 minutes each, with intervals of 2 minutes between the first and second periods (first half) and between the third and fourth periods (second half). During these intermissions all playing rules continue in force and no representative of either team shall enter the field unless he is an incoming substitute. See 13-1-5, p. 85.

Penalty: For illegally entering field: Loss of 15 yards from succeeding spot (13-1-6, pen., p. 85).

Timing the Intermissions

Article 2   The Field Judge is to time the two-minute intermissions and shall sound his whistle (or signal visibly) at 1 minute and 50 seconds. The Referee shall sound his whistle immediately thereafter for:

(a) play to start; and

(b) Clock operator to start the timing of 25 seconds. See 4-3-10-S.N. 1, p. 22.

Official Time

Article 3   The stadium electric clock shall be the official time. The clock operator shall start and stop the clock upon the signal of any official in accordance with the rules. The Line Judge (15-5-2, p. 102) shall be responsible for supervision of the timing and in case the stadium clock becomes inoperative, or for any reason it is not being operated correctly, he shall take over the official timing on the field.

Halftime

Article 4   Between the second and third periods, there shall be an intermission of 12 minutes. During intermission, play is suspended and the teams may leave the field. This is to be timed by the Line Judge. See 15-5-4, p. 102.

Note: See 13-1-1 to 4, p. 85, for fouls by non-players between halves.

Kickoff on Schedule

Article 5   Both teams must be on the field in ample time to kick off at the scheduled time for start of each half. Ample time prior to the start of the game is construed to be at least 15 minutes prior to the initial kickoff in order to insure sufficient time for proper warmup. Head coaches must be personally notified before the start of each half by designated members of the officiating crew.

Penalties: For delaying start of half:

(a) Loss of 15 yards from the spot of the kickoff as determined by Rule 4, Section 2, page 15.

Loss of Coin Toss Option

(b) Loss of coin toss option for both halves and 15 yards if a team is not on the field in ample time prior to the scheduled kickoff as indicated.

Sudden Death   **Article 6**   Provisions for the sudden death method of determining the winner in case of certain tie scores at the end of game will be found under Rule 16, p. 105.

Section 2   Starting Each Period

Toss of Coin

Article 1   Not more than three minutes before the kickoff, the Referee, in the presence of both team's captains (limit of six per team, all of whom must be uniformed members of the active list, shall toss a coin at the center of the field. The toss shall be called by the captain of the visiting team or by the captain designated by the Referee if there is no home team. The winner of the toss must choose one of two privileges and the loser is given the other. The two privileges are:

(a) which team is to receive; or

(b) the goal his team will defend.

Penalty: For failure to comply: Loss of coin toss option, both halves, and loss of 15 yards from spot of kickoff.

Second Half Choice

For the second half, the captain who lost the pregame toss is to have the first choice of the two privileges listed in (a) or (b) unless one of the teams lost its first and second half option under 4-1-5, p. 15. Immediately prior to the start of the second half, the captains of both teams must inform the Referee of their respective choices.

SUPPLEMENTAL NOTE

(1) When the teams first appear on field for the start of second half, the Referee is to assume a position on one side at the numbers and indicates which team will receive.

Change of Goals

Article 2   At the end of the first and third periods, the teams must change goals. Team possession, number of succeeding down, relative position of the ball on the field of play and of the necessary line remain unchanged.

Section 3   Timing

Time Out, Stop Clock

Article 1   The clock operator shall stop the game clock (time out) when upon his own positive knowledge or signal or upon a signal by any official:

(a) ball is out of bounds;

(b) a receiver catches after a fair catch signal (10-1-2, p. 65);

(c) ball is dead in touch;

(d) at end of down during which a foul occurs;

Status of Game Clock After Penalty Enforcement

Note: If the clock was stopped to assess and mark off a penalty, it will be started when the ball is declared ready for play unless the clock had been stopped otherwise by rule. In that case, clock starts on snap.

Exceptions:

(1) After a foul by either team in the last two minutes of the first half, the clock will start on the snap.

(2) After a foul by either team in the last five minutes of the second half, the clock will start on the snap;

(e) whenever a forward pass is incomplete;

(f) at the time of a foul, for which the ball remains dead or is dead immediately;

(g) upon his signal of two minutes remaining for a half;

(h) a period expires;

(i) any official signals a time out for any other reason;

(j) a kicked ball is illegally recovered and/or surrounded; or

(k) the completion of a down involving a change of possession.

A.R. 4.1   Second-and-10 on A30. Runner A1 goes to the A40 where he is tackled. During A1's run, A2 clipped B1 at the A35.
Ruling: A's ball second-and-20 on A20. Game Clock starts on ready to play signal after penalty is enforced.

A.R. 4.2   Second-and-10 on A30. Runner A1 goes to the A40 and steps out-of-bounds there. During A1's run, A2 clipped B1 at the A35.
Ruling: A's ball second-and-20 on A20. Game Clock starts with referee's ready signal as ball was dead when runner ran out-of-bounds.

Change of Possession

Notes: Change of possession includes:

(1) recovery of loose ball by team not putting ball in play;
(2) forward pass interception;
(3) free kick or kick from scrimmage recovered and/or advanced by the receiving team or that goes out of bounds; and
(4) legal touching, muff, or fumble by receiving team of any kicked ball that is recovered by the kicking team.

Time In, Start Clock	**Article 2** The clock operator shall start his clock (time in) when the ball is kicked off to start the game. Thereafter, following any time out (3-36, p. 14), the clock shall be started when the ball is next snapped or free-kicked.

Exceptions:

Timing for Last Two Minutes	1) After a field goal, safety, or touchdown, the clock is started at kickoff following a Try except as provided for the last two minutes of a half (6-3-1-Exception, p. 33).
	2) After the two-minute warning of a half, the clock is not started until a kickoff or safety kick is legally touched in the field of play (6-3-1, p. 33 and 11-5-3, p. 73).
Time In After Out of Bounds	3) Except in the last two minutes of the first half and the last five minutes of the game, on a play from scrimmage whenever a player goes out of bounds, the Game Clock is started when an official spots the ball at the inbounds mark and the Referee gives the ready signal.
Time In On Referee's Whistle	4) After the fourth team time out during a half (4-3-4, p. 18) by either team for any reason, after a Referee's time out (4-3-7, p. 19); or after an illegal substitution penalty (5-1-5, p. 25 and 5-2-1, p. 26), the clock is started with Referee's whistle (clock signal if the clock was running). See 4-3-10, p. 22, for Exception to Referee's time out.

> **A.R. 4.3** During the last two minutes of the game the offensive team safety kicks from the A20. **Ruling:** Time in starts when the safety kick is legally touched by any player in the field of play (6-3-1-Note, p. 33).
>
> No extension of the automatic time outs in Article 1 shall be allowed unless any player requests a team time out, or a Referee orders a team time out or suspends play himself.

Consecutive Time Outs	*Note 1: In case of consecutive time outs between downs, time is in according to the classification of the last time out (4-3-1-Exception 1, p. 16).*
	Note 2: Consecutive team time outs between downs by either team are allowed so long as it is not by the same team. Such a time out may follow an automatic time out (4-3-1, p. 16) or Referee's time out (4-3-7, p. 19) and maximum length of the second time out will be 40 seconds. No additional consecutive team time outs can be taken during the same dead ball period.

> **A.R. 4.4** Following a Referee's time out after a change of possession after a punt:
>
> a) Team B takes its third team time out.
> **Ruling:** Time in with snap.
>
> b) Team B takes its fourth team time out prior to last two minutes.
> **Ruling:** Team B is penalized 5 yards and time is in with snap.

Charged Time Outs	**Article 3** The Referee shall declare a charged team time out when he suspends play while the ball is dead:
	(a) After or upon a request for a time out by any player;
	(b) Should a player appear injured on the field, official will call time out for an injured player. Time out shall not be charged to team unless:
Time Out for Injury Not Charged	(1) players on field or from bench attempt to assist injured player from the field unless directed to by team physician or trainer in consultation with official;
	(2) injury occurs after two-minute warning of either half;

Exception: Time out is not charged if a foul committed by opponent caused the injury.

(3) injured player remains in the game.

Note: Members of both teams may go to the sideline for conference with coaches during an injury time out, but must be ready to play when Referee signals ball in play as soon as treatment is completed or injured player has left the field.

Exceptions: Following a time out as in (a) or (b), the Referee may order a charged time out for injury or for repair of legal equipment, but only in an obvious emergency (4-3-4 and 5, p. 18), and especially so during the last two minutes of a half (4-3-10, p. 22).

A.R. 4.5   Runner A1 is tackled and appears injured since he doesn't move.
Ruling: Official should call time out for injured player. Official should not try to determine if player is injured. Time out is not charged if conditions of 4-3-3-b, p. 17, are not violated.

Three Time Outs Allowed

Article 4   Three charged team time outs are allowed a team during each half without a distance penalty (4-3-5, p. 18). When any team time out occurs, the Field Judge shall start his watch and sound his whistle (or signal visibly) at the expiration of 1 minute and 50 seconds. The Referee shall not sound his whistle for play to start before such a signal from the Field Judge.

Exception 1: Whenever a team time out is called after the two-minute warning in a half, the time out shall last 40 seconds unless more time is required because of an injury or television utilizes a commercial opportunity.

Exception 2: The Referee may allow:

Injury and Equipment Time Out

(a) two minutes for an injured player or

(b) three minutes for repair of legal equipment if it is obviously needed.

Note: If such a player is not ready to play at the expiration of this time out, he must be withdrawn.

SUPPLEMENTAL NOTES

(1) In the case of extended team time outs ordered by the Referee for exceptions (a) and/or (b), the Field Judge shall not sound his whistle until the expiration of extra time is allowed.

(2) The Referee shall sound his whistle for play to start immediately upon Field Judge's signal for the expiration of any team time out.

(3) On all requested time outs, the Referee shall not signify that the ball will be put in play prior to 1 minute and 50 seconds of elapsed time, or 40 seconds during the last two minutes of a half.

Excess Time Outs Prior to Last Two Minutes

Article 5   Team time outs prior to the last two minutes of a half, in excess of three, for either team, is a foul unless the time out is for an injured player who is removed from the game (except injury time out caused by a foul, 4-3-3-Exc., p. 17).

Referee Whistle After Excess

After the fourth time out during a half by either team, time is in with the Referee's whistle for play to start (clock signal if time had been in). After the first three, all team time outs, regardless of the reason, are to be counted in determining the fourth or subsequent time outs. See 4-3-10, p. 22.

Excess Time Outs During Last Two Minutes

Article 6   Team time outs after two-minute warning of half.

(a) During the last two minutes of either half, additional time outs by either team after the third legal one are not allowed unless it is for an injured player who must be immediately designated and removed. A fourth time out under these conditions is not penalized. Subsequent requests (fifth or more) under these same conditions are allowed, but are penalized five yards. On all excess time outs against the defense, the play clock is reset to 40 seconds.

Excess Time Outs During Last Two Minutes, 10-Second Hold

(b) During the last two minutes of either half while time is in, if the score is tied or the team in possession is behind in the score and the offensive team has exhausted its legal time outs, an additional time out may be requested and granted under (a) above. However, the ball shall not be put in play until the time on the game clock has been reduced by 10 seconds. (The Referee, in a position between the center and the quarterback, will advise [by using the microphone] the game clock operator to take 10 seconds off the clock. During this time interval, the Umpire will be directly over the ball. After 10 seconds have been taken off the clock, both officials will back away with the Umpire raising his arm above his head. After a momentary delay, the Umpire will quickly lower his arm and give the wind-the-clock signal. This signal indicates to the game clock operator to restart the game clock and also to the offensive team that it may legally snap the ball). NOTE: There can never be a 10-second run off against the defensive team.

Penalty: For each excess time out: Loss of five yards from succeeding spot for delay. Necessary line and number of down remain the same.

SUPPLEMENTAL NOTES

(1) Either half can end during the 10-second period between time in and permissible play resumption, as well as during enforcement or declination of penalty for offensive team fouls.

(2) This applies to Sudden Death Rule (Rule 16, p. 105) in force for Wild Card Play-offs, Divisional Playoffs, Conference Championship Games, the Super Bowl, and the Pro Bowl.

Feigning Injuries

(3) The Rules Committee deprecates feigning injuries, with subsequent withdrawal, to obtain a time out without penalty and even so when done to conserve time. Coaches are urged to cooperate in discouraging this practice. The Referee should refuse such a request when it is an obvious evasion of the rules.

(4) The Referee must notify both captain and head coach when their team has been charged with three time outs, and no penalty is to be enforced for an excess time out unless such notice has been given. The Referee shall not delegate this notification to any other person.

A.R. 4.6 Offensive team A, with the score tied (or team A behind) in the last two minutes of the half and the clock running:

(a) Requests its fourth time out due to an injured player.
Ruling: Granted. No five yard penalty. Player has to be removed. Referee's ready signal starts the clock, but the ball is not put into play for at least 10 seconds.

(b) Requests its fifth time out due to an injured player.
Ruling: Granted. Five yard penalty. Player has to be removed. Referee's whistle starts the clock and the ball shall not be put into play for at least 10 seconds.

Referee's Time Out

Article 7 Play may be suspended by Referee (Referee's Time Out) at any time without penalty to either team when playing time is being destroyed because of delay not intentionally caused by either team, provided it does not violate some specific rule.

SUPPLEMENTAL NOTES

Automatic Referee's Time Out

The following situations are automatic Referee's time outs:

(1) Where there is a change of possession. The clock will start on the snap.

(2) Any possibility of a measurement for first down or in consulting a captain about one.

(3) Any time the player who originally takes the snap is tackled behind the line of scrimmage.

Exception:

Timing Last Two Minutes

During the last two minutes of a half, the Game Clock shall be restarted as soon as the ball has been spotted for the succeeding down, at which time the Referee is to give the ready signal. In all cases, a minimum of five seconds must have elapsed before the ball is made ready for play.

Note: Prior to the last two minutes of a half, the Referee will allow receivers to approach the line of scrimmage before giving the "wind the Game Clock" signal.

(4) Undue pileups on the runner or ball, or determining possession after a fumble during time in.

(5) Undue delay by officials in spotting ball for the next snap.

(6) Illegal recovery of any kicked ball from scrimmage.

(7) The snap made before the Referee can assume his position (not a repeated act). See 4-3-9-h, p. 22.

(8) Injury to an official or member of the chain crew.

(9) Captain's choice of a free kick or snap after a fair catch. See 11-5-3, p. 73.

(10) Officials' conference for a rules interpretation or an enforcement (15-1-6, p. 99). Clock starts as original status dictates.

(11) Repairing or replacing game equipment (not player equipment).

(12) Line Judge's signal of two minute warning for a half; the Game Clock starts on the snap.

Procedures for Crowd Noise

(13) Obvious inability of the offense to hear team signals due to crowd noise. When such situations prevail, the following procedures must be followed:

(a) If the quarterback (or other signal-caller) of the offensive team indicates to the Referee that his teammates cannot hear his signals, and the Referee deems it reasonable to conclude the players on the offense (other than wide receivers) cannot hear, the Referee will extend his right arm fully over his head to indicate disruptive crowd noise. The Referee then will signal a Referee's time out and ask the defensive captain to use best effort to quiet the crowd. The Referee then will announce over his wireless microphone that he has asked the defensive team to assist in quieting the crowd so that the game can continue. He then will return to his position behind the offensive team.

(b) If, after the public announcement described in (a) above, crowd noise conditions in that same ball possession are deemed by the Referee, with or without appeal by the offensive signal-caller, to be disruptive to the offense, he again will use the upraised-arm signal and will announce over his wireless microphone that any further crowd noise which is disruptive will result in forfeiture by the defense of one of its remaining time outs in the half or, in the absence of time outs, a five-yard penalty against the defense for delay of the game.

(c) If, after the public announcement described in (b) above, crowd noise conditions in that same ball possession are deemed by the Referee, with or without appeal by the offensive signal-caller, to be disruptive to the offense, he again will use the upraised-arm signal and will, if such signal does not quiet the crowd, assess the appropriate penalty provided for in (b) above.

(d) Thereafter if disruptive crowd noise recurs in the same ball possession, the Referee, with or without appeal from the offensive signal-caller, will use the upraised-arm signal while remaining in his normal position behind the offensive formation and without calling a Referee's time out. Following a momentary pause to confirm that disruptive noise conditions are continuing, he will assess the appropriate penalty provided for in (b) above.

(e) If, upon any appeal from the offensive signal-caller, the Referee deems that noise conditions are not sufficiently disruptive to apply the crowd-noise procedures, he will deny the appeal and proceed with normal game timing. The Referee's signal that he is denying the appeal will be to point toward the defensive team's goal line.

(f) During the time out described in (a) above, the offensive team may huddle. When the offensive team again attempts to run a play, the game clock will start on the snap. The 40/25-second clock will not be used.

(g) If, in any ball possession subsequent to the first possession of the game that involves disruptive crowd noise, the Referee, either with or without an appeal by the offensive signal-caller, deems it to be reasonable to conclude that the players on offense (other than wide receivers) cannot hear, the Referee will signal a Referee's time out and announce over his wireless microphone that the defensive team is now subject to appropriate crowd noise penalties. Any crowd-noise interruption thereafter in that same ball possession will result in the Referee using his upraised-arm signal, followed, if necessary, by a penalty against the defense.

(h) Once the procedures of (a) and (b) above have been followed in a given game, disruptive crowd-noise incidents in any subsequent ball possession will be handled by the procedures of (g). In effect, for each ball possession during which disruptive crowd noise occurs (with the exception of the first in the game), the Referee will make one public announcement after which he may assess a penalty, and he will thereafter always precede any such penalty by the upraised-arm signal but not by a public announcement. As specified in (a) and (b) above, he will make two public announcements before assessing a penalty on the first ball possession of the game during which disruptive crowd noise occurs.

(i) In any instance where the Referee is signaling with upraised arm, the offensive signal-caller may, if he chooses, continue to play. Such signal indicates that disruptive crowd-noise conditions prevail; it does not automatically stop play nor does it automatically result in a penalty. Conversely, if the Referee's arm is not upraised, the penalty situation does not prevail and the offense must attempt to continue play.

(14) On a play from scrimmage, if a fumble goes out of bounds forward by any player, the clock stops on the official's time out signal, then restarts on the wind of the clock signal. (See 7-5-6-Note, p. 44)

(15) On a play not from scrimmage, if a fumble goes out of bounds forward by any player, the clock stops on the official's time out signal and will restart at the snap.

Time In After Referee's Whistle

Article 8 After a Referee's time out, time in starts with his whistle (clock signal).

Exception: After a time out for a change of possession, notification of two minutes remaining for a half, stopping the clock for inability to hear signals, and after enforcement (when appropriate) time is in with the snap. See 11-5-3, p. 73 and 15-1-10, p. 100.

A.R. 4.7 Quarterback A1 drops back to pass and is tackled behind his line.
Ruling: Referee's time out. Stop the clock until the ball can be respotted at succeeding spot. (40 second clock starts when time out signal is given).

A.R. 4.8 Receiver B1 gives a fair catch signal and catches ball.
Ruling: Referee's time out. Stop clock. When ready for play, start clock with snap or fair catch kick.

A.R. 4.9 At the instant a runner is contacted by a defensive player, ball is inbounds. He then:

a) Slides across side line.
Ruling: Not a time out.

b) Loses possession after he touches ground and ball crosses sideline.
Ruling: Not a time out unless it is evident that undue time will be consumed in spotting ball (Referee's time out).

Delay of Game

Article 9 The ball must be put in play promptly and any action or inaction by either team that tends to prevent this is a delay of game. It is delay of game if the ball is not put into play within 40/25 seconds:

(a) by snap after the neutral zone starts (3-18, p. 10);

(b) after a Referee's time out.

Other examples of action or inaction that are to be construed as delay of game or attempts to consume or conserve playing time are:

(c) Repeatedly charging into the neutral zone prior to the snap when not otherwise ruled encroaching (7-2-2, p. 36).

(d) With time in, start of neutral zone is unduly delayed by failure of players of either team to assemble promptly.

Hurry Up
Offense
And Snap

Note: During last two minutes of half, once the ball has been respotted for the succeeding down and the Head Linesman has placed his bean bag on the ground at the new line of scrimmage, the Umpire, upon signal from the Referee, is to step away from the ball. At this point a snap may be made. If ball is snapped before all members of defensive team have taken their proper position on line of scrimmage, play is to be stopped immediately and that team penalized five yards for offside.

(e) When a player remains on a dead ball or on a runner who has been downed.

(f) Failure to play immediately when ordered.

(g) Player exercising rights of captain except in emergency.

(h) Repeatedly snapping ball after the neutral zone is established before the Referee can assume his position (7-3-3-c-2, p. 39).

(i) A runner repeatedly attempts to advance after he is so held that his forward progress is stopped.

(j) When one of the kickers recovers a kick (unless one recovered behind line other than a Try-kick), and carries it in any direction. See 9-1-4 Note, p. 59; 9-1-6, p. 60.

(k) Undue advance by a receiver who catches after a fair catch signal (valid or invalid) unless after touching kickers in fight. See 10-1-2-Exception, p. 65.

(l) Opponent taking ball from runner after it is dead, causes a loose ball or scramble that consumes playing time to re-spot the ball (7-4-1-d, p. 41).

(m) Undue delay in assembling after a time out.

(n) Substitute entering during play unless interference (12-2-15, p. 82).

Penalty: For delay of game: Loss of five yards:

(a) from succeeding spot if between downs and ball remains dead; or

(b) from previous spot if ball was in play. Number of down and necessary line remain the same.

Note: After an enforcement for delay of game by the defense, prior to or at the snap, number of down and necessary line remain the same. See 14-8-5, p. 97.

Action to
Conserve,
Consume
Time

Article 10   There shall be no unusual action or inaction during the last two minutes of a half to conserve or consume time.

Penalty: For attempts to conserve or consume time: Loss of five yards for delay. When efforts are made by the offensive team to conserve time, officials will run 10 seconds off the game clock before permitting the ball to be put in play on the ready signal. If the action is by the defense, the play clock will be reset to 40 seconds and the game clock will start on the ready signal. NOTE: There can never be a 10-second run off against the defensive team.

SUPPLEMENTAL NOTES

Play Clock
40/25-Second
Count

(1) The Play Clock operator shall time the 40/25-second intervals between plays upon signal from game official(s). The 40-second interval is to start when one play ends, unless certain administrative stoppages or other delays occur such as change of possession, team time out, referee's time out, injury, measurement, or any unusual delay that interferes with the normal flow of play. In these cases, a 25-second interval is to be used (even if the 40-second clock was already counting down). The 40/25-second clock is to start when:

a) neutral zone starts with Referee's whistle (3-18, p. 10);

b) referee's whistle indicates that play may start following any time out.

If the ball is not put in play within this time, he sounds his whistle for the foul and the ball remains dead. When the foul is prior to a snap, defensive team may decline distance penalty, in which case down is replayed. See 14-6 Exception (4), p. 96.

(2) More than two successive penalties, during the same down, after a warning is unsportsmanlike conduct (12-2-13-h, i; p. 83).

(3) When the ball is dead during time in, the Referee must immediately determine if a measurement is indicated, unless there has been a change of possession. If indicated, he declares a Referee's time out. Otherwise, he immediately signals start of neutral zone before approximating distance to be gained. The distance and the number of down are to be announced as he assumes his normal stance.

(4) Certain acts of delay may involve stopping the clock immediately. Repeated violations of substitution rule to conserve time are unsportsmanlike conduct (12-2-13-g, h; p. 83 and 4-3-9, p. 21).

Backward Pass Out of Bounds

(5) During a play from scrimmage a backward pass going out of bounds during the last two minutes of a half stops the clock. Time is in with the Referee's whistle (clock signal) when the ball is ready for play.

Note: Time for a half can expire before a ball can be put in play following Referee's whistle for play to start.

A.R. 4.10   With a short time remaining near end of a period during time in, either team delays establishment of neutral zone by failure to assemble promptly in an obvious attempt to consume time.
Ruling: Referee orders time out and penalizes for delay.

A.R. 4.11   Time is running out and only a few seconds remain when offensive guard A1 deliberately contacts defensive player or commits a false start in order to stop the clock.
Ruling: If Referee believes contact was deliberate and in an effort to conserve time, he will order clock to be run for 10 seconds after assessing a five-yard penalty.

Extension of Period

Article 11   If at the end of any period, time expires while the ball is in play, time is not called until down ends. During such a down:

Defensive Foul at End of Period

(a) If there is a foul (not one of a double foul) by defense, the offended team may choose to extend period by one down (enforcement as usual). If the first or third period is not so extended, any penalty (unless declined) is enforced before the start of the succeeding period.

Offensive Foul at End of Period

(b) If there is a foul by offense, there shall be no extension of the period. If the foul occurs on the last play of the half, no score made by offense is counted.

Exception: If offensive foul is (1) illegal touching of a kick, (2) fair catch interference, (3) palpably unfair act, or (4) foul followed by a change of team possession, the period may be extended by an untimed down, if defense so chooses.

A.R. 4.12   Fourth-and-10 on B40. On the last play of the first quarter offensive team misses an attempted field goal. Defensive team was offside. There is a strong wind at their back.
Ruling: Offensive team has option of extending period by an untimed down. It can put ball in play from the B35 and kick the same way. If the period is not extended, it would be fourth and five on B35 at start of second period.

A.R. 4.13   Third-and-10 on A45. Offensive team is offside. Quarterback A1 throws a legal pass which is complete to End A2 who runs for a score. Time for second half expired during play.
Ruling: No score and game over as it was an offensive foul on last play of half.

A.R. 4.14   Fourth-and-10 on A20. A punt is illegally touched by kicking team player A1 on the A45 who falls on the ball as time runs out in second half.
Ruling: One scrimmage down allowed, if desired, by receivers from the A45. Untimed down as it was an illegal touch.

A.R. 4.15   Defensive B1 intercepts at midfield on the last play of either half. On runback, B2 clips at the A40. A1 piles on after runner B1 is tackled on the A30.
Ruling: Extend the period with an untimed down from A40. B's ball. See 14-3-2, p. 93.

A.R. 4.16 The offensive team punts as time for the half expires. Defensive player B1 gives a valid fair catch signal and catches the ball on the A35.
Ruling: The receiving team may extend the period by a fair catch kick (6-1-2-b, p. 30). If the ball is illegally kicked out of bounds, the half is over.

Double Foul at End of Period

(c) If a double foul (14-3, p. 92) occurs on the last play of the first or third periods, the period is not extended. If a double foul occurs during the last play of either half, enforcement shall be as ordinarily (extend period by one down) if appropriate.

Touchdown on Last Play

(d) If a touchdown is made, the try-for-point shall be allowed (except during a sudden death period).

Fair Catch on Last Play

(e) If a fair catch is signaled or made, team may choose to extend the period by one free kick down (6-1-2-b, p. 30). If the first or third period is not so extended, the choice of a snap or free kick (10-1-6, p. 67) to start the succeeding down is not vitiated.

(f) If no fair catch signal is given and the kickers interfere with the receiver's opportunity to catch a scrimmage kick, the receiving team may extend the period by one down from scrimmage.

Extension of First or Third Periods

(g) If the first or third period is extended for any reason, or if a touchdown occurs during the last play of such a period, any additional play, including a Try, shall be completed before change of goal. If a period is extended for any reason, it shall continue until a down free from any foul specified in (a) to (f) is completed.

Safety on Last Play

(h) If a safety occurs during the last play of a half, the score counts. No safety kick is made unless it resulted from a foul, and even so unless receivers request that kick be made.

Defensive Fouls During Last 40/25 Seconds of Half

Article 12 In the last 40/25 seconds of either half, with the Game Clock running, and the defensive team behind with no time outs remaining, a defensive foul cannot prevent the termination of a half except for the normal options available to the offensive team.

Rule 5 Players, Substitutes, Equipment

Section 1 Number of Players

Number
of Players

Article 1 The game is to be played by two teams of 11 players each. If a snap or free kick is made while a team has:

(a) fewer than 11 players on field, ball is in play and there is no penalty;

(b) more than 11 players on field, ball is in play and there is a five-yard penalty (5-2-1, p. 25); or

(c) a player who fails to inform the Referee of a change of his eligibility when required by rule, no official is to notify team of this fact before play starts and there is a penalty (7-2-3, p. 37).

Team Captains **Article 2** Each team must designate its captain(s), and that player(s) is the sole representative of his team in all communications with Officials. See Rule 18, p. 109.

First Choice **Article 3** A captain's first choice from any alternative privileges which may be offered his team, before or during the game, is final and not subject to change.

Players
Numbered
by Position

Article 4 All players must wear numerals on their jerseys in accordance with Rule 5, Section 3, Article 3(c), and such numerals must be by playing position as follows: quarterbacks, punters, and placekickers, 1-19; running backs and defensive backs, 20-49; centers, 50-59 (60-79 if 50-59 unavailable); offensive guards and tackles, 60-79; wide receivers and tight ends, 80-89; defensive linemen, 60-79 (90-99 if 60-79 unavailable); and linebackers, 50-59 (90-99 if 50-59 unavailable).

If a player changes his position during his playing career in the NFL and such change moves him out of a category specified above, he must be issued an appropriate new jersey numeral.

Any request to wear a numeral for a special position not specified above (e.g., H-back) must be made to the Commissioner.

During the preseason period when playing rosters are larger, the League will allow duplication and other temporary deviations from the numbering scheme specified above, but the rule must be adhered to for all players during the regular season and postseason. Clubs must make numerals available to adhere to the rule, even if it requires putting back into circulation a numeral that has been retired or withheld for other reasons.

Players
Withdrawn
and
Substituted

Article 5 A player must be withdrawn and substituted for when:

(a) he is disqualified or suspended;

(b) his treatment for injury exceeds two minutes; or

(c) an attempt to repair legal equipment exceeds three minutes.

Unless disqualified or suspended, he may re-enter at any time (including between periods) except as specified for suspension (5-3, p. 27) and disqualification (12-2-6 and 13, pps. 78-81).

Penalties:

(a) For illegal return: Loss of five yards from succeeding spot after discovery.

(b) For return of a disqualified player: Loss of 15 yards and exclusion from playing field enclosure.

SUPPLEMENTAL NOTES

Coaches
Responsible
for Legal Subs

(1) Coaches are to assume full responsibility for the legality of substitutions, but this does not preclude a penalty if discovered before or after a substitute reports.

Enforcement
Spot for
Illegal Sub

(2) If it is not discovered until the end of a down but prior to the start of next one that a player had illegally returned, enforcement is from the previous spot when definitely known. Otherwise, enforcement is from succeeding spot as a foul between downs (14-5, p. 95).

Section 2 Substitutes

Legal Substitution

Article 1 Substitutes may not enter the field while the ball is in play. Any entering offensive substitute who participates in a play must enter while the ball is dead and must move onto the field as far as the inside of the field numerals; in addition, the player or players replaced must have cleared the field on their own side (between end lines) prior to the snap or free kick.

Quick Snap Following Substitution

Note: While in the process of substitution or simulated substitution, the offense is prohibited from rushing quickly to the line and snapping the ball with the obvious attempt to cause a defensive foul; i.e., too many men on the field. If in the judgment of the officials this takes place, the following procedure will be applied:

(1) If the play takes place and a defensive foul results, the flag will be picked up and the down replayed. At this time, the referee will notify the head coach that any further use of this tactic will result in an unsportsmanlike penalty being assessed.

Note: Covering official(s) will extend both arms horizontally to indicate that substitutions have been made.

(2) On a fourth down punting situation, the Referee and the Umpire will not allow a quick snap which would prevent the defense from having a reasonable time to complete their substitutions.

The above quick-snap rule will not be applicable in the last two minutes of either half.

Penalty: For illegal substitution: Loss of five yards (for delay) from previous spot and number of down and necessary line remain the same for:

(a) entry during play;

(b) withdrawn player on field at snap or free-kick; or

(c) clearing field on opponents' side or across end line (whether or not violation is discovered during down, or at end of down, 3-8-11, p. 7).

Interference with play during (a) to (c) is a palpably unfair act (12-3-3, p. 83).

SUPPLEMENTAL NOTES

(1) See 5-1-5, p. 25, for illegal return or withdrawal.

(2) If a substitute enters during dead ball with time in or after Referee's whistle following a time out, no Official is to signal his entry and Field Judge continues his timing of 40/25 seconds, if and when it has been started (4-3-10-S.N. 1, p. 22).

Exception: On an illegal return ball remains dead if discovered prior to snap.

(3) Under no circumstances is Referee to delay start of neutral zone because of an incoming substitute.

Substitute Becomes Player

(4) A substitute is not to report to an Official. He becomes a player when:

a) he informs a teammate that he is replacing him;

b) he participates in at least one play after communicating with a teammate;

c) a teammate voluntarily withdraws upon his entering; or

d) in the absence of any of the above a, b, or c he is on the field at snap or free kick.

(5) A player is legally in the game when he has participated in at least one play.

(6) A player is legally substituted for when he leaves the game for at least one play.

(7) If a player enters field of play, communicates with teammate(s) and then leaves without participating in one play, it shall be ruled Unsportsmanlike Conduct (12-3-1-f, p. 82) and so penalized, unless one of his teammates leaves the field of play. If this occurs, any teammate may replace him provided all other prescribed game rules are adhered to. Use of players who have not qualified either as legal players or substitutes for ulterior purposes defeats the purpose of the game.

(8) Referee shall sound his whistle for play to start immediately upon completion of a penalty for an illegal substitution, return, or withdrawal. Game clock will start as appropriate. See 4-3-10, p. 22.

Conserving
and
Consuming
Time

Article 2 After the two-minute warning of either half, a violation of the substitution rule occurs while ball is dead with time in by the team in possession.

(a) If the act is designed to conserve time, Referee stops play, penalizes, and will run off 10 seconds prior to allowing ball to be put in play. Clock starts when Umpire lowers his arm and gives wind-the-clock signal. See 4-3-10, p. 22.

(b) Repeated violations of substitution rule to conserve time are unsportsmanlike conduct (12-3-1-h, p. 83).

(c) If the act is designed to consume time, the clock is stopped immediately and is next started with the snap.

Section 3 Equipment, Uniforms, Player Appearance

General
Policy

Article 1 Throughout the game-day period while in view of the stadium and television audience, including during pregame warm-ups, all players must dress in a professional manner under the uniform standards specified in this Section 3. They must wear suitable padding and other equipment offering reasonable protection to themselves while reasonably avoiding risk of injury to other players. And they generally must present an appearance that is appropriate to representing their individual clubs and the National Football League. The term uniform, as used in this section, applies to every piece of equipment worn by a player, including helmet, shoulder pads, thigh pads, knee pads, and any other item of protective gear, and to every visible item of apparel, including but not limited to pants, jerseys, wristbands, gloves, stockings, shoes, visible undergarments, and accessories such as head coverings worn under helmets and hand towels. All visible items worn on game-day by players must be issued by the club or the League, or, if from outside sources, must have approval in advance by the League.

Team
Colors

Article 2 Pursuant to the official colors established for each NFL club in the League Constitution and Bylaws, playing squads are permitted to wear only those colors or a combination of those colors for helmets, jerseys, pants, and stockings; provided that white is also an available color for jerseys and mandatory color for the lower portion of stockings [see 5-3-3-(i), "Stockings," below]. Each player on a given team must wear the same colors on his uniform as all other players on his team in the same game. Before July 1 each year, home clubs are required to report to the League office their choice of jersey color (either white or official team color) for their home games of that forthcoming season (including postseason, in the event that the club should become a host for such a game), and visiting clubs must wear the opposite. For preseason or postseason games, the two competing teams may wear jerseys in their official colors (non-white), provided the Commissioner determines that such colors are of sufficient contrast.

Mandatory
Equipment,
Apparel

Article 3 All players must wear the equipment and uniform apparel listed below, which must be of a suitably protective nature, must be designed and produced by a professional manufacturer, and must not be cut, reduced in size, or otherwise altered unless for medical reasons approved in advance by the Commissioner; provided, however, that during pregame warm-ups players may omit certain protective equipment at their option, except that helmets must be worn. Where additional rules are applicable to specific categories of mandatory equipment or apparel, or where related equipment is optional, such provisions are also spelled out below.

Helmets, Face
Protectors

(a) Helmet with chin-strap fastened and face mask attached. Face masks must not be more than ⅝-inch in diameter and must be made of rounded material; transparent materials are prohibited. Plastic face shields, either clear or lightly tinted, for eye protection are optional, provided the League office is supplied in advance with appropriate medical documentation that the shield is needed. No visible identification of a manufacturer's name or logo on the exterior of a helmet or on any attachment to a helmet is permitted unless provided for under a commercial arrangement between the League and manufacturer; in no event is identification of any helmet manufacturer permitted on the visible surface of a rear cervical pad. All helmets must carry a small NFL shield logo on the rear lower-left exterior, which logo will be provided in quantity by the League.

Jerseys

(b) Jersey that covers all pads and other protective equipment worn on the torso and upper arms, and that is appropriately tailored to remain tucked into the uniform pants throughout the game. Tearaway jerseys are prohibited. Mesh jerseys with large fish-net material (commonly referred to as "bullet-hole" or "port-hole" mesh) are also prohibited. Surnames of players in letters a minimum of two and ½-inches high must be affixed to the exterior of jerseys across the upper back above the numerals; nicknames are prohibited; and in cases of duplicate surnames, the first initial of the given name must be used. All jerseys must carry a small NFL shield logo at the middle of the yoke of the neck on the front of the garment, which logo will be provided in quantity by the League.

Numerals

(c) Numerals on the back and front of jerseys in accordance with Rule 5, Section 1, Article 4. Such numerals must be a minimum of eight inches high and four inches wide, and their color must be in sharp contrast with the color of the jersey. Smaller numerals should be worn on the tops of the shoulders or upper arms of the jersey. Small numerals on the back of the helmet or on the uniform pants are optional.

Pants

(d) Pants that are worn over the entire knee area; pants shortened or rolled up to meet the stockings above the knee are prohibited. No part of the pants may be cut away unless an appropriate gusset or other device is used to replace the removed material. All pants must carry a small NFL shield logo on the front left groin area of the pants, midway between the fly opening and side seam, and ½-inch below the belt. The logo will be provided in quantity by the League.

Shoulder Pads

(e) Shoulder pads that are completely covered by the uniform jersey.

Hip Pads

(f) Hip pads that are covered by the outer uniform; provided, however, that punters and placekickers may omit such pads.

Thigh Pads

(g) Thigh pads; provided, however, that punters and placekickers may omit such pads.

Knee Pads

(h) Knee pads; provided, however, that punters and placekickers may omit such pads. Basketball-type knee pads are permitted but must be covered by the outer uniform.

Stockings

(i) Stockings that cover the entire area from the shoe to the bottom of the pants, and that meet the pants below the knee. Players are permitted to wear as many layers of stockings and tape on the lower leg as they prefer, provided the exterior is a one-piece stocking that includes solid white from the top of the shoe to no higher than the mid-point of the lower leg, and approved team color or colors (non-white) from that point to the top of the stocking. Uniform stockings may not be altered (e.g., over-stretched, or cut at the toes or stirrups) in order to bring the line between solid white and team colors higher than the mid-point of the lower leg. No other stockings and/or opaque tape may be worn over the one-piece, two-color uniform stocking. Barefoot punters and placekickers may omit the stocking of the kicking foot in preparation for and during kicking plays.

Shoes

(j) Shoes that are of a standard football design. Kicking shoes must not be modified, and any shoe that is worn by a player with an artificial limb on his kicking leg must have a kicking surface which conforms to that of a normal kicking shoe. Punters and placekickers may omit the shoe from the kicking foot in preparation for and during kicking plays. All players on the same team must wear the same color shoe (either all white or all black, with all-white or all-black laces, whichever are applicable), and the selection of such shoe color must be reported by clubs to the League office by July 1 each year. Punters and placekickers are permitted, only on plays in which they line up to kick, to deviate temporarily from this rule, e.g., by wearing one black and one white shoe, or two black shoes while the rest of the team wears white.

Other Prohibited Equipment, Apparel

Article 4 In addition to the several prohibited items of equipment and apparel specified in Article 3 above, the following are also prohibited:

Projecting Objects

(a) Metal or other hard objects that project from a player's person or uniform, including from his shoes.

Uncovered Hard Objects, Substances

(b) Hard objects and substances, including but not limited to casts, guards or braces for hand, wrist, forearm, elbow, hip, thigh, knee, shin, unless such items are appropriately covered on all edges and surfaces by a minimum of ⅜-inch foam rubber or similar soft material. Any such item worn to protect an injury must be reported by the applicable coaching staff to the Umpire in advance of the game, and a description of the injury must be provided. If the Umpire determines that an item in question, including tape or bandages on hands or forearms, may present undue risk to other players, he may prevent its use at any time before or during a game until the item is removed or appropriately corrected.

Detachable Toe

(c) Detachable kicking toe.

Torn Items

(d) Torn or improperly fitting equipment creating a risk of injury to other players, e.g., the hard surfaces of shoulder pads exposed by a damaged jersey.

Improper Cleats

(e) Shoe cleats made of aluminum or other material that may chip, fracture, or develop a cutting edge. Conical cleats with concave sides or points which measure less than ⅜-inch in diameter at the tips, or cleats with oblong ends which measure less than ¼- by ¾-inch at the end tips are also prohibited. Nylon cleats with flat steel tips are permitted.

Improper Tape

(f) Opaque, contrasting-color tape that covers any part of the helmet, jersey, pants, stockings, or shoes; transparent tape or tape of the same color as the background material is permissible for use on these items of apparel. Players may use opaque white tape on hands and arms, provided it conforms to 5-3-4(b) above ("Uncovered Hard Objects, Substances") and 5-3-4(h) below ("Improper Glove Color on Linemen"). Opaque tape on shoes is permitted, provided it is the same color as the shoe, and provided it does not carry up into the stocking area.

Items Colored Like Football

(g) Headgear or any other equipment or apparel which, in the opinion of the Referee, may confuse an opponent due to its similarity in color to that of the game football. If such color is worn, it must be broken by stripes or other patterns of sharply contrasting color or colors.

Approved Glove Color On Linemen

(h) Gloves, wrappings, elbow pads, and other items worn on the arms below or over the jersey sleeves by interior offensive linemen (excluding tight ends) which are of a color different from that which is mandatorily reported to the League office by the club before July 1 each year. Such reported color must be white or other official color of the applicable team, and, once reported, must not be changed throughout that same season.

Adhesive, Slippery Substances

(i) Adhesive or slippery substances on the body, equipment, or uniform of any player; provided, however, that players may wear gloves with a tackified surface if such tacky substance does not adhere to the football or otherwise cause handling problems for players.

Optional Equipment

Article 5 Among the types of optional equipment that are permitted to be worn by players are the following:

Rib Protectors

(a) Rib protectors ("flak jackets") under the jersey.

Wrist Bands

(b) Wrist bands, provided they are white or in official team colors.

Towels

(c) Towels, provided they are plain white with no logos, names, symbols, or illustrations. Such towels also must be attached to or tucked into the front waist of the pants, and must be no longer than 6 × 8 inches (slightly larger size may be folded to these limits for wearing in games). A player may wear no more than one towel. Players are prohibited from discarding on the playing field any loose towels or other materials used for wiping hands and the football. Streamers or ribbons, regardless of length, hanging from any part of the uniform, including the helmet, are prohibited.

Head Coverings

(d) Head coverings worn under the helmet, e.g., sweat bands and bandannas, are permissible and may be visible in the bench area, provided that they are of a solid color (white or official team color) and issued by the club, and further provided that no portion hangs from or is otherwise visible outside the helmet during play. Baseball-type caps may be worn in the bench area, provided they are in official team colors and issued by the club.

Logos and Commercial Identification

Article 6 Throughout the period on game-day that a player is visible to the stadium and television audience (including in pregame warm-ups, in the bench area, and during postgame interviews in the locker room or on the field), players are prohibited from wearing, displaying, or orally promoting equipment, apparel, or other items that carry commercial names or logos of companies, unless such commercial identification has been approved in advance by the League office. The size of any approved logo or other commercial identification involved in an agreement between a manufacturer and the League will be modest and unobtrusive, and there is no assurance that it will be visible to the television audience. Subject to any future approved arrangements with a manufacturer and subject to any decision by the Commissioner to temporarily suspend enforcement of this provision governing shoes, visible logos and names of shoes are prohibited, including on the sole of the shoe that may be seen from time to time during the game. When shoe logos and names are covered with appropriate use of tape [see 5-3-4(f) above], the logo or name of the shoe manufacturer must not be reapplied to the exterior of the tape unless advance approval is granted by the League office.

Personal Messages

Article 7 Throughout the period on game-day that a player is visible to the stadium and television audience (including in pregame warm-ups, in the bench area, and during postgame interviews in the locker room or on the field), players are prohibited from wearing, displaying, or otherwise conveying personal messages either in writing or illustration, unless such message has been approved in advance by the League office. Items such as armbands and jersey patches worn to celebrate anniversaries of events, to promote charities, to recognize causes and campaigns, or to honor or commemorate personages are also prohibited unless approved in advance by the League office. Further, such armbands and jersey patches must be modest in size, tasteful, non-commercial, and non-controversial; must not be worn for more than one football season; and if approved for use by a specific team, must not be worn by players on other teams in the League.

General Appearance

Article 8 Consistent with the equipment and uniform rules of this Section 3, players must otherwise present a professional and appropriate appearance while before the public on game-day. Among the types of activity that are prohibited are use of tobacco products (smokeless included) while in the bench area and use of facial makeup. The Referee is authorized to use his judgment in determining whether any other unusual appearance or behavior is violative of this Article 8.

Penalties:

(a) **For violation of this Section 3 before player has entered the game: player not permitted to enter game until violation corrected. If such violation occurs during pregame warm-ups: player must leave field and return to bench area or dressing room until violation corrected.**

(b) **For violation of this Section 3 discovered while player in game: suspension from succeeding play after discovery; player may re-enter when violation corrected.**

(c) **For repeat violation: disqualification from game.**

(d) **For illegal return of a player suspended under this Section 3: loss of five yards from succeeding spot and removal until properly equipped after one down.**

(e) **For violation of this Section 3 detected in the bench area: player and head coach will be asked to remove the objectionable item, properly equip the player, or otherwise correct the violation. The involved player or players will be disqualified from the game if correction not made promptly.**

SUPPLEMENTAL NOTE

In addition to the game-day penalties specified above, the Commissioner may subsequently impose independent disciplinary action on the involved player, up to and including suspension from the team's next succeeding game — preseason, regular season, or postseason, whichever is applicable.

Rule 6   Free Kick

Section 1   Putting Ball in Play

Kickoff

Article 1   A free kick called a kickoff (3-16, p. 9) puts the ball in play:

(a) at the start of each half;

(b) after a Try for point; and

(c) after a successful field goal.

Free Kick

Article 2   A free kick also puts the ball in play:

(a) after a safety (see 3-12-1b, p. 8);

(b) following a fair catch when this method is chosen (10-1-6, p. 67) (11-5-3, p. 73)

(c) when there is a replay for a short free kick (6-2-1, p. 31), and

(d) when enforcement for a foul during a free kick is from the previous spot (6-2-5, p. 32).

Note: the ball is put in play by a snap in all other cases (7-3-1, p. 39).

Spot of Free Kicks

Article 3   A free kick may be made from any point on or behind the offensive team's free kick line and between inbounds lines. A dropkick, placekick, or punt may be used.

Exceptions:

Types of Free Kicks

1) A punt may not be used on a kickoff.

2) During a placekick at the kickoff, the kicking team may use a manufactured tee that is 1, 2, or 3 inches in height and approved by the league.

3) A fair catch-kick must be made on or behind the mark of the catch (3-9-1, p. 7, and 10-1-6, p. 67) without the use of a "tee."

Note: When the mark of a fair catch is in a side zone, it is considered to be on the inbounds line.

Penalty: For illegal kick at free kick: New free kick lines are set five yards nearer A's goal line.

Initial Free Kick Lines

Article 4   The initial free kick lines during a given free kick shall be as follows (plus or minus any distance they might be moved because of a distance penalty enforced prior to the kick):
For the kicking team:

(a) Kickoff — offensive 35

(b) Safety kick — offensive 20

(c) Fair catch kick — the yard line through the mark of the catch.

For the receiving team:
A yard line 10 yards in advance of the offensive team's free kick line.

Note: Kicking team's final free kick line is a yard line through the spot of the ball when kicked.

A.R. 6.1   Receiver B1 makes a fair catch attempt with three seconds remaining and the score tied. The ball slips through his hands and touches the ground as the receiver falls on the ball.
Ruling: No fair catch allowed, as the ball has to be caught (3-9-1, p. 7). No fair catch option. The ball is in play with the snap if time remains.

A.R. 6.2   During the continuing action after a safety by the offensive team, defensive B1 punches an opponent.
Ruling: Disqualify B1. The initial free kick line for the kicking team is the 35 yard line (20 plus 15) and for the receivers it is the kicking team's 45 yard line. No tee is allowed, but a punt is permitted.

A.R. 6.3 The kicking team is offsides on a kickoff following a field goal. The penalty is accepted.
Ruling: New free kick lines are set. The kicking team's new free kick line is A30 and the receiving team's is A40. No punt is allowed, but a tee is permitted.

Whistle Prior to a Free Kick

Article 5 After the referee's whistle prior to a free kick:

(a) All receiving players (Team B) must be inbounds and behind their line until the kick.

(b) All kicking players (Team A) must be inbounds and behind the ball when kicked except the holder of the placekick (3-23, p. 12; 6-1-5, p. 31) may be beyond the line, and the kicker may be beyond the line but his kicking foot may not be.

Free Kick Violation

Penalty: For violation of free kick formation: The free kick is made again. New free kick lines are set five yards nearer the offender's end line unless a half-distance penalty is being enforced (14-2-1, p. 91).

A.R. 6.4 On a kickoff after a Try, the kicker (soccer-type) places his non-kicking foot beyond the ball with his kicking foot kicking the ball on the free kick line.
Ruling: Legal. (Kicking foot may not be beyond the line.)

A.R. 6.5 The kicking team punts from behind its goal line. Receiver B1 makes a fair catch on the A11. At the fair catch kick one of the receiving team is ahead of his free kick line.
Ruling: The kicking team's free kick line will be A6 yard line and that of receivers four yards behind their goal line. A second penalty by the receivers would only involve a 3-yard penalty (half-distance), and make the receiver's free kick line seven yards behind their goal line. The penalty is to be enforced although it results in placing B behind their goal line. A second such foul by B behind their goal line is penalized in the same manner.

Section 2 Ball in Play After Free Kick

Short Free Kick

Article 1 A free kick is short when it does not go to or across the receiving team's free kick line unless, before doing so, it is first touched by a player of the receiving team, or goes out of bounds. See 11-5-3-Exception p.73.

Penalties:

(a) **For the first short free kick: Loss of five yards from the previous spot.**

Kickoff Out of Bounds

(b) **For the second (or more) consecutive short free kick illegally touched or illegally out of bounds: The receiving team takes possession of the ball at the out of bounds spot or spot of illegal touch or recovery. If a re-kick is to be made, new free kick lines are set. See 6-3-1-Note, p. 33.**

A.R. 6.6 On a kickoff after a field goal, a kicking team player is first to touch the ball on his own 43-yard line (before it goes to or across the receiving team's free kick line). The ball rolls to the kicking team's 47-yard line where a receiving team player falls on it and is downed there.
Ruling: Receiving team's ball on the A47-yard line. (Receiving team has option to play or rekick from kicker's 30-yard line.)

A.R. 6.7 On a kickoff after a field goal, a kicking team player is first to touch the ball on the A43-yard line (before it goes to or across the receivers' restraining line). The ball rolls to the kicker's 48-yard line where a receiving team player picks it up, takes a few steps and fumbles. Kicking team recovers at A45.
Ruling: Rekick from kicker's 30. A five-yard penalty from the previous spot for a short free kick (if receiving team didn't fumble and kept possession, it has the option to keep the ball when it is dead).

A.R. 6.8 A receiving team player first touches a free kick after a Try on the kicking team's 44. The kicking team recovers on its own 43.
Ruling: Kicking team's ball on its own 43. No foul as the ball was touched first by a receiving team player. The ball is dead where it is recovered by the kicking team if it is muffed (no possession) by the receiving team.

A.R. 6.9 A kickoff after a Try is caught in the air by a kicking team player on the kicking team's 46-yard line:

(a) before any touching by the receiving team. A receiving team player could have caught the ball.
Ruling: Fair catch interference. 15-yard penalty from spot of foul, snap only (10-1-4, p. 66).

(b) before any touching by the receiving team. No receiving team player was near enough to have caught the ball.
Ruling: Legal play. A's ball first-and-10 on A46.

A.R. 6.10 A kickoff from the A35 bounces on the A43 and is in the air when A1 leaps from the A44 and catches the ball on the A46.
Ruling: Legal recovery. Not a short free kick, as the ball hit ground and ball was recovered after going 10 yards. A's ball, first-and-10 on A46.

Free Kick Recovery

Article 2 Free Kick Recovery

(a) If a free kick is recovered by the receiving team it may advance.

(b) If a free kick (legal or illegal) is recovered by the kicking team, the ball is dead. If the recovery is legal, the kicking team next puts the ball in play at the spot of recovery. Undue advance by the kicking team recovering (legal or illegal) is delay of game (4-3-9, p. 21, 11-5-3, p. 73).

(c) If a free kick is simultaneously recovered by two opposing players, the ball is awarded to the receiving team.

A.R. 6.11 A Kickoff after a Try is first touched by the receiving team on the kicker's 43-yard line before it reached the receiving team's restraining line. A member of the kicking team recovers, takes one step, is tackled, fumbles and the receiving team recovers on A43.
Ruling: No short free kick as ball touched by receiving team. Kicking team's ball on A43. The ball is dead when recovered.

A.R. 6.12 Kickoff after a Try goes to the kicking team's A44 and no one attempts to recover.
Ruling: Rekick from A30. Penalize five yards.

After Free Kick Ends

Article 3 All general rules apply when play continues after a free kick (loose ball) ends.

Player Out-of-Bounds During a Free Kick

Article 4 No player of the kicking team may touch or recover a kickoff or safety kick before:

(a) it is possessed by the receiving team (B) if that kicking team player has been out of bounds during the kick; or

(b) it has crossed the receiving team's restraining line, unless before doing so, it has first been touched by the receiving team.

Penalty: For illegal touching of a free kick by the kicking team: Loss of five yards from the previous spot. New free-kick lines are set if enforced.

A.R. 6.13 During a kickoff a kicking team player (A1) is blocked out-of-bounds (or steps out of bounds). A receiving team player (B1) muffs the kick and A1 re-enters and recovers the ball.
Ruling: Rekick — loss of five yards from the previous spot for illegal touching. The ball was never possessed by the receiving team.

A.R. 6.14 During a kickoff a kicking team player (A1) avoids a block and steps out-of-bounds (or is blocked out). He re-enters and uses his hands in a personal attempt to recover a muff by a receiving player (B1).
Ruling: Loss of 10 yards from the previous spot. Illegal use of hands.

Foul During A Free Kick

Article 5 If there is a foul other than unsportsmanlike conduct after a fair catch signal, fair catch interference or an invalid fair catch signal during a free kick, any enforcement, if made, is from the previous spot and the free kick must be made again (10-1-3, p. 65; 10-1-4, p. 66 and 10-1-1, p. 65).

A.R. 6.15 During a kickoff a kicking team player bats or kicks a ball muffed by the receiving team towards the receiver's goal line. The ball is recovered by the receiving team on its own 5-yard line.
Ruling: Previous spot foul. Loss of 10 yards (12-1-6, 7, p. 77). New free kick lines are set. Rekick — A25. Option for receivers, but they would take the penalty.

A.R. 6.16 During a kickoff a kicking team player (A1) is offside. The receiving team returns the ball to its 15-yard line (B15).
Ruling: Option for receiving team. Rekick — five-yard penalty or receiving team's ball on B15. New free kick lines are set if rekicked.

SUPPLEMENTAL NOTES

Legal Use
of Hands

(1) During a free kick a legal kicking team player within the first 10 yards may not block or use his hands or arms on an opponent or to push him out of the way in an actual legal attempt to recover the ball (12-1-2, Exception, p. 75), before the ball has gone 10 yards, unless it was touched by the receiving team (6-2-1, p. 31).

Running Into
Free Kicker

(2) Running into the kicker by the receiving team before he recovers his balance is a 5-yard penalty.

A.R. 6.17 On a kickoff after a try prior to the ball going 10 yards A1 blocks B1 above the waist on the A43. A2 falls on the ball on the A46.
Ruling: Re-kick from the A25. Kicking team members may not use hands, arms, or body prior to the ball going 10 yards unless ball was first touched by the receivers. See 6-2-5, S.N. 1, p. 33.

Section 3   Free Kick Out of Bounds or In Touch

Free Kick
Out-of-Bounds

Article 1   The kicking team may not kick a free kick out of bounds between the goal lines.

Receiving
Team Last
To Touch

Exception: If the receiving team is the last one to touch the kick before it goes out of bounds, it is not a foul by the kicking team, and the receiving team next puts the ball in play at the inbounds spot.

Penalties:

(a) Receivers' ball 30 yards from the spot of the kick or the team may elect the option of taking possession of the ball at the out of bounds spot.

While the receiving team may not waive the kicking team's obligations to rekick, it is not deprived of a choice of distance penalties in case of a multiple foul.

Exception: If the ball goes out of bounds or is short the first time an onside kick is attempted, the kicking team is to be penalized five yards and re-kick must be made (no declinations). New free kick lines are set.

(b) For the second (or more) consecutive free *onside* kick or onside kick out of bounds: Receiving team takes possession of the ball at the out of bounds spot or spot of illegal touch or recovery.

Free Kick
Timing,
Last Two
Minutes

Note: Time is in during the last two minutes of a half after legal touching or recovery of a kickoff or safety kick:

a) when the receiving team touches in field of play;

b) when the receiving team recovers in field of play;

c) when the receiving team recovers in end zone and immediately proceeds into field of play; and

d) when the kicking team legally touches in field of play.

Time is not in if:

a) the receiving team recovers in the end zone and makes no attempt to enter the field of play (including running laterally in end zone); or

b) the kicking team recovers in the field of play. (Referee's time out under change of possession rule (4-3-7-S.N. 1, p. 19).

c) the receiving team signals for and makes a fair catch.

A.R. 6.18 A free kick goes 12 yards and is first touched by a receiving team player. A kicking team player then touches the ball before it goes out of bounds on the 50.
Ruling: Kicking team player (A) last one to touch ball. Receiver's ball on the 50.

A.R. 6.19 A free kick is first touched by a kicking team player before it goes 10 yards. A receiving team player touches the ball before it rolls out of bounds on the A43.
Ruling: Option for the receiving team. Receiver's ball on the A43 or rekick — five-yard penalty for a short free kick (6-2-1, p. 31).

A.R. 6.20 A kickoff crosses the receiver's goal line and a receiving team player muffs the ball in the end zone. The kick is out of bounds on the receiving team's two-yard line after last touching a kicking player who tried to recover.
Ruling: Receiving team's ball 30 yards from spot of kick. See 6-3-1, p. 33.

A.R. 6.21 A kickoff crosses the receiving team's goal line and a receiving team player muffs the ball in the end zone. The kick rolls out of bounds on the receiving team's two-yard line without any other player touching the ball.
Ruling: Receiving team's ball on its two-yard line. (No rekick as the receiving team player was the last one to touch the ball).

Free Kick Behind Goal Line

Article 2 Rule 11, p. 69 governs if a free kick:

(a) goes out of bounds behind the receiving team's goal line;

(b) kickoff or safety kick becomes dead because the ball strikes the receiving team's goal post; or

(c) is downed in the end zone.

A.R. 6.22 A free kick is muffed by a receiving team player and the ball then rolls into the goal posts. A kicking team player then falls on it in the end zone.
Ruling: Touchback (11-6-1, p. 74). A ball hitting the goal post is out of bounds.

A.R. 6.23 A free kick is caught in the end zone by a receiving team player who goes to his one-yard line, is tackled and fumbles, and the ball rolls into the end zone and hits the goal post. A kicking team player falls on it in the end zone.
Ruling: (11-4-1-b, p. 70). Safety. Ball was out of bounds when it hit the goal post.

Rule 7 Scrimmage

Section 1 Necessary Gain on Downs

New Series,
First-and-10

Article 1 A new series (first-and-10) is awarded to the offensive team when the following conditions exist; subject, however, to the specific rules of enforcement (Rule 12, p. 75).

Necessary
Gain

(a) When, during a given series, the ball is declared dead in possession of offensive team while it is on, above, or across the necessary line, or unless a penalty places it there, or unless a touchback for them results.

Change of
Possession

(b) When the ball is dead in the field of play in the offense's possession, after having been in the defensive team's possession during the same down.

Defensive
Fouls

(c) When a foul is made by the defense, except as otherwise specified (14-8-5, p. 97), or when an impetus by them results in a touchback for offensive team.

Kick
Recovered
After Touch

(d) When the offensive team recovers a scrimmage kick anywhere in the field of play after it has *first* been touched *beyond* the line by the defense. See 9-1-6-Note, p. 60.

Forward Part
of Ball
Determines
Gain

Article 2 The *forward part of the ball* in its position when declared dead in the field of play shall be taken as the determining point in measuring any distance gained. *The ball shall not be rotated when measuring.*

Entire Ball
Out of
End Zone

Note: A ball in the end zone which is carried toward the field of play is still in touch. It is a safety or touchback if any part of the ball is on, above, or behind the goal line (plane) when dead. In such a case, the ball must be entirely in the field of play in order not to be in touch.

A.R. 7.1 Second-and-10 on B30. Runner A1 goes to the B25 where he is tackled, fumbles, and defensive player B1 recovers and runs to B28. B1 fumbles and A2 recovers on the B28 where he is downed.
Ruling: A's ball first-and-10 on B28. The ball is dead in the offensive team's possession after having been in the defensive team's possession during same down.

A.R. 7.2 Second-and-10 on B30. Quarterback A1 throws an incomplete pass. Defensive tackle held the tight end A2 on the line of scrimmage.
Ruling: A's ball first-and-10 on B25. Foul by defense is automatic first down for offensive team unless otherwise specified in 14-8-5, p. 97.

A.R. 7.3 Fourth-and-10 on A30. A punted ball is muffed by defensive B1 on the B35. A kicking team player A1 recovers on the B30.
Ruling: A's ball first-and-10 on the B30. Offensive team recovers kick first touched by defense *beyond* line. The ball is dead when recovered by A1 (9-1-6-Note, p. 60).

A.R. 7.4 Fourth-and-10 on A30. Punt is first touched by kicking team player A1 on B35 and then muffed by defensive B1. Offensive A2 recovers on B30.
Ruling: B's ball first-and-10 on B35. Illegal touch. It was first touched by the offensive and not the defensive team (9-1-4, p. 59).

A.R. 7.5 Fourth-and-10 on A30. A punt is blocked and rolls beyond line to A35 where defensive player B1 tries to recover but muffs it back to the A28 where punter A1 falls on it.
Ruling: A's ball first-and-10 on A28. Ball first touched beyond line by defense (9-1-6-Note, p. 60).

No First Down
for Offense

Article 3 If offensive team fails to advance ball to necessary line during a given series, it is awarded to defensive team for a new series at the spot:

(a) where dead at end of fourth down *or*

(b) where it is placed because of a combination penalty (14-8-2, p. 97) *or* a touchback for defensive team.

Exceptions: Ball is not awarded to defensive team when fourth down results either in:

(a) a safety by the offensive team *or*

(b) a touchback for the offensive team.

Section 2   Position of Players at Snap

Seven Men on Line

Article 1   The offensive team must have:

(a) seven or more players on its line (3-18, p. 10) at the snap.

(b) all players who are *not* on line, other than the snap receiver under center, must be at least one-yard behind it at snap, except as provided in 7-2-4, p. 37.

Note: Offensive lineman may lock legs.

Penalty: For violation of snap formation: Loss of five yards from previous spot.

A.R. 7.6   Fourth-and-10 on B35. On a field goal attempt offensive tackle A1 and offensive guard A2 lock their legs as they line up. The field goal is good.
Ruling: Field goal good, no foul.

Encroachment and Offside

Article 2   After the neutral zone starts, no player of either team at snap may:

(a) encroach upon it (3-18, p. 10); or

(b) be offside (3-19, p. 11).

Note: Officials are to immediately blow their whistles whenever a defender penetrates beyond the neutral zone prior to the snap and continues unabated toward the quarterback even though no contact is made by a blocker.

Penalty: For encroaching or being offside: Loss of five yards from previous spot. Number of down and necessary line remain the same.

SUPPLEMENTAL NOTES

(1) Unless both teams charge simultaneously, there cannot be a double foul.

Whistle on Contact

(2) If any player crosses his line and contacts an opponent, it is encroaching. *Blow whistle* immediately on contact.

Initial Action Responsible

(3) If a defensive player charges into the neutral zone, and the action draws an immediate charge forward by an offensive player directly opposite the action by the defense is encroachment.

(4) If a player charges into neutral zone without violating items (2) and (3), and returns to a legal position prior to the snap, it is not encroaching unless it is a repeated act after a warning.

A.R. 7.7   Second-and-10 on B30. Defensive tackle B1's initial charge into neutral zone makes offensive guard A1 directly across from him flinch and draw back.
Ruling: Blow the whistle immediately. Penalize A1 for false start, warn Team B. A1 would be legal if he went forward. A's ball second-and-15 on B35.

A.R. 7.8   Second-and-10 on B30. Defensive back B1 runs toward the line of scrimmage as if he is going right over guard A1. He stops on the defensive side of the neutral zone but guard A1 in a three-point stance picks up.
Ruling: Penalize offensive A1 for false start. A's ball second-and-15 on B35. Blow the whistle immediately.

A.R. 7.9   Second-and-10 on A30. Defensive player B1 jumps across the line and contacts offensive player A1 prior to the snap.
Ruling: Blow whistle immediately and kill play. A's ball second-and-five on A35.

A.R. 7.10   The offensive team uses a double shift (first, second, or third time during the game). At the start of the second shift, a defensive player B1 charges into the neutral zone and is in the neutral zone at the snap.
Ruling: Loss of five yards for offside against defensive team.

A.R. 7.11   The offensive team uses a double shift. At the start of the second shift, defensive player B1 charges into the neutral zone and makes contact.
Ruling: A legal shift. Penalize the defensive team five yards for encroachment.

A.R. 7.12 Offensive upback A2 moves *abruptly* (simulating the snap) when he goes in motion prior to the snap.
Ruling: Loss of five yards for false start. Blow whistle immediately.

Reporting
Change of
Position

Article 3 An offensive player who comes into game wearing an illegal number for the position he takes must report to the referee who in turn will report same to the defensive captain. The clock shall not be stopped and the ball may not be put in play until the referee takes his normal position.

Penalties:

Failure
To Report

a) **Five yards for illegal substitution if player in above category enters the game and/or his team's huddle without reporting and later reports his player position status to the Referee prior to snap. In such cases the clock shall start with the Referee's whistle (clock signal) immediately upon enforcement of penalty, if clock had previously been running.**

b) **For failure to notify Referee of change in eligibility or ineligibility status (when required) prior to snap: Loss of five yards for illegal substitution.**

SUPPLEMENTAL NOTES

(1) It is not necessary for entering substitutes or players legally in the game to report to the Referee under the following conditions:

Legal
Position
Changes

a) players wearing eligible pass receiver number playing in eligible pass receiver positions; or

b) players wearing ineligible pass receiver numbers playing in ineligible pass receiver positions.

(2) When a player is legally designated (Referee informed) as being eligible or ineligible (Article 3), he must participate in such a position until legally withdrawn.

Player
Returning
To Original
Position

Exception: If the change in playing position status is followed by: 1) a touchdown; 2) a completed kick from scrimmage (a punt, drop kick, or place kick); 3) a foul; 4) a team time out; 5) the end of a quarter; or 6) time out for the two-minute warning, the said player may return to his originally eligible or ineligible playing position without restriction. However, if the kick is not completed or a touchdown not made, the said player must remain in his new position until legally withdrawn (5-1-5, p. 25). If withdrawn, he is to re-enter to the position indicated by his number unless he again informs the Referee that he is assuming a position other than that designated by his number.

Notify
Referee on
Position
Change

(3) Coaches must instruct those players wearing numbers not qualifying them for designated positions to report to the Referee, *prior to the huddle,* their change in eligibility or ineligibility status. This rule prevails whether player is already in the game or is an entering substitute and whether it is a play from scrimmage; an attempted field goal; or a Try-for-Point after touchdown.

(4) The Referee especially must be alert to the above situation at all times and be certain that the defensive captain is notified of the change of any player position status.

Article 4 At the snap, a center, guard, or tackle of the offensive team may be anywhere on his line, but he may not be behind it unless he is at least one-yard behind it and has informed the Referee of his change of position to that of an eligible receiver (7-2-3, p. 37).

Penalty: For center, guard, or tackle not on the line at the snap: Loss of five yards from the previous spot.

A.R. 7.13 Offensive tackle A1 is legally shifted to the backfield and is then withdrawn. He returns before the next snap to a tackle position.
Ruling: Illegal. He must stay out one play, or have his team request a team time out. See 5-2-1-S.N.6, p. 26, and 7-2-3 Exception, p. 37.

**Player
Movement
at Snap**

Article 5 At the snap, all offensive players must be stationary in their positions:

(a) without any movement of feet, head or arms;

(b) without swaying of body; and

(c) without moving directly forward *except that one* player only and he, playing in a backfield position, may be in motion provided he is moving, parallel to, obliquely backward from, *or* directly backward from the line of scrimmage at snap.

**Illegal
Motion**

Note 1: No player is ever permitted to be moving obliquely or directly forward toward his opponent's goal line at snap.

Note 2: Non-abrupt movement of head and/or shoulders by offensive players prior to the snap is legal. Players must come to a stop before ball is snapped. If officials judge the action of the offensive players to be abrupt, false start foul is to be called.

Penalty: For player illegally in motion at snap: Loss of five yards from previous spot. In case of doubt, this penalty shall be enforced.

A.R. 7.14 Third-and-one on the B40. Quarterback A1 stops about a foot behind the center and then moves forward and takes the snap and goes to the B38.
Ruling: Illegal motion. Can't be moving forward at snap. A's ball third-and-six on B45.

A.R. 7.15 At the snap offensive back A1 is on the line of scrimmage and in motion along line.
Ruling: A1 is illegally in motion as he was not playing a backfield position.

A.R. 7.16 The offensive Team A has eight players on the line. End A1 on line runs behind line to lead interference and at the snap is three yards behind the line.
Ruling: Illegal motion as end A1 was not playing in a backfield position at the snap. The distance behind the line at the snap has no bearing on the validity of this situation.

A.R. 7.17 After a huddle or shift, offensive halfback A1 assumes a position on the end of the line and offensive end A2 assumes a position one yard behind the line (no change in their eligibility status). End A2 only in motion parallel to line at snap.
Ruling: End A2 legally in motion as he was playing in a backfield position at the snap.

A.R. 7.18 After a huddle or shift offensive halfback A1 assumes a position on the end of the line and offensive end A2 assumes a position one yard behind the line (no change in their eligibility status). Halfback A1 only is in motion parallel to line at snap.
Ruling: A1 illegally in motion as he was not playing in a backfield position at the snap.

**Complete
Stop
One Second**

Article 6 After a shift or huddle all offensive players after assuming a set position must come to an absolute stop. They also must remain stationary in their position without any movement of their feet, head or arms, or swaying of their body for a period of at least one second before snap.

Penalty: For illegal pause or motion after a shift: Loss of five yards from previous spot. In case of doubt the penalty is to be enforced.

SUPPLEMENTAL NOTES

(1) A single man in motion is not a shift, but if he is moving directly forward at the snap, it is illegal motion (7-2-5-c, p. 38).

(2) After a shift if all players come to a legal stop and then one or more men start again before snap, the play may result in encroaching (7-2-2, p. 36), illegal motion (7-2-5, p. 38), a second shift (7-2-6, p. 38), or a false start (7-3-4, p. 40).

A.R. 7.19 Team A shifts and comes to a stop for one second. Offensive End A1 then goes out along his line and stops. Back A2 then moves backward and the ball is snapped less than one second after End A1 stops.
Ruling: Legal play. Movement of End A1 and Back A2 are not simultaneous.

A.R. 7.20   After a shift or a huddle the offensive players come to a stop and remain stationary. Before the lapse of one second Back A1, who did not shift or huddle, starts and is in motion backward at snap.
Ruling: Illegal shift. All eleven players must come to an absolute stop for one second.

A.R. 7.21   After a legal pause following a shift:

(a) offensive Backs A1 and A2 move forward just prior to snap. They regain their positions and are stationary at the snap.
Ruling: A second shift and one second rule again applies.

(b) offensive Back A1 charges forward just prior to snap. He regains his position at snap but B1 contacts Guard A3 as a result of the movement of A1.
Ruling: Loss of five yards from previous spot against A1 for false start. Blow whistle on contact.

A.R. 7.22   Following a shift or huddle all offensive players except offensive Tackle A1 make a legal pause prior to snap. Tackle A1 moves into the neutral zone but regains a stationary position less than one second prior to snap.
Ruling: Illegal shift unless Tackle A1 is penalized for false start.

Out of
Bounds
at Snap

Article 7   No player may be out of bounds at the snap.

Penalty: For player out of bounds at snap: Loss of five yards from the previous spot.

Section 3   Putting the Ball in Play

Put Ball
in Play

Article 1   The offensive team must put the ball in play by a snap at the spot where previous down ended, unless otherwise specifically provided for, *unless* a free kick is prescribed or is chosen after a fair catch (6-1-2-b, p. 30).

Penalty: For not using a snap when prescribed: Loss of five.

No Snap
Until
Enforcement

Article 2   When a foul occurs, the ball shall *not* be put in play again until the penalty (Rule 14, p. 87):

(a) has been enforced;

(b) declined;

(c) offset;

(d) been annulled by a choice; or

(e) disregarded.

Snap
Provisions

Article 3   The snap (3-31, p. 13) may be made by any offensive player who is on the line but must conform to the following provisions:

(a) The snap must start with ball on ground with its long axis horizontal and at right angles to line, and

(b) The impulse must be given by one quick and continuous motion of hand or hands of snapper. The ball must actually leave or be taken from his hands during this motion.

(c) The snapper may *not:*

Snapper
Restrictions

(1) move his feet abruptly from the start of snap until the ball has left his hands;

(2) have quick plays after the neutral zone starts if the Referee has not had a reasonable time to assume his normal stance. The ball remains dead. No penalty unless for a repeated act after a warning (delay of game).

Penalty: For illegally snapping ball: Loss of five yards from spot of snap for false start.

False Start

Article 4 From the start of the neutral zone until the snap, no offensive player, if he assumed a set position, shall charge or move in such a way as to simulate the start of a play (false start).

Penalty: For false start: Loss of five yards from spot of snap.

SUPPLEMENTAL NOTES

Movement of Interior Linemen

(1) When interior lineman of the offensive team (tackle to tackle) takes or simulates a three-point stance and then moves after taking that stance, the offensive team shall be penalized for a false start. The official *must* blow his whistle immediately.

(2) The penalty for a false start (Article 4) shall be enforced regardless of whether snap is made or not. The distance penalty for the false start may be declined.

No Offensive Movement

(3) Any quick, abrupt movement by a single offensive player or by several offensive players in unison, which simulates the start of the snap is a false start.

Exception: This does not apply to an offensive player under the center who turns his head or shoulders (only) provided he receives a hand to hand snap. Any obvious attempt by the quarterback to draw an opponent offside is to be penalized as a false start.

Extension of Hands

(4) Any extension of hands by a player under center as if to receive the snap is a false start unless he receives the snap. This includes any player under or behind the center placing his hands on his knees or on the body of the center.

(5) Any offensive backfield player, not under center, including a kicker or a place kick holder who extends his hands, does not have to receive the snap, nor must he retract them prior to the snap.

A.R. 7.23 Second-and-10 on the B40. Quarterback A1 bobs his head in an exaggerated manner prior to the snap and draws the defense into the neutral zone.
Ruling: Penalize five yards for false start. Blow the whistle immediately.

A.R. 7.24 Second-and-10 on A30. Offensive interior lineman A1 simulates a three-point stance after a huddle. He then moves to a regular three-point stance. Defensive player charges and contacts player not directly opposite him.
Ruling: False start against offense. Blow whistle immediately to kill play. Defensive action ignored. A's ball second-and-15 on A25.

A.R. 7.25 Second-and-10 on A30. Offensive team breaks from huddle and all linemen except Tackle A1 assume a three-point stance. Tackle A1 rests his elbows on his knees in a crouched position. After a second A1 assumes a three-point stance. When he started his move to a three-point stance defensive B1 charges across line and contacts Tackle A1.
Ruling: Penalize B1 for encroachment. A1's move was legal. Blow the whistle immediately. A's ball second-and-five on A35.

A.R. 7.26 Second-and-10 on A30. Offensive interior lineman moves his feet abruptly after taking a three-point stance to make himself more comfortable. The ball is then snapped and defensive player B1 gets quarterback A2 to fumble and B1 recovers on A25.
Ruling: False start. Blow whistle immediately on lineman's movement.

A.R. 7.27 Third-and-10 on A30. Offensive quarterback A1 places his hands on side of snapper. Ball goes through A1's legs to Back A2 who completes a pass to the A40.
Ruling: False start. Five yard penalty. Snap must go to quarterback A1. A's ball third-and-15 on A25. Blow whistle immediately.

A.R. 7.28 The offensive team comes out of a huddle into a T formation. Quarterback A1 extends his hands under the center, after which the offensive team shifts into a spread formation, with Quarterback A1 assuming a blocking halfback position. Offensive back A2 assumes a tailback position with hands extended for the snap. During the shift into the spread formation by the offensive team, defensive B1 is drawn offside.
Ruling: False start against the offensive team. Blow whistle immediately. Loss of five. If the defensive team were not offside, it would be a legal play.

Defense Can't Touch Ball

Article 5 Prior to the snap no defensive player shall enter the neutral zone and touch the ball.

Penalty: For actions interfering with the ball prior to or during the snap: Loss of five yards for delay from the spot of the snap. Blow whistle immediately on contact.

Legal Snap

Article 6 The snap must be to a player who was *not* on his line at the snap, unless it has first struck the ground. The play continues as after any other backward pass (8-4-1-Exception, p. 54) if the snap either:

(a) first touches the ground, or

(b) first touched or is caught by an eligible backfield receiver.

Penalty: For snapping to ineligible snap receiver: Blow whistle. Loss of five yards from the spot of snap.

A.R. 7.29 Fourth-and-10 on A30. The snap first touches the ground and goes off kicker A1's hands. A defensive player picks it up on the A20 and scores.
Ruling: Touchdown (8-4-1, p. 54).

A.R. 7.30 Fourth-and-10 on A30. Snap is high and punter A1 jumps high and muffs the ball, which rolls to the A20. A defensive player B1 picks up the ball on the A20 and scores.
Ruling: Touchdown. (8-4-1, p. 54).

Snap at Inbounds Spot

Article 7 Ball is next put in play (snap) at inbounds spot by the team entitled to possession (7-1-1 and 3, p. 35, and 7-3-1, p. 39) when:

(a) a loose ball is out of bounds between goal lines;

(b) a runner is out of bounds between goal lines;

(c) the ball is dead in a side zone;

(d) the ball is placed there as the result of an enforcement; or

(e) the mark of a fair catch is in a side zone (6-1-3-Note, p. 30).

Exceptions: The ball is next put in play at the previous spot if:

(a) a forward pass goes out of bounds;

(b) an incompletion; or

(c) a foul by the defense occurs in a side zone during an unsuccessful try.

Section 4 Dead Ball

Dead Ball Declared

Article 1 An official shall declare dead ball and the down ended:

(a) when a runner is out of bounds, cries "down," or falls to the ground and makes no effort to advance.

Quarterback Kneel

(b) any time a quarterback immediately drops to his knee (or simulates dropping his knee) to the ground behind the line of scrimmage during the last two minutes of a half. The game clock will not stop during this action.

Player Slide Feet First

(c) whenever a player declares himself down by sliding feet first on the ground. The ball is dead at the spot of the ball at the instant the runner so touches the ground.

(d) when a runner is so held or otherwise restrained that his forward progress ends.

Contacted by Defense

(e) when a runner is contacted by a defensive player and he touches the ground with any part of his body except his hands or feet, ball shall be declared dead immediately. The contact by the defensive player must be the cause of runner going down (7-3-1, p. 39).

Notes: The ball is dead at the spot of the ball at the instant the runner so touches the ground, irrespective of the condition of the field. A runner touching the ground with his hands or feet while in the grasp of an opponent may continue to advance.

Grabbing of Ball From Player

(f) when an opponent takes a ball (hand in hand) in possession of a runner who is down on the ground.

(g) when any forward pass (legal or illegal) is incomplete (8-1-5, p. 47).

(h) when any legal kick touches receivers' goal posts or crossbar unless it later scores a goal from field (9-1-14, p. 62).

(i) when any scrimmage kick crosses receivers' goal line from the impetus of kick and no attempt is made to run it out, or if it is lying loose in the end zone from the impetus of the kick.

(j) when any legal kick or a short free kick is recovered by the kickers, except one kicked from behind line which is recovered behind line (not a Try-kick). See 9-1-4-Note, p. 59 for exception.

(k) when defense gains possession during a try, or a Try-kick ceases to be in play.

(l) when a touchdown, touchback, safety, field goal or Try-for-point has been made.

(m) when any receiver catches after a fair catch signal (valid or invalid) before kick is touched in flight by an opponent.

(n) when any official sounds his whistle, even though inadvertently.

(o) when any fourth down fumble by offensive team is recovered by any offensive player other than the fumbling player. See 8-4-2-Exception, p. 55 and S.N., p. 55.

Note: An opponent may take or grab a ball (hand to hand) in possession of a runner provided the runner is on his feet or is airborne.

A.R. 7.31 Second-and-10 on A30. Offensive End A1 catches a legal forward pass on the A40 where he is stopped by B1 but A1 breaks away and goes back to the A38 in an attempt to break loose. He is tackled on the A38 by B2.
Ruling: A's ball third-and-two on A38. No forward progress is given as he was not stopped. He broke away before he was downed.

A.R. 7.32 Second-and-10 on A30. Both eligible offensive A1 and defensive B1 leap in the air to catch a forward pass and collide during a legal attempt to catch ball on the 50. A1 catches the pass and falls to the ground.
Ruling: Ball is dead at spot. A's ball first-and-10 on the 50.

A.R. 7.33 Second-and-10 on A30. Runner A1 breaks clear and is on the 50 when he slips and falls down. B1 takes the ball from A1's hands when A1 is on the ground.
Ruling: Blow whistle to kill play. May not take ball unless runner is on his feet. A's ball first-and-10 on the 50.

A.R. 7.34 Second-and-10 on A30. A backward pass from the A25 hits the ground on the A20 where a defensive player recovers and runs for a score.
Ruling: Touchdown (8-4-1, p. 54).

A.R. 7.35 Second-and-goal on B4. Runner A1 gets to the goal line and ball touches goal line when he is tackled. He fumbles and defensive B1 recovers in end zone.
Ruling: Touchdown. Ball dead as soon as ball touches goal line in player possession (11-2-1-a, p. 69).

Loose Ball Becomes Dead

Article 2 If a loose ball comes to rest anywhere in field and no player attempts to recover, official covering the play should pause momentarily before signaling dead ball (official's time out). Any legal kick is awarded to receivers and any other ball to team last in possession. When awarded to a team behind the goal line, the ball is placed on its 1 yard line. See 7-4-5 and Note, p. 43.

A.R. 7.36 Second-and-goal on B2. Runner A1 goes to the line of scrimmage where he is tackled and fumbles. The ball rolls into the end zone when the Referee inadvertently blows his whistle as the ball is loose in the end zone. Defense then falls on the ball.
Ruling: Ball dead when whistle blew. A's ball third-and-one on B1. Place ball on one yard line.

A.R. 7.37 A player recovers a loose ball in play by falling on it. He then arises and advances.
Ruling: Legal advance unless he has recovered a legal kick made by his team.

Inadvertent Whistle

Whistle During Run

Article 3 If an official inadvertently sounds his whistle during a play, the ball becomes dead immediately:

(a) If during a run, it is the offensive team's ball at the spot of the ball at the time of the whistle.

Whistle During Backwards Pass or Fumble	(b) If during a backward pass or fumble, it is the offensive team's ball at the spot of the ball at the time of the whistle. Exception: The ball is placed on the one-yard line if the whistle sounds when the ball is loose in either end zone.
Whistle During Kick	(c) If during a kick, it is the receiver's ball at the spot of the ball at the time of the whistle.
Whistle During Forward Pass	(d) If during a forward pass from behind the line, the ball reverts to the passers at the previous spot. It is an incomplete pass. If a penalty is called, the penalty is assessed from the previous spot.

(e) If during a forward pass from beyond the line, the ball reverts to the passers at the spot of the pass. It is an illegal pass. The penalty is assessed from the spot of the pass.

(f) If during a forward pass not from scrimmage, the ball reverts to the passers at the spot of the pass. The penalty is assessed from the spot of the pass.

A.R. 7.38 Second-and-10 on A30. Runner A2 fumbles a hand off from QB A1 on the A25. The ball is on the A22 when the Referee inadvertently blows his whistle.
Ruling: A's ball third-and-18 on A22. Offensive team's ball at the spot of the ball at whistle.

A.R. 7.39 Second-and-five on A30. During a forward pass while the ball is in the air the line judge inadvertently blows his whistle. Prior to the whistle Guard A1 held B1 on the A25.
Ruling: Option for B. Either an incomplete pass (A's ball third-and-five on A30) or foul for holding against A (second-and-15 on A20). Any enforcement is as ordinary.

A.R. 7.40 A forward pass first touches ineligible A1 beyond line. While the pass is still in flight, a whistle sounds. The pass is incomplete.
Ruling: Loss of down or 10 yards from previous spot. See 8-1-5-(e), p. 47.

Ball Put in Play	**Article 4** When the ball is dead, it is next put in play (7-3-1, p. 39) at spot designated by official so declaring it. This is usually the spot of the ball when his whistle sounded, but may be some other spot, in case Referee is informed by an official that the ball should have been dead at another spot or in case the rules prescribe otherwise (15-2-3, p. 100).
Ball Touches Official	**Article 5** The ball is not dead because of touching an official who is inbounds or because of a signal by an official other than a whistle.

Note: When a foul occurs, any official observing it immediately sounds his whistle if it is one for which ball remains dead or is dead immediately. Otherwise he signals it by means of dropping his flag (15-1-4-Note, p. 99) at the spot of the foul unless distance precludes it. In such case, he still indicates the foul in the same manner, but approximates spot, and notes any pertinent circumstances. Unless a whistle sounds, ball continues in play until otherwise dead (7-4-1, p. 41).

Section 5   Possession of Ball After Out of Bounds

Kick Out of Bounds	**Article 1** If any legal kick, except for a free kick, is out of bounds between the goal lines, ball is next put in play at inbounds spot by the receivers, *unless* there is a spot of illegal touching nearer kickers' goal line. For free kick out of bounds, see 6-3-1, p. 33.
Fourth Down Out of Bounds	**Article 2** If it is a play from scrimmage, any possession by offensive team after an out of bounds during fourth down is governed by the location of the necessary line (7-1-3, p. 35).
Runner Out of Bounds	**Article 3** If a runner (3-27, p. 12) is out of bounds between goal lines, the ball is next put in play by his team at inbounds spot.
Forward Pass Out of Bounds	**Article 4** If a forward pass is out of bounds between the goal lines, the ball is next put in play by passing team as provided for an incompletion or for an illegal pass. See 8-1-5, p. 47.

Backward Pass Out of Bounds

Article 5 If a backward pass is out of bounds between the goal lines, the ball is next in play at the inbounds spot by the team last in possession.

Fumble Not Recovered

Article 6 A fumble by the offensive team cannot result in an advance by that team if the ball is not recovered in the field of play or end zone.

(a) A fumble that goes forward and out of bounds is to return to that team at the spot of the fumble.

Fumble Out of Bounds and Clock

Note: If, on a play from scrimmage, a fumble goes out of bounds forward, the Game Clock is to be stopped but is to be restarted when the ball can be made ready for play at the spot of the fumble. If the ball goes out of bounds behind the spot of the fumble, Game Clock is to be stopped and is to be restarted when the ball is snapped for the next down.

(b) A fumble in the field of play that goes backward and out of bounds belongs to the offense at the out of bounds spot.

Fumble Out of Bounds in End Zone

(c) A fumble in the field of play that goes forward into the opponent's end zone and over the end line or sideline results in the ball being given over to the defensive team and a touchback awarded.

(d) A fumble which occurs in a team's own end zone and goes forward into the field of play and out of bounds will result in a safety *if that team provided the impetus that put the ball into the end zone. If the impetus was provided by the opponent, the play will result in a touchback.*

(e) A fumble which occurs in a team's own end zone or in the field of play and the ball goes out of bounds in the end zone will result in a safety *if that team provided the impetus that put the ball into the end zone. If the impetus was provided by the opponent, the play will result in a touchback.*

A.R. 7.41 Second-and-goal on B4. Runner A1 fumbles at line of scrimmage where ball rolls out of bounds:

a) at one-yard line.
Ruling: A's ball third-and-goal on B4.

b) over end line.
Ruling: B's ball first-and-10 on B20.

A.R. 7.42 Second-and-14 on A2. Runner A1 fumbles in end zone. Ball rolls out of bounds.

a) at one-yard line.
Ruling: Safety

b) in end zone.
Ruling: Safety

A.R. 7.43 Second-and-14 on A2. B1 intercepts a forward pass on the A20, runs to the A3, and fumbles. The ball rolls into the end zone. A1 picks up the ball in the end zone, is tackled there, and fumbles ball in end zone. The ball rolls out of bounds over the end line.
Ruling: Touchback; A's ball — first-and-10 on A20. (See 7-5-6-(d)).

A.R. 7.44 Third-and-12 on B22. B1 intercepts forward pass in end zone. Tries to run it out and fumbles in end zone. Ball rolls out of bounds:

a) on B3.
Ruling: Touchback (see 7-5-6-(e))

b) over the end line
Ruling: Touchback (see 7-5-6-(e))

Out of Bounds Behind Goal Line

Article 7 If a pass, kick, or fumble is out of bounds behind a goal line, Rule 11, p. 69, governs.

Rule 8   Forward Pass, Backward Pass, Fumble

Section 1   Forward Pass

One Forward Pass Legal

Article 1   The offensive team may make *one* forward pass from behind the line during each play from scrimmage provided the ball does not cross the line and return behind line prior to the pass.

Illegal Pass

(a) Any other forward pass by either team is illegal and is a foul by the passing team.

Illegal Pass Intercepted

(b) When any illegal pass is intercepted, the ball may be advanced and the penalty declined.

Penalties:

a) **For a forward pass not from scrimmage: Loss of five yards from the spot of the pass. It is a safety when the spot of the pass is behind the passer's goal line.**

b) **For a second forward pass from behind line, or for a pass that was thrown *after* the ball returned behind the line: Loss of down from the previous spot. (This is an offset foul.)**

c) **For a forward pass from beyond the line: Loss of down and five yards from the spot of the pass. See 14-8-2, p. 97. See S.N. 3 below.**

SUPPLEMENTAL NOTES

Illegal Passes and Pass Interference

(1) Eligibility and pass interference rules apply to a second pass from behind the line or a forward pass that was thrown from behind the line after the ball returned behind the line. On all other illegal passes, eligibility rules do not apply.

(2) For a second pass from behind the line that is incomplete behind the defensive team's goal line, see 8-1-5, p. 47, Penalty a.

Spot of Enforcement of Illegal Passes

(3) The penalty for a forward pass beyond the line is to be enforced from the spot where any part of the passer's body is beyond the line of scrimmage when the ball is released.

Necessary Yardage

(4) When a distance penalty in Penalty c) leaves the ball in advance of the necessary line, it is first-and-10 for the offensive team.

Intentional Fumble Forward

(5) An intentional fumble forward is a forward pass. See 8-4-2-Exc. 1, p. 55.

Incomplete Illegal Passes

(6) For when any legal or illegal pass becomes incomplete, see 8-1-5, p. 47.

(7) For team possession during a forward pass (loose ball) or when it ends, see 3-2-3, p. 4.

A.R. 8.1   Second-and-10 on A40. A forward pass is batted back by a defensive player. The ball goes back in the air to the quarterback behind his line. He throws it again to his end who catches it on the B40 and goes for a score.
Ruling: No score. Loss of down. Third-and-10 on A40.

A.R. 8.2   Second-and-18 on A4. A second forward pass from behind the line is caught by offensive end A1 in his end zone. He is downed in his end zone.
Ruling: The ball is dead when A1 catches. Loss of down at the previous spot. Not a safety. A's ball third-and-18 on A4.

A.R. 8.3   Second-and-10 on A40. A second forward pass from behind the line is intercepted by the defensive team at midfield. A defensive player returns it for a touchdown.
Ruling: Touchdown. Illegal passes may be intercepted.

A.R. 8.4 A punt is caught on the defensive team's 20 yard line. The player who caught the ball attempts to throw a backward pass but the ball goes forward and hits the ground. The kicking team falls on it.
Ruling: Incomplete pass. The ball is dead when it hits the ground. Penalize from the spot of the pass as it was an illegal pass (8-1-1, Pen. a — p. 45). B's ball first-and-10 on B15.

A.R. 8.5 A forward pass is intercepted by a defensive player in his end zone. While in the end zone, he attempts to pass backward. The pass goes forward, hits the ground on the one-yard line and is recovered by the first passing team.
Ruling: Safety. Forward pass not from scrimmage in the end zone.

A.R. 8.6 Third-and-10 on B35. A second forward pass is thrown from behind the line to flanker A1. Defensive player B1 interferes with A1 on the B20, but A1 catches it anyway and is downed on the B20.
Ruling: Double foul. Illegal pass by the offensive team and interference by the defensive team. Interference rules apply on the second forward pass from behind the line (14-3-1, p. 92). A's ball third-and-10 on B35 (replay).

A.R. 8.7 Third-and-15 on A30. During a forward pass from beyond the line on the A40, offensive player A1 clips on the A40. The pass is incomplete.
Ruling: Choice for defensive team. Loss of down and five from the spot of the pass or loss of 15 from the spot of the pass (unless offensive player fouls behind that spot — spot of foul). A's ball fourth-and-10 on A35 or third-and-20 on A25.

A.R. 8.8 Third-and-15 on A30. During a forward pass from beyond the line on the A40, defensive player B1 clips on the A40. The ball falls incomplete.
Ruling: Double foul (14-3-1, p. 92). Replay at the previous spot. A's ball third-and-15 on A30.

Legal Touching of Forward Pass

Article 2 A forward pass from behind the line may be touched or caught by any eligible player. (Pass in flight may be tipped, batted, or deflected in any direction by any eligible player at any time. See 12-1-6-Exc. and Note, p. 77).

Eligible Receivers

(a) Defensive players are eligible at all times.

(b) Offensive players who are on either end of the line (other than a center, guard, or tackle) are eligible. See 5-1-4, p. 25; 7-2-4, p. 37.

(c) Offensive players who are at least (legally) one yard behind the line at the snap are eligible, except T-formation quarterbacks. See 7-2-4, p. 37.

Eligibility Lost

Article 3 An eligible receiver becomes ineligible if he

(a) goes out of bounds (prior to or during a pass) and remains ineligible until an eligible receiver or any defensive player touches the pass.

Eligibility Regained

Note: All offensive players become eligible once a pass is touched by an eligible receiver or any defensive players.

Ineligible Receivers

Article 4 An ineligible offensive player is one who:

(a) was originally ineligible;

(b) loses his eligibility through going out of bounds (8-1-5 Penalty-b, and Note 2, p. 47); or

Failure to Report Eligibility

(c) fails to notify the referee of being eligible when indicated (7-2-3, Penalty, p. 37); or

(d) is a T-formation quarterback who, takes his stance behind center,

(1) receives a hand-to-hand pass or snap from him while moving backward;

(2) does not receive a hand-to-hand pass or snap from him and is not legally one yard behind the line of scrimmage; or

(3) ever receives a forward pass (handed or thrown) from a teammate during a play from scrimmage.

Eligibility for T-Formation QB

Note: To become an eligible pass receiver, a T-formation quarterback must assume the position of a backfield player (as in a single wing, double wing, box or spread formation) at least one yard behind his line at the snap. In case of doubt, the penalty for an ineligible player receiving a forward pass shall be enforced.

Incomplete Pass

Article 5 Any forward pass (legal or illegal) becomes incomplete and the ball is dead immediately if the pass:

(a) strikes the ground, goes out of bounds, or touches the goal post of either team;

(b) is illegal and is caught by the offensive team (cannot continue);

(c) is caught by any offensive player after it has touched an ineligible offensive player before any touching by any eligible receiver; or

Loss of Down

(d) The pass first touches or is caught by an ineligible offensive player on or behind the line; is a second such pass from behind the line or a pass that was thrown from behind the line after the ball crossed the line.

Penalty: Loss of down at previous spot. (This foul offsets a foul by the defense.)

Loss of 10 Yards or Loss of Down

(e) The pass is first touched or caught by an ineligible offensive player beyond the line.

Penalty: Loss of 10 yards or loss of down from the previous spot. (This foul offsets a foul by the defense.)

Note 1: See 8-3-1, p. 52 for intentional grounding.

Note 2: If a legal receiver goes out of bounds (accidentally) or is forced out by a defender and returns to first touch or catch a pass inbounds, the play is to be treated as an incomplete pass, unless after it is touched, it is intercepted by B. The interception is legal. See 8-1-3-a, p. 46.

Completed Passes

Article 6 A legal forward pass thrown from behind the line is complete and may be advanced if it is:

(a) caught by an eligible offensive player before any illegal touching by a teammate;

(b) caught by any offensive player after it is first touched by any eligible player; or

(c) intercepted by the defense (defense may also intercept and advance an illegal forward pass).

SUPPLEMENTAL NOTES

Muffed Forward Handoff

(1) A ball handed forward (no daylight) to an eligible receiver behind the line is treated as a fumble if he muffs it (3-21-2-Exc., p. 11). A ball handed forward (no daylight) to an ineligible receiver behind the line is treated as a forward pass and is incomplete when caught or muffed (unless intercepted by B in which case the play continues). See 8-1-5 penalty, p. 47.

(2) The penalty for an incompletion may not be declined unless there was another foul by the passing team. This does not preclude the ball being dead (14-4, p. 94).

(3) The bat of a pass in flight by any player (even when illegal touching) does not end a pass nor does it change the impetus if the act sends it in touch.

Simultaneous Catch

(4) If a pass is caught simultaneously by two eligible opposing players who both retain it, the ball belongs to the passers. It is not a simultaneous catch if a player gains control first and retains control, regardless of subsequent joint control with an opponent. If the ball is muffed after simultaneous touching by two such players, all the players of the passing team become eligible to catch the loose ball.

Both Feet Inbounds

(5) A pass is completed or intercepted if the player has both feet or any other part of his body, except his hands, inbounds prior to and after the catch.

Forced Out of Bounds

(6) A pass is completed or intercepted if the player inbounds would have landed inbounds with both feet but is carried or pushed out of bounds while in possession of the ball in the air or before the second foot touches the ground inbounds by an opponent.

(7) A pass is not intercepted if the defensive player does not have both feet inbounds prior to the interception (as well as after the interception).

A.R. 8.9 Third-and-10 on B40. A forward pass from behind the line goes off eligible offensive end A1's hands and flanker back A2 catches it in the end zone.
Ruling: Touchdown.

A.R. 8.10 While in midair, a receiver firmly takes hold of a pass, but loses possession of the ball when his shoulder lands on the ground with or without being contacted by an opponent.
Ruling: Incomplete pass. Receiver must hold onto the ball when he alights on the ground in order to complete the reception.

A.R. 8.11 A runner (in full possession of the ball) is contacted by an opponent while he is attempting to gain yardage. The contact causes the runner to hit the ground, at which time the ball comes loose.
Ruling: Play is dead when the impact jars the ball loose. No fumble.

A.R. 8.12 Second-and-15 on A4. A second forward pass from behind the line is caught by eligible end A2 after the ball had touched eligible end A1. He is downed in the end zone.
Ruling: The ball is dead when A2 caught it. No safety (8-1-5-Pen. 1, p. 47). Loss of down from the previous spot. A's ball third-and-15 on A4.

A.R. 8.13 Third-and-10 on B40. On a legal forward pass, eligible end A1 is blocked out of bounds on the B36. He returns to the field of play, catches pass, and scores.
Ruling: No score. Loss of down as the player became an ineligible receiver by going out of bounds. A's ball fourth-and-10 on B40.

A.R. 8.14 Third-and-10 on B40. On a legal forward pass, eligible end A1 is blocked out of bounds on the B20. He returns to the field of play and catches a pass after a defensive player touched it. He scores.
Ruling: Touchdown. Legal play as all ineligible receivers become eligible after the defense touches the ball.

A.R. 8.15 Third-and-10 on B40. Eligible end A1 touches a legal forward pass on the B35 and the ball is then touched by ineligible receiver A2 on B35. A defensive player intercepts. He runs it back to the B45 where he fumbles and passing Team A recovers.
Ruling: Legal touch. A's ball first-and-10 on B45.

A.R. 8.16 Second-and-five on B20. A forward pass from behind the line barely touches the crossbar. Eligible offensive end A1 catches the ball in the end zone.
Ruling: No score. The ball is dead immediately upon touching the crossbar (or goal posts). Loss of down from the previous spot. A's ball third-and-five on B20.

A.R. 8.17 Second-and-10 on B30. A legal forward pass is caught by offensive flanker A1 near the sideline. His second step touches the sideline.
Ruling: Incomplete pass. Both feet have to alight inbounds. A's ball third-and-10 on B30.

A.R. 8.18 Second-and-10 on B30. A legal forward pass is intercepted by defensive player B1. As he lands with the ball in his possession, he straddles the sideline.
Ruling: Incomplete pass. Both feet have to touch inbounds. A's ball third-and-10 on B30.

A.R. 8.19 Second-and-10 on B30. A legal forward pass is caught by offensive flanker A1 near the sideline on the B10. While in the air he is driven out backwards by a defensive player at B11. Neither foot touched inbounds but both feet would have landed inbounds if he weren't driven out.
Ruling: Completed pass. A's ball first-and-goal on B10, wind clock.

A.R. 8.20 Second-and-10 on B30. A legal forward pass is intercepted by defensive player B1 who jumped in from out of bounds to intercept pass. Both feet touch inbounds after interception.
Ruling: Incomplete pass. Both feet have to be inbounds prior to interception. A's ball third-and-10 on B30. See 8-1-6-S.N. 7, p. 48.

A.R. 8.21   Second-and-10 on B30. Eligible offensive A1 jumps in air (behind or beyond line) to receive a forward pass and then passes backward to ineligible offensive A2 before he alights.
Ruling: Legal catch.

A.R. 8.22   Second-and-20 on A40. QB A1 receives a hand-to-hand snap from center and hands off to back A2 who runs to his right and throws a legal forward pass from behind the line to QB A1. QB A1 catches the pass on the A38.
Ruling: The ball is dead when caught by ineligible man. T-quarterback is an ineligible receiver. Loss of down at previous spot. Third-and-20 on A40.

A.R. 8.23   Second-and-10 on A40. A legal forward pass touches ineligible guard A1 behind the line. The ball is then intercepted by a defensive player who returns it to the A20.
Ruling: Pass not incomplete when A1 touched by ball. Pass continues in play. B's ball first-and-10 on A20.

A.R. 8.24   Second-and-10 on A40. A legal forward pass touches ineligible guard A1 behind the line. The ball is then intercepted by the defensive team which returns it to the A20, fumbles, and the ball is recovered by the passing team.
Ruling: Loss of down penalty for touching ineligible receiver behind the line. Pass not incomplete when ineligible receiver touches it. A's ball third-and-10 on A40.

A.R. 8.25   Second-and-10 on A40. A legal forward pass is touched by ineligible guard A1 behind the line and is then caught by eligible back A2 who runs to the 50.
Ruling: The ball is dead when caught. A pass touched by an ineligible player behind the line is loss of down. A's ball third-and-10 on A40.

A.R. 8.26   Fourth-and-two on B4. A legal forward pass touches ineligible receiver A1 in the end zone and falls incomplete.
Ruling: B will accept option of loss of down at previous spot rather than loss of 10 yards. B's ball first-and-10 on B4.

A.R. 8.27   Fourth-and-two on B4. A legal forward pass accidentally touches ineligible receiver A1 on the B3 and falls incomplete.
Ruling: Loss of down penalty as touching was beyond the line. B's ball first-and-10 on B4. See 8-1-5-e, p. 47.

A.R. 8.28   Second-and-15 on A8. A legal forward pass is batted back by a defensive player and the ball lands in the end zone. A defensive player falls on it in the end zone.
Ruling: Incomplete pass. A's ball third-and-15 on A8.

A.R. 8.29   First-and-10 on A30. A legal forward pass is touched simultaneously by two opposing eligible players, A1 and B1. The pass goes in the air where ineligible A2 catches it on the A40 and runs to midfield.
Ruling: Legal completion.

Section 2   Pass Interference/Ineligible Player Downfield

Pass
Interference
Not Allowed

Article 1   There shall be *no pass* interference beyond line of scrimmage when there is a forward pass thrown from behind the line. This applies whether or not the pass crosses the line.

Pass
Restrictions

(a) The restriction for the offensive team begins with the snap.

(b) The restriction for the defensive team begins when the ball leaves the passer's hands.

Ineligible
Player
Downfield

Article 2   It is a foul when an ineligible offensive player, prior to a legal forward pass:

   (a) advances beyond his line, after losing contact with an opponent at the line of scrimmage;

   (b) loses contact with an opponent downfield after the initial charge and then continues to advance or move laterally;

   (c) moves downfield without contacting an opponent at the line of scrimmage.

The above restrictions end when the ball leaves the passer's hand.

Penalty: Ineligible offensive player downfield: loss of 5 yards from previous spot.

Not Ineligible Player Downfield

Article 3   It is *not* a foul for an ineligible receiver downfield when ineligible receivers:

(a) immediately retreats voluntarily behind the line after legally crossing the line;

(b) are forced behind their line;

(c) move laterally behind their line (before or after contact of their initial charge) provided they do not advance *beyond* their line until the ball leaves the passer's hands; or

(d) have legally crossed their line in blocking an opponent (eligible offensive player A1 may complete a pass between them and the offensive line).

Ineligibles Legally Downfield

Article 4   *After* the ball leaves the passer's hand, ineligible forward pass receivers can advance:

(a) from behind their line;

(b) from their own line; or

(c) from their initial charge position, provided they do *not* block or contact a defensive player(s) *until* the ball is touched by a player of either team. *Such prior blocking and/or contact is forward pass interference.*

When an ineligible lineman, who has legally crossed his line in blocking an opponent, is touched by a forward pass while beyond his line, enforcement is for Penalty (e) under 8-1-5, p. 47 (loss of down or 10 yards).

Pass Interference by Either Team

Article 5   It is pass interference by either team when any player movement beyond the offensive line significantly hinders the progress of an eligible player or such player's opportunity to catch the ball during a forward pass. When players are competing for position to make a play on the ball, any contact by hands, arms, or body shall be considered incidental unless prohibited. Prohibited conduct shall be when a player physically restricts or impedes the opponent in a manner that is visually evident and materially affects the opponent's opportunity to gain position or retain his position to catch the ball. If a player has gained position, he shall not be considered to have impeded or restricted his opponent in a prohibited manner if all of his actions are a bona fide effort to go to and catch the ball.

Provided an eligible player is not interfered with in such a manner, the following exceptions to pass interference will prevail:

Incidental Contact

(a) If both players are looking for the ball or if neither player is looking for the ball and there is incidental contact in the act of moving to the ball that does not materially affect the route of an eligible player, there is no interference. If there is any question whether the incidental contact materially affects the route, the ruling shall be no interference.

Note: Inadvertent tripping is not a foul in this situation.

(b) Any eligible player looking for and intent on playing the ball who initiates contact, however severe, while attempting to move to the spot of completion or interception will not be called for interference.

(c) Any eligible player who makes contact, however severe, with one or more eligible opponents while looking for and making a genuine attempt to catch or bat a reachable ball will not be called for interference.

Restriction Lifted

The restriction for pass interference ends for both teams when the pass is touched.

Players Right to Ball

Note: During a forward pass it must be remembered that defensive players have as much right to the path of the ball as eligible players.

Legal Use of Hands During Pass

(d) After a legal forward pass has been *touched* by an eligible player, any player may use his hands to push an opponent out of the way during an actual personal attempt to catch the ball, and is irrespective of his original eligibility. This does *not* preclude a penalty against the offensive team for illegal touching prior to touching an eligible player.

No Interference

(e) Pass interference by the defense or the offense is not to be called when the forward pass is clearly uncatchable by the involved receiver and defender.

Note: There is no defensive pass interference behind the line.

A.R. 8.30 Second-and-10 on A30. On a screen pass, Defensive B1 blocks eligible A1 behind the line of scrimmage while the ball is in the air.
Ruling: It is legal play.

Penalties:

Pass
Interference
Penalties

a) **Pass interference by offense: Loss of 10 yards from previous spot.**

b) **Pass interference by defense: First down for offensive team at the spot of any such foul. If the interference is also a personal foul (12-2, p. 77), the usual distance penalty for such a foul is also enforced (from spot of foul). If the interference is behind the defensive goal line, it is first down for the offensive team on the defense's one yard line, or, if the previous spot was inside the two yard line, then halfway between the previous spot and the goal line.**

See 8-3-3, 4, p. 53 for optional penalty in case of a personal foul (12-2, p. 77-82) by opponents prior to any completion or interception.

A.R. 8.31 Second-and-10 on A30. Center A1 blocks his man and drives him to the A32 where he loses contact. He then moves laterally to his right before the ball is thrown and completed to eligible end A2 who is downed on the A45.
Ruling: Ineligible man moved laterally beyond the line after losing contact. Loss of 5 yards. A's ball second-and-15 on A25 (8-2-1, p. 49).

A.R. 8.32 Second-and-10 on A30. Ineligible offensive tackle A1 charges, driving lineman B1 back from his line. The pass is completed on the A45.
Ruling: Not ineligible player downfield. A's ball first-and-10 on A45 (8-2-1, p. 49).

A.R. 8.33 Second-and-10 on A30. On a swing pass from behind the line, a defensive man blocks eligible end A1 on the A32 while the ball is in the air. The pass is incomplete behind the line.
Ruling: Defensive pass interference. It is defensive pass interference whether the pass crosses the line or not once the ball is thrown. A's ball first-and-10 on A32.

A.R. 8.34 Second-and-10 on A30. Eligible tight end A1 goes across his line on the snap and blocks defensive player B1 on the A35 before eligible flanker A2 catches it on the A34. Flanker A2 goes to the A45.
Ruling: Offensive pass interference. Can't block beyond the line prior to the ball being touched. A's ball second-and-20 on A20.

A.R. 8.35 Second-and-10 on A30. Eligible offensive player A1 touches the ball on the A45 and the ball goes off his hands. Defensive player B1 then blocks eligible A2 and prevents him from catching the ball on the 50.
Ruling: Legal block. The ball was touched. No pass interference. A's ball third-and-10 on A30.

A.R. 8.36 Second-and-10 on A30. On a quick pass over the center, defensive player B1 touches the ball on the A35 and it goes high in the air. Defensive player B2 is about to catch the ball when offensive end A1 pushes B2 out of the way and catches the ball and goes to the A45.
Ruling: Legal play as the ball was touched by the defense. Interference rules ended when defensive player touched the pass. A's ball first-and-10 on A45.

A.R. 8.37 Second-and-10 on A30. Eligible offensive player A1 and B1 both make a bona fide attempt to catch a pass on the A45. There is contact between them and the pass falls incomplete on the A45.
Ruling: Incomplete pass. Legal play as it was a simultaneous and bona fide attempt by opposing players. A's ball third-and-10 on A30.

A.R. 8.38 Second-and-10 on A30. Tight end A2 blocks B1 on the A35 as the quarterback is looking for an open receiver. A2 then runs to the 50. The quarterback then throws a pass which A2 catches as no one is near him.
Ruling: Offensive pass interference. A's ball second-and-20 on A20.

Face
Guarding

A.R. 8.39 Second-and-10 on A30. Defensive player B1, beyond the line, has his back to the ball during a forward pass. He makes no attempt to catch it but waves his arms in close proximity to an eligible opponent on the A45.
Ruling: Pass interference for face-guarding.

A.R. 8.40 Fourth-and-1 on B4. Offensive end A1 pushes a defensive player out of the way in the end zone to catch a legal pass.
Ruling: Loss of 10 yards from previous spot. A's ball fourth-and-11 on B14.

A.R. 8.41 Second-and-10 on B30. A defensive player pushes eligible offensive player A1 out of the way in the end zone and catches a pass. He returns it to the 50.
Ruling: Defensive pass interference in the defensive end zone. A's ball first-and-goal on B1.

A.R. 8.42 Fourth-and-10 on B15. On a fake field goal attempt place-kick holder A1 stands up and throws a pass to eligible end A2 who pushes defensive player B1 out of the way in the end zone to catch the pass there.
Ruling: Offensive pass interference. A's ball fourth-and-20 on B25.

A.R. 8.43 Second-and-10 on A30. A defensive player clips eligible offensive player A1 on the A45 as he is about to catch a pass. The pass falls incomplete on the 50.
Ruling: Interference is also a personal foul and penalize for both. A's ball first-and-10 on B40.

A.R. 8.44 Second-and-10 on A30. During a pass, defensive player B1 grabs the face mask of offensive eligible player A1 on the A35. The ball is thrown to the 50 where defensive B2 interferes with eligible A2. The pass falls incomplete.
Ruling: Additional yardage would have been tacked on if the personal foul (face mask) was the pass interference at the 50 (Penalty b, p. 51) or if the pass had been completed (8-3-3, p. 53). A's ball first-and-10 on 50.

A.R. 8.45 Second-and-10 on A30. On a legal forward pass which is unintentionally thrown too high and too far for End A1 to catch, B1 pushes A1 as the ball is already beyond him and A1 obviously couldn't reach the ball. Ball hits ground 12 yards away from A1.
Ruling: No pass interference. Ball wasn't catchable.

Section 3   Fouls on Passes and Enforcement

Intentional
Grounding

Article 1   Intentional grounding will be called when a passer, facing an imminent loss of yardage due to pressure from the defense, throws a forward pass without a realistic chance of completion.

Note 1: The penalty is the sole responsibility of the referee and the protection of the quarterback is his primary responsibility; the flight of the ball is secondary. If there is any question, the referee should not call intentional grounding.

> *Note 2: Intentional grounding will not be called when a passer (the quarterback), while out of the pocket and facing an imminent loss of yardage, throws a forward pass that lands near or beyond the line of scrimmage, even if no offensive player(s) have a realistic chance to catch the ball (including if the ball lands out of bounds over the sideline or endline).*

Note 3: A passer, after delaying his passing action for strategic purposes, is prohibited from throwing the ball to the ground in front of him, even though he is under no pressure from defensive rusher(s).

Note 4: A passer is permitted to stop the clock legally to save time if immediately upon receiving the snap he begins a continuous throwing motion and throws the ball directly forward into the ground.

Penalty: For intentional grounding: loss of down and 10 yards from the previous spot, or if foul occurs more than 10 yards from line of scrimmage, loss of down at spot of foul, or safety if passer is in his end zone when ball is thrown.

Note: The penalty for intentional grounding may be declined and the result of the play is an incomplete pass.

A.R. 8.46   Second-and-20 on A4. An offensive quarterback drops back into his end zone. Just before he is tackled in his end zone, he intentionally grounds the ball by throwing a pass directly in front of him. A defensive player falls on it.
Ruling: Intentional grounding. Safety.

A.R. 8.47   Second-and-10 on A30. Quarterback intentionally grounds ball forward as he stands on A16 to keep from being tackled.
Ruling: Loss of down at spot of foul as quarterback is more than 10 yards behind the line. Third-and-24 on A16.

A.R. 8.48   Second-and-10 on B20. Quarterback deliberately throws the ball out of bounds to stop the clock.
Ruling: The pass was not thrown away to prevent loss of yardage. A's ball third-and-10 on B20. See 8-3-1-Note 4, p. 52.

Enforcement Spot on Forward Pass Fouls

Article 2   If there is a foul (including an incompletion) by either team from the time of the snap until a forward pass from behind the line ends, the penalty is enforced from the previous spot.

Exceptions:

1) Pass interference by the defense is enforced from the spot of the foul.

2) A personal foul prior to interception or completion of a pass from behind the line, enforcement is from the spot chosen (8-3-3, 4, p. 53).

A.R. 8.49   Third-and-10 on A30. During a run prior to an incompleted pass, offensive player A1 holds a defensive player on the A25.
Ruling: Choice for defense. Fourth-and-10 on A30 or third-and-20 on A20 (from previous spot).

A.R. 8.50   Third-and-10 on A30. During a run prior to an intended pass by quarterback A1, defensive player B1 holds flanker A2 on the A45. QB A1 doesn't throw the ball and is downed on the A20.
Ruling: Enforce from the previous spot. A's ball first-and-10 on A35.

Personal Foul Prior to Completion

Article 3   When a team commits a personal foul **prior** to a completion of a legal forward pass from behind the line, the offended team shall have the choice of either:

(a) the usual penalty — 15 yards from the previous spot, *or*

(b) a 15-yard penalty enforced from the spot where the ball is dead.

Exception: If the passing team is fouled and loses possession **after** a completion, enforcement is from the previous spot and the ball will be retained by the offended team after enforcement of the personal foul.

Personal Foul Prior to Interception

Article 4   When a team commits a personal foul prior to an interception of a legal forward pass from behind the line, the offended team will have a 15 yard penalty enforced from the spot where the ball is dead.

Exception: If the intercepting team is fouled and loses possession after the interception, enforcement is from the spot where the interception occurred and the ball will be retained by the offended team after the enforcement of the personal foul.

Note: Personal fouls do not include holding, illegal use of hands, illegal batting, kicking the ball, or tripping. See Rule 12-2, p. 77-82.

A.R. 8.51 Third-and-10 on A40. Defensive player B1 roughs the passer prior to a pass completion to eligible end A1 on the B45. A1 runs to the B40 where he is downed.
Ruling: Personal foul prior to completion of a legal forward pass. 15-yard penalty enforced from the spot where the ball is dead. A's ball first-and-10 on B25.

A.R. 8.52 Third-and-10 on A40. A defensive player roughs the passer as he throws a short swing pass to back A1 who is downed on the A35. The foul is prior to the completion of the pass.
Ruling: Enforce from the previous spot as the usual penalty on a pass. A's ball first-and-10 on B45.

A.R. 8.53 Third-and-10 on A40. Offensive guard A1 clips defensive player B1 as he tries to reach the passer. B2 intercepts the pass and returns it to the A30.
Ruling: Enforce from the spot where the ball is dead. Personal foul prior to interception. B's ball first-and-10 on A15.

A.R. 8.54 Third-and-10 on A40. Defensive player B1 roughs the passer prior to a completed pass to end A1 on the 50. A1 runs to the B40 where he is tackled, fumbles and the defensive team recovers on the B35.
Ruling: Personal foul prior to completion. Enforce from the previous spot and the ball reverts to the offended team. A's ball first-and-10 on the B45.

A.R. 8.55 Third-and-10 on A30, B1 intercepts forward pass at B30, runs to the B35, fumbles and team A recovers. Prior to pass, A3 crackbacks on A26.
Ruling: B's ball first-and-10 on B45.

A.R. 8.56 Third-and-10 on A40. Defensive player B1 roughs the passer prior to a completion to eligible end A1 on the B40. A1 goes for a score.
Ruling: Touchdown. Loss of 15 on the kickoff. Kickoff on 50. See 14-1-14, p. 91.

Defensive Foul and Incomplete Pass

Article 5 If there is a foul by the defense from the start of the snap until a legal forward pass ends, it is *not* offset by an incompletion by the offensive team.

Exceptions: Any foul by the offensive team would offset a foul by the defensive team (14-3-1, p. 92).

A.R. 8.57 Second-and-10 on A30. During a forward pass the ball goes off eligible end A1's fingers and flanker A2 catches it on the B40. The defensive team was offside.
Ruling: A's ball first-and-10 on B40.

A.R. 8.58 Second-and-10 on A30. A forward pass is caught by ineligible tackle on A28. B1 was offside.
Ruling: Penalties offset. Second-and-10 on A30.

A.R. 8.59 Second-and-10 on A30. A forward pass is caught by ineligible A2 beyond the line. Prior to or during the pass, defensive player B1 strikes A1.
Ruling: Disqualify B1. Replay at previous spot.

Section 4 Backward Pass and Fumble

Article 1 A runner may pass backward at any time (3-21-4, p. 11).

(a) An offensive player may catch a backward pass or recover it after the pass touches the ground and advance.

(b) A defensive player may catch a backward pass or recover it after the pass touches the ground and advance.

Note: A direct snap from center is treated as a backward pass.

A.R. 8.60   Third-and-10 on B30. A backward pass hits the ground on the B35. A defensive player recovers it and runs to the B45.
Ruling: Legal recovery and advance. B's ball first-and-10 on B45 (8-4-1-b, p. 54).

Fumble Recovery

Article 2   Any player of either team may recover or catch and advance a fumble

(a) before the fumble strikes the ground, *or*

(b) after the fumble strikes the ground.

Note: A fumble is legally recovered or caught in bounds by a player if the player had both feet in bounds prior to the recovery or catch. See 7-5-6, p. 44 for fumble out of bounds and 11-4-1-Exc.; p. 70, for a fumble in end zone following intercepting momentum.

Exceptions:

Intentional Fumble

1) If a runner *intentionally* fumbles forward, it is a forward pass (3-21-2-a and Note, p. 11).

Fourth Down Fumble and Legal Advance

2) If a fourth down fumble occurs during a play from scrimmage and the fumbling player recovers the ball, he only

a) may advance, or

b) hand and/or pass the ball forward or backward (as prescribed by rule).

Dead Ball on Fourth Down Fumble

3) If a fourth down fumble occurs during a play from scrimmage and the recovery or catch is by another offensive player, the spot of the next snap is:

a) the spot of the fumble unless

b) the spot of recovery is behind the spot of the fumble and it is then at the spot of recovery. See 8-4-4, p. 56.

4) If a fourth down fumble occurs during a play from scrimmage and the ball rolls out of bounds from field of play, the ball is next put in play at the spot of the fumble, unless the spot of out of bounds is behind the spot of the fumble, then it is at that spot (Rule 7-5-6, p. 44). See 11-6-1, p. 74.

SUPPLEMENTAL NOTE

Fumble After Two Minute Warning Applies to Both Teams

After the two-minute warning, any fumble that occurs during a down (including Try-for-Point), the fumbled ball may only be advanced by the offensive player who fumbled the ball, or any member of the defensive team. See 11-3-1-b, p. 69.

A.R. 8.61   Fourth-and-10 on A40. A high snap from center glances off the kicker's hands as he muffs the ball on the A28. The ball rolls to the A25. A defensive player picks it up and goes for a score.
Ruling: Touchdown. (8-4-1-Note, p. 54).

A.R. 8.62   A's ball fourth-and-10 on B20. Direct snap from center on an attempted field goal glances off placekick holder's hands at the B27. Field goal kicker recovers the ball at B30 and *runs for a touchdown.*
Ruling: Legal touchdown. See 8-4-2-Exc. 5, p. 55.

A.R. 8.63   Second-and-10 on B14. On last play of game Team A is behind by four points. QB A1 falls back to pass, fumbles, and ball eventually winds up in B's end zone. A2 falls on it.
Ruling: No score. Game over. See 8-4-2, S.N., p. 55.

A.R. 8.64   Fourth-and-four on B9. Offensive player A1 fumbles (forward unintentionally) on the B9. A1 recovers and goes to the B4.
Ruling: Legal advance as the fumbling player recovered. A's ball first-and-goal on B4.

A.R. 8.65   Fourth-and-four on B9. Offensive player A1 fumbles on the B9 (forward unintentionally). His teammate A2 recovers on the B7 and goes to the B4.
Ruling: Player other than the fumbling player recovered. The spot of the snap is the spot of the fumble (B9). B's ball first-and-10 on B9.

A.R. 8.66 Fourth-and-four on B9. Offensive player A1 fumbles on the B9 and A2 recovers on the B12 and goes to the B4.
Ruling: Other player than the fumbler recovered and spot of next snap is the spot of recovery as it is behind the spot of the fumble. B's ball first-and-10 on B12.

A.R. 8.67 Fourth-and-four on B9. Offensive player A1 fumbles on the B9. Defensive player B1 touches the ball and then offensive player A2 recovers on the B7.
Ruling: Ball is returned to spot of fumble (B9). B's ball first-and-10 on B9.

A.R. 8.68 Fourth-and-four on B9. A1 fumbles on the B9 and the ball rolls out of bounds on the B4 without any player touching it.
Ruling: The ball is next put in snap at the spot of the fumble. B's ball first-and-10 on B9.

Simultaneous Recovery

Note: When a backward pass or fumble is a simultaneous or hidden ball recovery by two opposing players, the ball is awarded to the team making the pass or fumble.

Backward Pass Out of Bounds

Article 3 If a backward pass goes out of bounds between the goal lines, the ball is next put in play at the inbounds spot by the team in last possession. The ball is dead (7-5-5, p. 44). Rule 11, p. 69, governs if a backward pass is declared dead behind the goal line.

Enforcement Spot During Backward Pass or Fumble

Article 4 When a foul occurs during a backward pass or fumble, the basic spot of enforcement is the spot of the fumble or the spot of the backward pass. If the offensive team fouls behind the spot of the fumble or backward pass, the spot of enforcement is the spot of the foul (4-1-5-c, p. 87).

Exceptions: When the spot of a backward pass, fumble or foul is behind the line, the penalty is enforced from the previous spot. See 11-4-2, p. 71, for Safety.

Note: When the spot of the foul by B is behind A's goal line (during a scrimmage down) 11-6-3, p. 74 and 14-1-11, p. 89 do not apply. Enforcement is from the previous spot.

SUPPLEMENTAL NOTES

Backward Pass or Fumble Touching Goal Posts

(1) When a backward pass or fumble touches a goal post, ball is dead as it is out of bounds.

(2) For team possession during a backward pass or fumble (loose ball) or when it ends, see 3-2-3, p. 4 and 3-21-2-Note, p. 11.

Use of Hands on Backward Pass or Fumble

(3) After a backward pass or fumble touches the ground, any offensive player may legally block or otherwise use his hands or arms to push or pull an opponent out of the way but only in an actual personal attempt to recover (12-1-2 and 3, p. 75).

(4) A backward pass going out of bounds during the last two minutes of a half stops the clock (4-3-10-S.N. 5, p. 23).

A.R. 8.69 First-and-10 on A40. Runner A1 advances to the 50 where he passes backward. During the backward pass A2 holds on the A45. The ball goes out of bounds on the A48.
Ruling: Enforcement is from the spot of the foul as it is behind the basic spot (14-1-5-d, p. 87). A's ball first-and-15 on A35.

A.R. 8.70 Fourth-and-15 on A8. A punt is blocked and the ball is in the end zone when defensive player B1 pushes A1 out of the way to allow his teammate B2 to recover the ball in the end zone.
Ruling: The spot of enforcement is the previous spot as the foul by the defense occurred behind this line. A's ball first-and-10 on A13.

A.R. 8.71 Second-and-10 on B30. QB A1 fumbles on the B32. A defensive player bats the loose ball in flight to the B40 where A1 recovers.
Ruling: The enforcement spot is the previous spot as the foul is behind the line. Illegal bat (12-1-6, p. 77). A's ball first-and-10 on B20.

A.R. 8.72 Second-and-10 on B30. QB A1 passes backward and a defensive player bats the pass in flight. The ball goes to the B40 where A1 recovers.
Ruling: Legal bat (12-1-6-Exc., p. 77). A's ball third-and-20 on B40.

A.R. 8.73 Second-and-10 on B30. A backward pass or fumble hits the ground on the B35 and a defensive player bats the ball to the B40 where he recovers.
Ruling: Illegal bat of a loose ball. Enforcement is from the previous spot as it is behind the line. A's ball first-and-10 on B20.

A.R. 8.74 B1 intercepts a forward pass in his end zone and advances to his 2 where he fumbles. B1 recovers. During the fumble B2 fouls

a) in his end zone.
Ruling: Safety. Enforcement is from the spot of the foul as it is not from scrimmage. See 11-4-2, Page 71 and 14-1-11b, page 89.

b) on his five-yard line.
Ruling: B's ball first-and-10 on B1. Enforcement is from the spot of the fumble.

A.R. 8.75 Third-and-15 on B30. B1 intercepts a pass in the end zone and runs it out to the B20 where he throws a backward pass which hits the ground on the B15. A1 recovers on the ground and scores.
Ruling: Legal recovery and advance by A1. Touchdown A (8-4-1-b, p. 54).

A.R. 8.76 A backward pass or fumble by offensive Team A on its four-yard line comes to rest on the two-yard line. Offensive player A1 blocks B1 into the ball and causes it to cross the goal line.

a) A2 recovers in the end zone.
Ruling: Safety if A2 is downed in the end zone. May advance if he can (3-14-3, Note, p. 9).

b) B2 recovers in the end zone.
Ruling: Touchdown.

A.R. 8.77 Second-and-10 on B30. A ball is handed forward by QB to eligible receiver A2 who is behind his line. Receiver A2 muffs ball and defensive player B recovers on the B35 and goes to the 50.
Ruling: Legal advance. It is not a forward pass (3-21-2, Exception, p. 11), and it is treated as a fumble. B's ball first-and-10 on 50.

A.R. 8.78 Second-and-10 on B30. A ball is handed backward (no daylight) to ineligible receiver A1 on the B35. A1 muffs the ball and B1 recovers and goes to the 50.
Ruling: Legal recovery. A ball which is handed backward from one player to another (no daylight) and is dropped, shall be treated as a fumble. Either team may recover and advance B's ball first-and-10 on 50.

Rule 9   Scrimmage Kick

Section 1   Kick from Scrimmage

Article 1   The kicking team, behind the scrimmage line, may:

Punt

(a) punt;

(b) drop kick; or

(c) placekick.

Penalty: For a punt, drop kick, or placekick not kicked from behind the line of scrimmage: 10 yards from the spot of the kick.

Note: This is not considered illegally kicking the ball.

A.R. 9.1   The kicking team's punt is blocked and the kicker picks up the ball behind the line of scrimmage and throws a forward pass to end A1.
Ruling: Legal play (8-1-1, p. 45).

A.R. 9.2   A field goal attempt inside the B20 is blocked and bounces back toward the kicker. The kicker then kicks the loose ball on the ground from behind the line of scrimmage. The ball goes over the crossbar.
Ruling: No field goal. Illegal. Option of 10-yard penalty from the previous spot for kicking a loose ball (12-1-7, p. 77 and 14-1-5. Exception 1, p. 87), or touchback (11-6-1-b, p. 74).

Receivers
Recover

Article 2   If the receivers recover any kick, they may advance. For fair catch exception, see 10-1-2, p. 65.

Note: For team possession during a scrimmage kick (loose ball) or when it ends, see 3-2-3, p. 4.

Players on
Line During
Kick

Article 3   During a kick from scrimmage, only the end men as eligible receivers on the line of scrimmage at the time of the snap, are permitted to go beyond the line before the ball is kicked.

Cover
Men on
Kicks

Exception: An eligible receiver who, at the snap, is aligned or in motion behind the line and more than one yard outside the end man on his side of the line clearly making him the outside receiver, *replaces* that end man as the player eligible to go downfield after the snap. All other members of the kicking team must remain at the line of scrimmage until the ball has been kicked, unless kick is made from beyond the line.

Penalty: Loss of five yards from the previous spot for leaving before the ball is kicked.

A.R. 9.3   Fourth-and-12 on A40. On a poor snap from center, kicker A1 picks up the ball and gets the punt off. B1 catches the ball on the B10, and is tackled by center A2, who had crossed the line of scrimmage prior to the ball being kicked.
Ruling: Fourth-and-17 on A35. It is illegal for the center to cross the line prior to the ball being legally kicked. Five yard penalty from the previous spot. The defensive team would have the option of the ball on the B10, but would decline that option and take the penalty.

Illegal
Touching

Article 4   No player of the kickers may illegally touch a scrimmage kick before it has been touched by a receiver (first touching).

Legal
Touching by
Offense

Exception: When a kick is from behind the line, any touching behind the line by any offensive player is legal and any player may recover and advance.

Penalty: For illegal touching of a scrimmage kick: Receivers' ball at any spot of illegal touching or possession. Officials' time out when the ball is declared dead. This illegal touch does not offset a foul by the receivers during the down. See 4-3-1, p. 16; 4-3-7, p. 19; and 14-3-1-Exception 4, p. 92.

Note: When any player of the kicking team illegally recovers or catches a scrimmage kick inside the defensive five-yard line, carries it across the defense's goal line, it is a touchback. There is no penalty for delay. (This creates Exception to 4-3-9-k, p. 22, and 7-4-1-k, p. 42.)

A.R. 9.4   Fourth-and-10 on A40. A punt rolls to the receiving team's 25-yard line (B25) where a kicking team player illegally touches it. The ball rolls to the B15 where B1 picks it up and returns it to his 20-yard line.
Ruling: Receiver's ball on its 25-yard line where the kickers illegally touched it.

A.R. 9.5 Fourth-and-10 on A40. A punt is illegally touched by A1 on the B30. B1 picks it up, returns to the B35 and fumbles. A1 recovers there.
Ruling: B's ball on the B30 where the kicking team illegally first touched.

A.R. 9.6 Fourth-and-12 on A40. A punt is blocked. The kicker picks up the ball behind the line of scrimmage on the A30 and advances to midfield.
Ruling: Legal recovery and advance. Didn't make yardage for a first down. B's ball at midfield. See 9-1-4, Exception, p. 59.

A.R. 9.7 Fourth-and-10 on A40. Kicking team player A1 illegally touches a punt from the scrimmage on the B25. B1 then recovers and runs to the B35.

a) During a run, kicking team player A1 holds on the B30.
Ruling: Enforce from the end of the run (14-1-5-b, p. 87). B's ball first-and-10 on B40.

b) During a run, receiving team player B1 holds on the B30.
Ruling: Enforce from the spot of the foul (14-1-5-d, p. 87). B's ball first-and-10 on B20.

A.R. 9.8 Fourth-and-10 on A40. A punt is blocked and does not cross the line.

a) Receiver B1 bats or muffs the ball across the line (3-18-3, p. 11) where kicking team player A1 is the first player to touch the ball and recovers on the A45.
Ruling: Illegal touching of kick by A1. B's ball at the spot of illegal touching on A45 (officials' time out).

b) Receiver B1 deliberately kicks the ball across the line where A1 is the first player to touch the ball on the A45 and recovers it.
Ruling: Loss of 10 from the previous spot. Illegal touching is not an offset foul (14-3-1-Exception 4, p. 92). A's ball first-and-10 on the 50. See 9-1-4, p. 59.

A.R. 9.9 A punt is illegally touched by a kicking team player on the B4. He then carries it across the goal line.
Ruling: Touchback.

A.R. 9.10 A punt is illegally touched by A1 on the receiver's four-yard line. B1 tries to pick up the ball but muffs and A2 grabs it on the three-yard line and carries it across the line.
Ruling: Illegal touching. No touchback as second touching by A2 was not illegal touching. B's ball on its four-yard line.

A.R. 9.11 A punt is illegally touched on the B4 by kicking team player A1. He carries it into the end zone. During his run to the end zone, B1 clips in the end zone.
Ruling: Spot of enforcement is B20. B's ball first-and-10 on B10.

Kicker Out of Bounds

Article 5 No player of the kicker's team, who has been out of bounds, may touch or recover a scrimmage kick beyond the line until after it has been touched by B.

Penalty: Loss of five yards from the previous spot.

Kickers Recover Kick Made From Behind Line

Article 6 A ball is dead if the kickers recover a kick made from behind the line (other than one recovered behind the line unless a try-kick) (9-1-4, Exception, p. 59).

Kick Recovery Beyond Line

Note: When the kickers recover a legal kick from scrimmage anywhere in the field of play after it has first been touched by the receiving team beyond the line, it is first-and-10 for A. See 7-1-1-d, p. 35 and 9-1-4, Exception, p. 59.

A.R. 9.12 Fourth-and-five on A10. A punt crosses the line, touches B1 on the A12, and rebounds behind the line where A1 picks it up and is downed on the A14.
Ruling: The ball had first touched Team B beyond the line and wherever A recovers it would be a first down where the ball is finally dead. If the recovery by A is behind the line, A may advance. If the recovery is beyond the line, the ball is dead at the spot of recovery. First down for A in either situation. A's ball first-and-10 on A14.

Kick Touched at or Behind Line by Offense

Article 7 If a kick from behind the line is touched in the immediate vicinity of the neutral zone or behind A's line by B, such touching does not make A eligible to recover the kick beyond the line.

A.R. 9.13 Fourth-and-five on A10. A punt is partially blocked behind the line of scrimmage by B1. The ball bounces around behind the line and then rolls beyond the line of scrimmage where A2 recovers on the A16.
Ruling: Though B touched the ball, it was behind the line and legal. A2 illegally touched the ball beyond the line at the A16. Ball awarded to B at that spot. B's ball first-and-10 on A16.

Kick Rebounds Behind Line and Is Touched by Kickers

Article 8 Any touching behind the line by a kicking team player is legal, even if the kick crosses the line and returns behind the line before touching a receiver beyond the line.

Kick Simultaneously Recovered

Article 9 When a legal kick is simultaneously recovered by two eligible opposing players, or if it is lying on the field of play with no player attempting to recover, it is awarded to the receivers. See 7-4-2, p. 42.

A.R. 9.14 Fourth-and-10 on A40. A punt is first muffed by B1 on the B20 and then simultaneously recovered by B2 and A1 on the B15.
Ruling: Simultaneous recovery of a kick by two eligible opponents belongs to the receivers. B's ball first-and-10 on B15.

Article 10 Ordinarily there is no distinction between a player touching a ball or being touched by it.

Blocked Into Kick

Exception: If he is pushed or blocked into a kick by an opponent he is *NOT* considered to have touched it (3-14-3-Note, p. 9).

A.R. 9.15 Fourth-and-five on A30. A scrimmage kick comes to rest on B's 45.

    a) A1 blocks B1 into the ball and A2 recovers on the B40.
    Ruling: A2 illegally touched as B1 is not considered to have touched it. B's ball first-and-10 on B40.

    b) A1 pushes B1 into the ball and A2 recovers on the B40.
    Ruling: Illegal use of hands by kickers. Receiving team has option of taking illegal touch on the B40. A's ball fourth-and-15 on A20.

Offensive Use of Hands During Kick

Article 11 During a kick a kicking team player, after he has crossed his scrimmage line, may use his hands to ward off, push or to pull aside a receiver who is legally or illegally attempting to obstruct him. See 12-1-2-Exc. 3, and Note, p. 75.

Note: Illegal touching of a scrimmage kick does not offset a foul by the receivers during the down (9-1-4, p. 59).

Kick Recovered Behind Line by Offensive Team

Article 12 When a scrimmage kick from behind the line is recovered by the kicking team behind the line, it may advance.

Exception: If the kicking team recovers a kick behind the line during a Try-kick the ball is dead immediately (11-3-1, p. 69).

A.R. 9.16 Fourth-and-10 on A30. A punt crosses the line and before being touched by the receiving team, the ball rebounds behind the line. A1 recovers and advances to the A35.
Ruling: Legal recovery but necessary yardage for the first down for Team A not made. B's ball first-and-10 on A35.

A.R. 9.17 Fourth-and-10 on A30. A punt crosses the line and is first touched by receiver B1 beyond the line at the A35. Kicking team member A1 recovers beyond the line and advances.
Ruling: The ball is dead where A1 recovered. First-and-10 for A irrespective of the necessary line (9-6-1-Note, p. 60). A's ball first-and-10 on A35.

Kick Crosses Receivers' Goal Line

Article 13 When a kick from scrimmage, or unsuccessful field goal crosses the receivers' goal line from the impetus of the kick, it is a touchback *unless:*

(a) there is a spot of illegal touching by the kickers outside the receivers' 20 yard line; *or*

(b) the receivers after gaining possession, advance with the ball into the field of play; *or*

(c) kickers recover in end zone after receivers first touch ball in field of play.
    Ruling: Kickers' ball at spot of first touch in the field of play; *or*

d) kickers recover in end zone after receivers first touch ball in end zone.
Ruling: Kickers' ball at the 1 yard line.

Note: Receiving team players may advance any kick (scrimmage or unsuccessful field goal attempt) whether or not the ball crosses the receiver's goal line, Rule 9 (Kicks From Scrimmage) applies until the receiving team has gained possession. See 11-5-2, p. 72.

A.R. 9.18　Kicking team member A1 illegally touches a kick on the B10. Receiver B1 muffs on his five-yard line and A2 recovers in B's end zone.
Ruling: B's ball at spot of illegal touch (B10).

A.R. 9.19　On a scrimmage kick receiver B1 touches or muffs the ball on his 2 yard line.

　　a) B1 recovers and is downed in the end zone.
　　Ruling: Touchback.

　　b) Kicking player A1 recovers in the end zone.
　　Ruling: A's ball first-and-Goal on B's 2 yard line.

A.R. 9.20　On a scrimmage kick receiver B1 touches or muffs the ball in the end zone. The ball rebounds to B's three-yard line.

　　a) B1 recovers there.
　　Ruling: B's ball first-and-10 on B3.

　　b) Kicking team player A1 recovers on the B3.
　　Ruling: A's ball first-and-goal on B3.

A.R. 9.21　On a scrimmage kick receiver B1 gains possession in the end zone after touching the ball in the field of play.

　　a) B1 is tackled and downed in the end zone.
　　Ruling: Touchback.

　　b) B1 runs to the B4.
　　Ruling: B's ball first-and-10 on B4.

　　c) B1 fumbles and A1 recovers in the end zone.
　　Ruling: Touchdown.

A.R. 9.22　On a scrimmage kick receiver B1 gains possession and is downed in the end zone.

　　a) During the run B2 clips in the end zone.
　　Ruling: Safety (14-1-11, p. 89).

　　b) During the run B2 clips in the field of play.
　　Ruling: Receiver's ball first-and-10 on B10 (enforcement is from the succeeding spot after a touchback).

A.R. 9.23　Fourth-and-10 on B45. A1 first touches a punt on B's 5. In attempting to recover he forces the ball into B's end zone (new impetus) where B1 recovers and goes to the B10.
Ruling: B has the option of the spot of first touching (B5) but takes his advance on the B10. B's ball first-and-10 on B10.

Kick Touching Receivers' Goal Posts

Article 14　If a scrimmage kick *touches the receivers' goal posts* or crossbar either before or after touching a player of either team, it is a touchback unless it later scores a field goal. See 3-20-2, p. 10 and 11-5-1, p. 72.

A.R. 9.24　A kickoff to start the game hits the goal post before possession by the receivers.
Ruling: Touchback. Any legal kick (scrimmage or free kick) which touches the receivers' goal posts or crossbar other than one which scores a field goal is a touchback. See 11-6-1-d, p. 74 and 11-5-1, p. 72.

Kick Touching Kickers' Goal Posts

Article 15　If a scrimmage kick *touches the kickers' goal post or crossbar* (irrespective of where it was made from, or how it occurred), it is a safety. Goal post is out of bounds. See 11-4-1-b, p. 70.

A.R. 9.25　Fourth-and-10 on A10. A punt is blocked and the ball rebounds, hits the goal post, and rolls into the end zone where receiver B1 falls on it.
Ruling: Safety. Ball out of bounds.

Kick Out of Bounds

Article 16　For a scrimmage kick out of bounds between goal lines, see 7-5-1, p. 43. If the kick becomes dead behind a goal line, Rule 11-6, p. 74, governs.

Scrimmage Kick Spots of Enforcement

Article 17 If there is a foul from the time of the snap until a legal scrimmage kick ends, enforcement is from the previous spot. This includes a foul during a run prior to the legal kick (14-1-13-S.N. 1, p. 90), and running into or roughing the kicker (12-2-6, p. 78).

Spot Foul

Exception 1: Illegal touching of kick, fair catch interference, invalid fair catch signal, or unsportsmanlike conduct (blocking) after fair catch signal are all enforced from the spot of the foul.

Post-Possession Foul

Exception 2: If the receiving team commits a foul after the ball is kicked (ball crosses the scrimmage line) during a scrimmage down and the receivers possess and keep the kicked ball, the penalty for their infraction will be ruled as a foul after possession (post-possession) and must be assessed from:

1) The spot where possession was gained;
2) The spot where ball becomes dead; or
3) The spot of the foul.

Post-Possession Foul, Illegal Touch

Exception 3: In cases of illegal touch by kicker, and a post-possession foul by the receiving team, if the receiving team then loses possession, the ball reverts to the receivers and the spot of enforcement will be assessed from:

1) The spot where possession was gained;
2) The spot of the foul.

Note: See 14-3-1-Exc. 4, p. 92.

A.R. 9.26 Fourth-and-10 on A30. A1 fumbles behind the line, recovers, runs, and then punts from the A35. The ball goes out of bounds at B20.
Ruling: Enforcement is from A35. Ten yard penalty. A's ball fourth-and-15 A25.

A.R. 9.27 Kicking team member A1 illegally touches a punt on the B10. Receiver B1 recovers, advances, fumbles, and A2 recovers.
Ruling: The ball is awarded B on its 10 — the spot of illegal touch.

A.R. 9.28 Fourth-and-10 on 50. Receiver B1 illegally pulls the center to allow B2 the opportunity to block the kick. A2 successfully punts.
Ruling: First-and-10 on B45. B penalized for foul prior to the kick.

A.R. 9.29 Fourth-and-10 on 50. Punter A1 kicks and after the ball has crossed the scrimmage line, receiver B1 clips at the B40. B2 gains possession at the B16, runs to the B20, and is downed.
Ruling: B's ball first-and-10 on B8. Enforce from the spot of the possession. It is a post-possession foul and is considered an offensive foul.

A.R. 9.30 Fourth-and-10 on 50. Punter A1 kicks and after the ball crosses the scrimmage line, receiver B1 clips at the B40. The ball then goes out of bounds at the B8.
Ruling: B's ball first-and-10 on the B4. It is a post-possession foul.

A.R. 9.31 Fourth-and-10 on 50. Punter A1 kicks and after the ball has crossed the scrimmage line, receiver B1 clips at the B22. A2 touches the ball at the B18. A3 recovers on the B8.
Ruling: B's ball first-and-10 on the B4.

A.R. 9.32 Fourth-and-10 on 50. Punter A1 kicks and after the kick has crossed the scrimmage line, receiver B1 clips on the B30. Kicking team member A2 touches the ball at the B18. Receiving team member B2 muffs the kick on the B15. Kicking team member A3 recovers on the B10.
Ruling: Penalize B 15 yards from the previous spot. Team B did not gain possession and recovery by A3 was legal (touching by A2 was illegal). Not a post-possession foul.

Rule 10   Fair Catch

Section 1   Fair Catch

Valid Fair Catch

Article 1   A fair catch signal is valid beyond the line while kick is in flight when one arm is fully extended above the head and waved from side to side.

Shielding Eyes

Note: A receiver may legally raise his hand(s) to his helmet (but not above the helmet) in order to shield his eyes from the sun.

Penalty: For invalid fair catch signal: Snap by receivers five yards behind the spot of the signal. See 11-4-2, p. 71.

A.R. 10.1   Receiver B1 gives a fair catch signal on the B30 and catches the ball on the B28.

> a) B1's signal was arm fully extended straight up.
> **Ruling:** Invalid signal. B's ball first-and-10 on B25 (5 yards from signal).

> b) B1's signal was arm straight fully extended and waved from side to side.
> **Ruling:** Valid signal. B's ball first-and-10 on B28.

Dead Ball on Fair Catch

Article 2   If a receiver signals (valid or invalid) for a fair catch during any kick except one which does not cross the line, the ball is dead when caught by any receiver (Article 2, Exception). If the catcher did not signal, the ball is put in play by the receivers at the spot of the catch. See 10-1-6, p. 67.

Exceptions: Any receiver may recover and advance after a fair catch signal if the kick either:

1) touches the ground, or

2) touches one of the kickers in flight.

Delay Penalty for Undue Advance

Note: Undue advance by any receiver who catches (except as provided in above Exception) is delay of the game but does not preclude the fair catch. No specific distance is specified for undue advance as the ball is dead at the spot of the catch (3-9-1, p. 7) when caught (time out). If the catcher comes to a reasonable stop, there is no penalty for delay. Any penalty is enforced from the spot of the catch.

A.R. 10.2   Receiver B1 signals for a fair catch and then muffs. He recovers on the ground and then runs for a score.
Ruling: Touchdown. Legal advance as the ball touched the ground. If the kicking team recovered after the muff, the ball is dead at the spot of recovery.

A.R. 10.3   Receivers B1 and B2 signal for a fair catch. B1 muffs. B2 catches and comes to a legal stop.
Ruling: Fair catch. Either man may catch but not advance.

A.R. 10.4   Receiver B1 signals for a fair catch, muffs and B2 who did not signal catches ball.
Ruling: Not a fair catch. The ball is dead at the spot where it was caught. No option for fair catch and the ball is put in play by snap.

A.R. 10.5   Receiver B1 makes a valid fair catch signal on the B15. He catches on his 20, advances unduly and fumbles. Kicking team player A1 recovers.
Ruling: Five-yard penalty for delay from the spot where the ball was caught. The ball is dead when caught. B's ball first-and-10 on B15.

A.R. 10.6   Receiver B1 signals for a fair catch. The kick in flight strikes A1 after which it is caught by B2 who advances.
Ruling: Legal advance if any fair catch interference penalty is declined (choice).

Illegal Block After Fair Catch Signal

Article 3   If a player signals (valid or invalid) for a fair catch, he may not until the ball touches a player:

(a) block, *or*

(b) initiate contact with one of the kickers.

Penalty: For illegal block after a fair catch signal. Snap by receivers 15 yards from the spot of the foul.

A.R. 10.7   Receiver B1 signals a fair catch on the B28. He disregards the ball and blocks A2 on the B30 as the ball goes over his head and before touching any player and rolls out of bounds at B18.
Ruling: B's ball first-and-10 on B15.

A.R. 10.8   Receiver B1 signals a fair catch on the B12. He disregards the ball and blocks kicking team player A2 on the B8:

a) before or after the ball rolls into the end zone or out of bounds.
Ruling: B's ball first-and-10 on B4.

Fair Catch
Interference

Article 4   During any kick (except one which fails to cross the scrimmage line), if any receiver could reach the kick in flight, no player of the kickers shall interfere with either:

a) the receiver;

b) the ball; or

c) the receiver's path to the ball.

Penalty (a): For fair catch interference following a signal: Loss of 15 yards from the spot of the foul. Fair catch also awarded irrespective of a catch. See Article 5-Note, and Article 6, p. 67.

Penalty (b): For interference with the opportunity to make a catch (no prior signal made): Loss of 15 yards from the spot of the foul and offended team is entitled to put the ball in play by a snap from scrimmage. See 4-3-11-f, p. 24.

SUPPLEMENTAL NOTES

Receiver's
Right
to Ball

(1) A receiver running toward a kick in flight has the right of way and opponents must get out of his path to the ball. Otherwise it is interference irrespective of any contact or catch or whether any signal (valid or invalid) is given or not.

Fair Catch
Opportunity

(2) After a fair catch signal, the opportunity to make a catch does not end when a kick is muffed. The player who signaled fair catch must have a reasonable opportunity to catch the ball before it hits the ground without being interfered with by the members of the kicking team.

Intentional
Muff Prior to
Fair Catch

(3) An intentional muff forward prior to a catch in order to gain ground is an illegal bat (see 12-1-6, p. 77).

A.R. 10.9   Receiver B1 is about to catch a punt. Just before the ball reaches his hands, he is tackled by A1 on the B30, but he catches the ball while falling.
Ruling: Fair catch interference and fair catch awarded and 15 yards from the spot of the foul even though B1 did not signal. Same ruling would apply if B1 fumbles or muffs; however, the ball continues in play. B's ball first-and-10 on B45. B did not signal, so team B puts the ball in play by snap from scrimmage. See S.N., p. 67.

A.R. 10.10   Receiver B1 does not signal for a fair catch and runs toward the punted ball in an attempt to catch it. A1 is in his way on the B30 and B1 can't get to the ball. The ball rolls to the B20 where it is downed by B2.
Ruling: A 15-yard penalty from the spot of the foul for fair catch interference. No fair catch signal given. B's ball first-and-10 on B45. Ball in play by snap from scrimmage. See S.N., p. 67.

A.R. 10.11   Offensive end A1 goes downfield under a punt. He is struck by the kick in flight on the B30 while standing in front of B2 who is ready to catch. B2 had signalled a fair catch.
Ruling: Fair catch interference and B awarded fair catch whether the catch is made or not. Team B can advance the ball if it gets it and has option of yardage gained or penalty for fair catch interference. B's ball first-and-10 on B45. B2 signalled fair catch and gets option of fair catch kick or putting ball in play by snap from scrimmage. See S.N., p. 67.

A.R. 10.12   Receiver B1 signals for a fair catch and then muffs the ball on the B30. A1 catches at the B30 and advances. B1 could have caught the muffed ball.
Ruling: Fair catch interference as opportunity to make the catch does not end when the kick is muffed. The ball is dead when A1 catches the ball. B's ball first-and-10 on B45. (See 10-1-4, S.N. 2, p. 66).

**Receiver's
Rights on
Fair Catch**

Article 5   After a receiver has made a fair catch following a valid signal, an opponent:

(a) may not tackle him;

(b) may not block him; and

(c) must avoid contact with him.

Penalty: For running into the maker of a fair catch: Loss of 15 yards from the mark of the catch (snap or free kick). See 6-1-3 Note, p. 30.

**Fair Catch
in End Zone**

Note: Following a signal a receiver may make or be awarded a fair catch (for interference) in his end zone, but it is a touchback. See Article 4, Penalty (b), p. 66 for interference with the opportunity to make a catch.

A.R. 10.13   Fourth-and-10 on A20. Receiver B1 makes an invalid fair catch signal and catches on B40. He comes to a legal stop on B42 and is tackled by A1.
Ruling: B's ball first-and-10 on B35 (10-1-1, p. 65).

**Choices
After
Fair Catch**

Article 6   When a fair catch is declared for a team, the captain must choose (and his first choice is not revocable) either:

(a) A fair catch kick (punt, drop kick, or placekick without "Tee"), or

(b) A snap to next put the ball in play.

SUPPLEMENTAL NOTES

(1) If, with time remaining, receiver signals and makes a fair catch, receiver's captain has option of attempting a fair catch kick or putting ball in play by a snap from scrimmage.

(2) At the end of a period, if time expired when receiver signals and makes a fair catch, receiving team's only option is to fair catch kick.

(3) If, with time remaining, receiver signals for a fair catch, and is interfered with, and time remains, receiving team will be awarded a 15-yard penalty and has option of a fair catch kick or putting ball in play by a snap from scrimmage.

(4) At the end of a period, if time expired during a play in which receiver signalled for a fair catch, and he is interfered with, receiving team will be awarded a 15-yard penalty and has option of a fair catch kick or putting ball in play by a snap from scrimmage.

(5) If, with time remaining, receiver does *not* signal for a fair catch, and he is interfered with, receiving team will be awarded a 15-yard penalty, but must put the ball in play by a snap from scrimmage.

(6) At the end of a period, if time expires during a down and receiver does *not* signal for a fair catch, but he is interfered with, receiving team will be awarded a 15-yard penalty, but must put the ball in play by a snap from scrimmage.

(7) If time expired, and receiver did not signal for a fair catch and there was no foul, the period is over.

Rule 11   Scoring

Section 1   Value of Scores

Scores

Article 1   The team that scores the greater number of points during the entire game is the winner. Points are scored as follows:

(a) Touchdown .... 6 points
(b) Successful Try-for-Point .... 1 point
(c) Field goal .... 3 points
(d) Safety by opponents .... 2 points

Sudden Death

Article 2   To insure a winner in all NFL games the sudden death method of deciding a tie game is Rule 16, page 105.

Section 2   Touchdown

Touchdown Plays

Article 1   It is a touchdown:

(a) when a runner (3-38, p. 14) advances from the field of play and the ball touches the opponents' goal line (plane), *or*

(b) while inbounds any player catches or recovers a loose ball (3-2-3, p.4) on or behind the opponents' goal line.

SUPPLEMENTAL NOTES

Dead Ball

(1) The ball is automatically dead at the instant of legal player possession on, above, or behind the opponents' goal line.

Palpably Unfair Act

(2) The referee may award a touchdown when a palpably unfair act deprives the offended team of one.

Foul After Touchdown

(3) For a foul after a touchdown (between downs), see 3-11-2-d, p. 8 and 14-5, p. 95.

A.R. 11.1   Third-and-goal on B2. Runner A1 goes to the goal line with the ball over the plane of the goal line. He is tackled and fumbles and the defensive team recovers in the end zone.
Ruling: Touchdown. The ball is automatically dead at the instant of legal player possession on the opponent's goal line.

Section 3   Try-for-Point (Try)

Try-for-Point Attempt

Article 1   After a touchdown, the scoring team is allowed a Try-for-Point. This Try is an attempt to score one additional point, during one scrimmage down with the spot of snap.

(a) anywhere between the inbounds line *and*

(b) which is also two or more yards from the defensive team's goal line.

Note: All general rules for fourth-down fumbles apply to the try. (See 8-4-2-Exc 2, p. 55.)

During this Try:

Try Good

(a) if a Try-kick is legally kicked, one point is scored. (The conditions of 11-5-1 must be met.)

Try No Good

(b) if a kick cannot score, the ball becomes dead as soon as its failure is evident.

Try Point Awarded

(c) if there is no kick and the Try results in what would ordinarily be a safety by the defense or a touchdown by the offense, the point is awarded.

Whistle on Contact

(d) if there is illegal movement by offensive interior linemen and/or contact fouls which normally cause play to be whistled dead during ordinary scrimmage plays, they are to be handled the same way during Try-for-Point situations. Blow whistle immediately. See 7-3-4, p. 40.

A.R. 11.2   An attempted Try-kick is blocked. Offensive A1 recovers behind the line and advances across the goal line or recovers in defensive's end zone.
Ruling: No score in either case. The ball is dead as soon as its failure as a kick to score a try-for-point is evident.

A.R. 11.3 During a Try, placekick holder A1 fumbles. B1 kicks, bats, or muffs the loose ball (new impetus) on his 2 and it goes out of bounds behind the goal line.
Ruling: Ordinarily a safety (11-4-1, p. 70). Award point.

Start of Try

Article 2 The Try begins when the referee sounds his whistle for play to start.

Note: See 3-11-1-d, Exception, p. 7 for a foul after a touchdown and before the whistle.

A.R. 11.4 Offensive player A1 clips after runner A2 had scored a touchdown.
Ruling: Penalty is enforced from the succeeding spot which is the spot of the next kickoff. Spot of ball for Try is from 2 or more yards from B's goal line. Penalty is not enforced on Try.

Article 3 During a Try:

Unsuccessful Try

(a) if any play or a foul by the offense would ordinarily result in a touchback or loss of down, the try is unsuccessful and there shall be no replay.

Defensive Foul Results in Score

(b) if any play or a foul by the defense would ordinarily result in a safety, the point scores for the offensive team.

Replay Try

(c) if a foul by the defense does not permit the try to be attempted, the down is replayed and the offended team has the option to have the distance penalty assessed on the next try or on the ensuing kickoff.

Defensive Foul on Unsuccessful Extra Point

(d) if the defensive team commits a foul and the try is attempted and is unsuccessful, the offensive team may either accept the penalty yardage to be assessed or decline the distance penalty before the down is replayed.

(e) all fouls committed by the defense on a successful try will result in the distance penalty being assessed on the ensuing kickoff. See A.R. 14.27, p. 91.

Note: See 12-3-1-j, k, l, n, o, p, p. 83, that apply during a try.

A.R. 11.5 During a Try, runner A1 is downed on B's 2 in a side zone. During the run, B1 commits a personal foul.
Ruling: Replay from the previous spot or from the spot after enforcement.

A.R. 11.6 During a Try which is unsuccessful, defensive B1 commits a foul.
Ruling: Replay at previous spot or one yard line.

A.R. 11.7 During a Try which is successful, defensive B1 fouls.
Ruling: Try good and loss of yardage on kickoff against B (14-1-14, p. 91).

Double Foul Replayed

Article 4 If fouls are signalled against both teams during a Try, it must be replayed (14-3-1, p. 92).

No Score for Defense

Article 5 During a Try the defensive team can never score. When it gains possession, the ball is dead immediately.

Kickoff After Try

Article 6 After a Try the team on defense during the Try shall receive (6-1-1-b, p. 30).

Section 4 Safety

Safety

Article 1 When an impetus by a team sends the ball in touch (3-14-1, p. 8) behind its own goal, it is a safety if the ball is either:

(a) dead in the end zone in its possession, or

(b) out of bounds behind the goal line.

Intercepting Momentum

Exception: If the intercepting momentum of a pass interception carries the defensive player and the ball into the end zone, the ball is next in play at the spot of the interception by the defense, unless the intercepting defensive player without fumbling the ball advances it into the field of play. This is irrespective of any other act (muff, fumble, pass, or recovery) by the intercepting team.

(a) If a player of the team which intercepts the ball commits a foul in the end zone, it is a safety.

(b) If a player who intercepts the ball throws an illegal forward pass in the end zone, it is a safety. If his opponent intercepts the illegal pass thrown from the end zone, the ball remains alive (8-1-1-b, p. 45). If he scores, it is a touchdown.

(c) If a player of the team which intercepts the ball commits a foul in the field of play and the ball becomes dead in the end zone, the basic spot is the spot of the interception.

(d) If spot of interception is inside the B1-yard line, ball is to be spotted at B1.

SUPPLEMENTAL NOTES

Impetus

(1) The impetus is always attributed to the offense (team which passed, kicked, or fumbled) unless the defense creates a new impetus by a muff, bat, or illegal kick as specified (3-14-3, p. 9).

(2) See 8-1-1-S.N.3, p. 45 and Penalties under 8-1-2 to 5, pp. 46-47 for Exceptions to (b) of 11-4-1, p. 70, when there is an incompletion or pass violation by the offense behind its goal line during a forward pass from behind the line.

A.R. 11.8 Second-and-10 on A6. QB A1 throws a backward pass which is batted by defensive B1. The ball goes out of bounds behind the goal line.
Ruling: Safety. Legal bat and no change of impetus.

A.R. 11.9 Defensive B1 muffs a punt on his five-yard line. In attempting to recover he forces the ball (new impetus) into his end zone. See 3-14-3, p. 9.

a) where he recovers and is downed there.
Ruling: safety.

b) where he recovers and advances.
Ruling: legal advance.

c) where kicking team player recovers.
Ruling: Touchdown.

A.R. 11.10 Defensive B1 catches a punt on his four-yard line. He fumbles the ball on the B4 and kicking team player A1 bats the loose ball. The ball rolls over the end line.
Ruling: Touchback. See 11-6-1, p. 74 and 12-1-6, p. 77.

A.R. 11.11 Defensive B1 fumbles a punt on the B5 and it crosses his goal line. Kicking team player A1 recovers while he is touching or outside the side line at the instant of touching the ball.
Ruling: Safety. If it had been a muff (no new impetus or change of possession) and the same situation, it would be a touchback (11-6-1, p. 74).

A.R. 11.12 Second-and-10 on B20. Defensive B1 intercepts a legal forward pass on his two-yard line. His intercepting momentum carries him into the end zone where he is downed.
Ruling: B's ball first-and-10 on B2.

A.R. 11.13 Second-and-10 on B20. Defensive B1 intercepts a legal forward pass on the B4 and his intercepting momentum carries him into the end zone. He then runs it out to the B35.
Ruling: He is the only one who can advance it. B's ball first-and-10 on B35.

A.R. 11.14 Second-and-10 on B20. Defensive B1 intercepts a pass on the B6 and the intercepting momentum carries him into the end zone where he is tackled, fumbles and passing team player A1 recovers there.
Ruling: B's ball first-and-10 on B6.

A.R. 11.15 Second-and-10 on B20. Defensive B1 intercepts a legal forward pass on the B4 and his intercepting momentum carries him into the end zone where is is downed.

a) B2 clipped in the end zone.
Ruling: safety.

b) B2 clipped on the B2.
Ruling: B's ball first-and-10 on B1.

Foul Behind Offensive Goal

Article 2 It is a safety when the offense commits a foul (anywhere) and the spot of enforcement is behind its own goal line.

A.R. 11.16 Second-and-15 on A4. Runner A1 fumbles a handoff on his five-yard line. The ball rolls into the end zone where A1 bats or kicks the ball across the end line to prevent a recovery by the defense.
Ruling: Safety, whether the penalty is enforced from the spot of the foul or is declined. If the foul obviously deprives defensive B1 of recovery, it is a touchdown (11-2-1-S.N. 2. p. 69).

A.R. 11.17 Receiver B1 recovers a free kick in his end zone. While advancing, he fumbles while still in the end zone. The fumble is on the ground on the B2 where B3 deliberately kicks it.
Ruling: Safety (8-4-4, p. 56). The spot of enforcement is from the spot of the fumble.

A.R. 11.18 B1 catches a kickoff and makes a forward pass from behind his goal line.
Ruling: Safety. Team A may intercept and advance.

A.R. 11.19 Second-and-15 on A2. Runner A1 is downed two yards behind his goal line.

   a) A2 holds anywhere in the field.
     Ruling: Safety (14-1-11, p. 89).

   b) B1 holds on A1.
     Ruling: A's ball first-and-10 on A6 (12-1-4-Pen., p. 76 and 14-1-12-Exc. 7, p. 90).

A.R. 11.20 Second-and-16 on A4. QB A1 drops back to pass and throws a legal forward pass complete to end A2 who runs for a touchdown. Prior to the completion offensive tackle A3 holds in the end zone.
Ruling: No touchdown. Safety.

Ball in Play After Safety

Article 3 After a safety, the team scored upon must next put the ball in play by a free kick (punt, dropkick or placekick). No tee can be used. See 6-1-2 and 3, p. 30.

Exception: Extension of period (4-3-11, pp. 23-24).

Section 5 Field Goal

Legal Field Goal

Article 1 A field goal is scored when all of the following conditions are met:

   (a) The kick must be a placekick or dropkick made by the offense from behind the line of scrimmage or from the spot of a fair catch (fair catch kick).

   (b) The ball must not touch the ground or any player of the offensive team before it passes through the goal.

Entire Ball Through Goal

   (c) The entire ball must pass through the goal. In case wind or other forces cause it to return through the goal, it must have struck the ground or some object or person before returning.

Missed Field Goals

Article 2 All field goals attempted and missed from a scrimmage line beyond the 20-yard line will result in the defensive team taking possession of the ball at the scrimmage line. On any field goal attempted and missed from scrimmage inside the 20-yard line, the ball will revert to the defensive team at the 20-yard line.

Exception 1: If a field goal attempt is missed and the ball is touched or possessed by the receivers beyond the line of scrimmage in the field of play, the ball will not come back to the previous spot. All general rules for a kick from scrimmage will apply. If a foul occurs during the missed field goal attempt, Rule 9-1-17, p. 63 governs.

Exception 2: If a blocked field goal attempted from anywhere on the field is recovered behind the line of scrimmage by a defensive player and is not advanced, or if the blocked field goal attempt goes out of bounds behind the line of scrimmage, it is the receiving team's ball at that spot.

SUPPLEMENTAL NOTES

   (1) If a missed field goal is first touched by the receivers beyond the line in the field of play and the ball then goes out of bounds, it is the receivers' ball at the out of bounds spot.

   (2) If a missed field goal goes into the end zone and the ball then bounces back into the field of play, it is the receivers' ball at the previous spot if they did not touch the ball in the field of play (touchback if kick is made from inside B20).

   (3) If on a missed field goal the ball first touches a receiver in the end zone and returns to the field of play where it is not covered and then declared dead, the ball belongs to B at the previous spot (touchback if kick is made from inside B20).

Exception: If a receiver is the first to touch a missed field goal in the field of play, and the ball then rolls into the end zone where it is declared dead (no new impetus) in possession of B, it is a touchback.

A.R. 11.21 Fourth-and-10 on B35. On a field goal attempt the kick is wide and goes over the end line.
Ruling: B's ball first-and-10 on B35. The defensive team takes possession at the previous spot.

Note: See 12-3-1-j, k, l, n, p. 83, that apply during a field-goal attempt.

A.R. 11.22 Fourth-and-10 on B35. A field goal attempt is missed and:

> a) the ball rolls dead on the B10.
> **Ruling:** B's ball first-and-10 on B35.

> b) B1 touches and downs the ball on the B10.
> **Ruling:** B's ball first-and-10 on B10.

> c) B1 fair-catches the ball on the B10.
> **Ruling:** B's ball first-and-10 on B10.

A.R. 11.23 Fourth-and-10 on B35. On a field goal attempt B1 catches the ball on the B10 and:

> a) returns the ball to the B24.
> **Ruling:** B's ball first-and-10 on B24. If the defensive team runs a missed field goal, it continues as any other play.

> b) returns the ball to the 50.
> **Ruling:** B's ball first-and-10 on 50.

A.R. 11.24 Fourth-and-10 on B35. A field goal attempt is partially blocked behind the line and the ball rolls out of bounds on the B5:

> a) without touching any receiver beyond the line of scrimmage.
> **Ruling:** B's ball first-and-10 on the B35 (the previous spot).

> b) after touching a receiver beyond the line of scrimmage.
> **Ruling:** B's ball first-and-10 on the B5 (the spot of out of bounds).

A.R. 11.25 Fourth-and-10 on B35. A missed field goal hits in the end zone and bounces back into the field of play to the B3 where:

> a) no receiver touches the ball.
> **Ruling:** B's ball first-and-10 on the B35 (the previous spot).

> b) receiver B1 falls on the ball at the B3.
> **Ruling:** B's ball, first-and-10 on the B3.

> c) B1 picks up the ball on the B3 and runs to the B10.
> **Ruling:** B's ball first-and-10 on the B10.

> d) B1 picks up the ball, runs to the B10, is tackled and fumbles. A1 recovers and is downed on the B8.
> **Ruling:** A's ball first-and-goal on the B8.

A.R. 11.26 Fourth-and-10 on B35. On a missed field goal attempt B1 touches the ball on the B4 and the ball then rolls into the end zone (or over the end line) where it is declared dead in possession of team B.
Ruling: Touchback. B's ball first-and-10 on B20.

A.R. 11.27 Fourth-and-two on B10. A field goal is good. B1 punched A2 on the scrimmage line.
Ruling: Option for team A. Score for field goal or A's ball first-and-goal on B5. See 14-6. Disqualify B1. If a score taken, it is 15-yard penalty against B on kickoff (14-1-14, p. 91).

Fair Catch Kick

Article 3 On a free kick following a fair catch all general rules apply as for a field goal attempt from scrimmage. The clock starts when the ball is kicked.

Exception: The ball is no longer a free kick ball. The kicking team can't get the ball unless it had been first touched or possessed by the receivers.

A.R. 11.28 On a free kick from the B45 following a fair catch, offensive A1 touches and falls on the ball on the B33 without any defensive player touching the ball.
Ruling: B's ball first-and-10 on the B45 (the previous spot). The clock is started when the ball is kicked.

A.R. 11.29 On a free kick from the B45 following a fair catch, the ball goes out of bounds on the B10:

> a) without touching any player.
> **Ruling:** B's ball first-and-10 on the B45. The clock starts when the ball is kicked.

> b) after touching any offensive player.
> **Ruling:** B's ball first-and-10 on the B45. The clock starts when the ball is kicked.

No Artificial Media

Article 4 No artificial media shall be permitted to assist in the execution of a field goal and/or Try-For-Point after touchdown attempt.

Kickoff
Team

Article 5 After a field goal, the team scored upon will receive. See 6-1-2 and 3, p. 30.

Section 6 Touchback

Note: A touchback, while not a score, is included in this rule because, like scoring plays, it is a case of a ball dead in touch (3-14-2, p. 9).

Touchback
Situations

Article 1 When an impetus (3-14-3, p. 9) by a team sends a ball in touch behind its opponents' goal line, it is a touchback:

(a) if the ball is dead in the opponents' possession in their end zone; or

(b) if the ball is out of bounds behind the goal line (see 7-5-6-c, p. 44).

(c) if the impetus was a scrimmage kick unless there is a spot of first touching by the kickers outside the receivers' 20-yard line or if the receivers after gaining possession advance with the ball into the field of play (9-1-13-b, p. 61); or

(d) if any legal kick touches the receivers' goal posts or crossbar other than one which scores a field goal.

New Impetus

Note: The impetus is not from a kick if a muff, bat, juggle, or illegal kick of any kicked ball (by a player of either team) creates a new momentum which sends it in touch. See 3-14-1, Note, p. 9, for a specific ball-in-touch ruling.

A.R. 11.30 QB A1 throws a legal pass which is intercepted in the end zone by defensive B1. B1 tries to run it out and is downed in the end zone.
Ruling: Touchback. B's ball first-and-10 on B20.

A.R. 11.31 A punt is caught in end zone by defensive B1 who tries to run it out. He is tackled, fumbles and kicking team player A1 recovers in end zone.
Ruling: Touchdown for A1.

Article 2 It is a touchback:

Fair Catch
Interference
in End Zone

(a) when the kickers interfere with a fair catch behind the receivers' goal line (10-1-5-Note, p. 67); or

First
Touching
in End Zone

(b) when the kickers first touch a scrimmage kick behind the receivers' goal line.

(c) when a kicking team player illegally recovers or catches a punt inside the receiver's five-yard line and carries the ball across the defender's goal line. (See 9-1-4-Note, p. 59.)

A.R. 11.32 Fourth-and-10 on B35. A1 is touching the goal line with his foot when he downs the punted ball on the 1 yard line in the field of play.
Ruling: Touchback.

Defensive
Foul Behind
Offensive
Goal Line

Article 3 When the spot of enforcement for a foul by the defense is behind the offensive goal line, the distance penalty is enforced from the goal line (14-1-11, p. 89). See 8-4-4 for Exception, p. 56.

A.R. 11.33 Receiver B1 fumbles a punt and the ball rolls into his end zone where he recovers. B1 runs but is downed in the end zone. During B1's run A1 commits a personal foul.
Ruling: B1's ball first-and-10 on B15.

A.R. 11.34 Second-and-15 on A4. A backward pass or fumble by offensive A1 on the A2 strikes ground. Defensive B1 deliberately bats or deliberately kicks the ball into the end zone.

a) where A2 recovers.
Ruling: Touchback (or loss of 10 from previous spot). A's ball first-and-10 on A20.

b) where B2 recovers.
Ruling: Loss of 10 from the previous spot. A's ball first-and-10 on A14.

Article 4 After a touchback, the touchback team next snaps from its 20 (any point between the inbounds lines and the forward point of the ball on that line).

Rule 12   Player Conduct

Note — The spot of enforcement (when not stated), or the actual distance penalty, or both, are subordinate to the specific rules governing a foul during a fumble, pass, or kick, and these in turn are subordinate to the general provisions of Rule 14, page 87.

Section 1   Use of Hands, Arms, and Body

Article 1   No offensive player may:

Assisting Runner

(a) assist the runner except by individually blocking opponents for him.

Interlocked Interference

(b) use interlocking interference. Interlocked interference means the grasping of one another by encircling the body to any degree with the hands or arms; or

Pushing or Lifting Runner

(c) push the runner or lift him to his feet.

Penalty: For assisting runner or interlocked interference: Loss of 10 yards.

A.R. 12.1   Second-and-goal on B2. Runner A1 gets to the line of scrimmage and is stopped but A2 who is behind him pushes him from behind and shoves him over the goal line. **Ruling:** No score. Illegally assisting runner. A's ball second-and-goal on B12.

Legal Use of Hands

Article 2   A runner may ward off opponents with his hands and arms, but no other offensive player may use them to obstruct an opponent, by grasping with hands or encircling with arm in any degree any part of body, during a block.

Exceptions:

Legal Block

1) During a legal block (3-3, p. 5, 12-1-5, p. 77), when such hand or the hand of such arm is in contact with his own body.

Use of Hands During Loose Ball

2) During a loose ball, an offensive player may use his hands/arms legally to block or otherwise push or pull an opponent out of the way in a **personal legal** attempt to recover. See specific fumble, pass or kick rules and especially 6-2-5-S-N. 1, p. 32.

3) During a kick, an offensive player may use his hands/arms to ward off or to push or pull aside a receiver who is legally or illegally attempting to obstruct him beyond the line.

4) A runner may lay his hand on a teammate or push him into an opponent but he may not grasp or hold on to him.

Use of Hands Beyond Line

*Note: During a scrimmage kick, an offensive player may not use his hands to push or pull aside a receiver who is attempting to obstruct him **until** he has crossed his line. First touching of a scrimmage kick does not offset a foul by receivers during the down. See 9-1-4, p. 59 and 14-3-1, Exception 4, p. 92.*

Illegal Use of Body

Article 3   No player on offense may push or throw his body against a teammate either:

(a) in such a way as to cause him to assist runner, *or*

(b) to aid him in an attempt to obstruct an opponent or to recover a loose ball, *or*

(c) to trip an opponent, *or*

(d) in charging, falling, or using hands on the body into the back from behind above the waist of an opponent.

Penalty: For holding, illegal use of hands, arms or body of offense: Loss of 10 yards.

Note: Tripping by either team: Loss of 10 yards.

Defensive Holding

Article 4   A defensive player may not tackle or hold any opponent other than a runner. Otherwise, he may use his hands, arms, or body only:

(a) to defend or protect himself against an obstructing opponent;

Legal Contact Within Five Yards of Line

Exception 1: An eligible receiver is considered to be an obstructing opponent only to a point five yards beyond the line of scrimmage unless the player who receives the snap clearly demonstrates no further intention to pass the ball. Within this five-yard zone, a defensive player may make contact with an eligible receiver which may be maintained as long as it is continuous and unbroken. The defensive player cannot use his hands or arms to push from behind, hang onto, or encircle an eligible receiver in a manner that restricts movement as the play develops.

Illegal Contact

Beyond this five-yard limitation, a defender may use his hands or arms only to defend or protect himself against impending contact caused by a receiver. In such reaction, the defender may not contact a receiver who attempts to take a path to evade him.

(b) to push or pull him out of the way on line of scrimmage to cross it;

(c) in an actual attempt to get at or tackle runner;

(d) to push or pull him out of the way in an actual legal attempt to recover a loose ball;

(e) during a legal block on an opponent who is not an eligible pass receiver; or

(f) when legally blocking an eligible pass receiver above the waist.

Exception 2: Eligible receivers lined up within two yards of the tackle, whether on or behind the line, may be blocked below the waist *at* or *behind* the line of scrimmage. *No* eligible receiver can be blocked below the waist after he goes beyond the line.

Note 1: Once the quarterback hands off, is tackled, pitches the ball to a back, or if the quarterback leaves the pocket area (see 3-24, p. 12), the restrictions on the defensive team relative to offensive receivers will end, provided the ball is not in the air.

Note 2: Whenever a team presents an apparent punting formation, defensive action that would normally constitute illegal contact (chuck beyond five yards) will no longer be considered a foul.

Penalty: For illegal use of hands, arms or body by defense: Loss of five yards.

SUPPLEMENTAL NOTES

(1) An eligible pass receiver who takes a position more than two yards outside of his own tackle may not be blocked below the waist.

(2) The unnecessary use of the hands by the defense, except as provided in Article 4, is illegal and is commonly used in lieu of a legal block (Article 5).

(3) Any offensive player who pretends to possess the ball and/or one to whom a teammate pretends to give the ball, may be tackled provided he is crossing his scrimmage line between the offensive ends of a normal tight offensive line.

A.R. 12.2 Second-and-10 on B40. Defensive B1 holds offensive end A1 on the line of scrimmage. QB A2 can't throw the ball and is tackled at the 50.
Ruling: Not a forward pass. Enforcement is from the previous spot. A's ball first-and-10 on B35.

A.R. 12.3 Second-and-10 on A40. Eligible end A1 goes downfield to the B45 and is contacted (chucked) by defender B1 as A1 attempts to evade him. The pass falls incomplete.
Ruling: A's ball first-and-10 on A45. Illegal contact. Eligible receiver A1 is not considered an obstructing player as he was more than five yards beyond line of scrimmage.

A.R. 12.4 Second-and-10 on A40. Eligible receiver A1 is chucked by B1 at the scrimmage line. B1 then chucks back A2 on the A44 prior to the pass. The pass then falls incomplete.
Ruling: Legal use of hands as A1 and A2 were not the same player.

A.R. 12.5 Second-and-10 on A30. Eligible pass receiver A1 takes a position three yards outside his own tackle and is blocked below the waist at line of scrimmage. The pass falls incomplete.
Ruling: Illegal contact as eligible receiver was more than two yards outside of his tackle. Five yard penalty. A's ball first-and-10 on A35.

A.R. 12.6 Second-and-10 on A30. Eligible pass receiver A1 lines up one yard outside of his own tackle and is blocked below the waist at the line of scrimmage. Pass falls incomplete.
Ruling: Legal block as receiver was lined up within two yards of the tackle. A's ball third-and-10 on A30.

A.R. 12.7 During a pass *behind* the line (forward or backward) B1 uses his hands on potential receiver A1 who is *behind* A's line. B1 is not using his hands to ward off A1, to push or pull A1 out of the way in order to get to the runner (passer) or to push or pull him out of the way in an actual attempt to catch or recover a loose ball.
Ruling: Illegal use of hands by the defense. Loss of five yards and first down for A (14-8-5, p. 97).

Legal and Illegal Block

Article 5 A player of either team may block at any time provided it is not:

   (a) pass interference (8-2-1, p. 49);

   (b) fair catch interference (10-1-4, p. 66);

   (c) kicker (12-2-6, p. 78) or passer interference (12-2-11, p. 80);

   (d) unnecessary roughness (12-2-8, p. 79); or

   (e) illegal cut

A.R. 12.8 Defensive B1 blocks offensive A1 which allows B2 to recover a loose ball.
Ruling: Legal block. Can't use hands unless it is a personal attempt to recover but may block (12-1-5, p. 77).

Illegal Bat

Article 6 A player may not bat or punch:

   (a) a loose ball (in field of play) toward opponent's goal line;

   (b) a loose ball in any direction if it is in either end zone;

   (c) a ball in player possession.

Exceptions: *A forward pass in flight may be tipped, batted, or deflected in any direction by any player at any time. A backward pass in flight may not be batted forward by an offensive player.*

Note: A pass in flight that is controlled or caught may only be thrown backward.

Penalty: For illegal batting or punching the ball: Loss of 10 yards. For enforcement, treat as a foul during a backward pass or fumble (see 8-4-4, p. 56).

Illegally Kicking Ball

Article 7 No player may deliberately kick any loose ball or ball in player's possession.

Penalty: For illegally kicking the ball: Loss of 10 yards. For enforcement, treat as a foul during a backward pass or fumble (see 8-4-4, p. 56).

SUPPLEMENTAL NOTES

   (1) If a loose ball is touched by any part of a player's leg (including knee), it is not considered kicking and is treated merely as touching.

   (2) If the penalty for an illegal bat or kick is declined, procedure is the same as though the ball had been merely muffed. However, if the act (impetus) sends the ball in touch, 3-14-3, p. 9, applies.

   (3) The penalty for Article 6 and 7, p. 83, does not preclude a penalty for a palpably unfair act, when a deliberate kick or illegal bat actually prevents an opponent from recovering.

   (4) The ball is not dead when an illegal kick is recovered.

   (5) The illegal kick or bat of a ball in player possession is treated as a foul during fumble (8-4-4, p. 56).

A.R. 12.9 Second-and-15 on A2, Quarterback A1 fumbles a snap in the end zone. While the ball is loose on the ground there, A1 deliberately kicks it. The ball is last touched by B1 before going out of bounds on A's 2-yard line.
Ruling: Safety. See 7-5-6-d, p. 44; 11-4-2, p. 71 and 12-1-7, p. 77.

Section 2   Personal Fouls

Striking, Kicking or Kneeing

Article 1 All players are prohibited from:

   (a) striking with the fists;

   (b) kicking or kneeing; or

   (c) striking, swinging, or clubbing to the head, neck, or face with the heel, back, or side of the hand, wrist, forearm, elbow, or clasped hands. See 12-2-3, p. 78.

Note: It also is illegal for an opponent to club the passer's arm.

Penalty: For fouls in a, b, and c: Loss of 15. If any of the above acts is judged by the official(s) to be flagrant, the offender may be disqualified as long as the entire action is observed by the official(s).

Head
Slap

Article 2   A defensive player shall not contact an opponent above the shoulders with the palm of his hands except to ward him off on the line. The exception applies only if it is not a repeated act against the same opponent during any one contact.

Legal
Contact

Article 3   A defensive player may use the palm of his hands on an opponent's head, neck or face only to ward off or push him in an actual attempt to get at a loose ball.

No
Striking

Article 4   A player in blocking shall not strike an opponent below the shoulders with his forearm or elbows by turning the trunk of his body at the waist, pivoting or in any other way that is clearly unnecessary.

Penalty: For illegal use of the palm of the hands or for striking an opponent below the shoulders with the forearm or elbow: Loss of 15 yards.

Note: Any impermissible use of elbows, forearms, or knees shall be penalized under the unnecessary roughness rule; flagrantly unnecessary roughness shall be penalized under the same rule and the player disqualified.

A.R. 12.10   Second-and-10 on A30. Defensive player B1, on his initial charge, head slaps an offensive tackle on the helmet once with his open hand trying to get at runner A1. A1 is downed on the A35.
Ruling: Illegal. A's ball first-and-10 on the 50.

A.R. 12.11   Second-and-10 on A30. Defensive player B1, on his initial charge, head slaps an offensive tackle on his helmet repeatedly with his open hand in trying to get at a runner. The runner is downed on the A35.
Ruling: Illegal. Loss of 15 yards. A's ball first-and-10 on the 50.

Grasping
Face Mask

Article 5   No player shall grasp the face mask of an opponent.

Penalty: Incidental grasping of the mask — five yards. Not a personal foul (if by the defense there is no automatic first down). Twisting, turning, or pulling the mask — 15 yards. A personal foul. The player may be disqualified if the action is judged by the official(s) to be of a vicious or flagrant nature.

A.R. 12.12   Third-and-10 on A30. Runner A1 runs to the A33, where he is tackled by B1, who incidentally grasps A1's face mask on the tackle, but it is not a twist, turn, or pull.
Ruling: A's ball, third-and-two, on A38. It is not an automatic first down. Five-yard penalty.

Running
Into Kicker

Article 6   No defensive player may run into or rough a kicker who kicks from behind his line unless such contact:

(a) is incidental to and after he has touched the kick in flight.

(b) is caused by the kicker's own motions.

(c) occurs during a quick kick;

(d) occurs during a kick or after a run behind the line, or:

(e) occurs after the kicker recovers a loose ball on the ground:

(f) is caused because a defender is blocked into the kicker.

Running,
Roughing
Kicker

Penalty: For running into the kicker: Loss of five yards from the previous spot, no automatic first down. (This is not a personal foul). For roughing the kicker, loss of 15 yards from the previous spot. (This is a personal foul, and also disqualification if flagrant).

SUPPLEMENTAL NOTES

(1) Avoiding the kicker is a primary responsibility of defensive players if they do not touch the kick.

(2) Any contact with the kicker by a defensive player who has not touched the kick is running into the kicker.

(3) Any unnecessary roughness committed by defensive players is roughing the kicker. Severity of contact and potential for injury are to be considered.

(4) When two defensive players are making a bona fide attempt to block a kick from scrimmage (punt, drop kick, and/or placekick) and one of them runs into the kicker after the kick has left the kicker's foot at the same instant the second player blocks the kick, the foul for running into the kicker shall *not* be enforced, unless in the judgment of the referee, the player running into the kicker was clearly the direct cause of the kick being blocked.

(5) If in the judgment of the referee any of the above action is unnecessary roughness, the penalty for roughing the kicker *shall* be enforced from the previous spot as a foul during a kick.

A.R. 12.13 Kicker A1 in punt formation muffs a snap. He recovers on the ground and then kicks. A1 is run into, blocked or tackled by B1 who had started his action when A1 first recovered.
Ruling: Legal action by B1.

A.R. 12.14 A1 receives a snap. He starts to run but after a few strides, he kicks from behind his line. As A1 kicks, he is tackled or run into.
Ruling: The kicker is to be protected, but the referee should use his judgment when ordinary line play carries an opponent into such a kicker or at any time when it is not obvious that a kick is to be made (quick kick).

A.R. 12.15 Fourth-and-12 on B30. On a field goal attempt which is not good, receiver B1 runs into the kicker without touching the ball.
Ruling: A's ball fourth-and-7 on B25. Running into the kicker. If the field goal has been good, no penalty would be enforced on the succeeding kickoff, since it was not a personal foul.

No Piling On

Article 7 There shall be no piling on (3-22, p. 12).

Penalty: For piling on: Loss of 15 yards.

Note: An official should prevent piling on a prostrate or helpless runner before the ball is dead. When opponents in close proximity to such a runner are about to pile on, and further advance is improbable, the official covering should sound his whistle for a dead ball, in order to prevent further play and roughness. See 7-4-1-d, p. 41.

A.R. 12.16 The holder of a Try-kick is run into or piled on and the act is not incidental to blocking the kick.
Ruling: Unnecessary roughness. Such a player is obviously out of play unless the kick is blocked, and even then until he arises and participates in play. See 11-3-1, p. 69, 14-1-14, p. 91 and 14-6, Exception 6, p. 96.

Unnecessary Roughness

Article 8 There shall be no unnecessary roughness. This shall include, but will not be limited to:

Striking

(a) striking an opponent anywhere above the knee with the foot or any part of the leg below the knee;

Roughing Runner

(b) tackling the runner when he is clearly out of bounds;

(c) throwing the runner to the ground after the ball is dead;

(d) running or diving into, or throwing the body against or on a ball carrier who falls or slips to the ground untouched and makes no attempt to advance, before or after the ball is dead;

(e) running or diving into, or throwing the body against or on a player obviously out of the play, before or after the ball is dead;

Tackling Runner Out of Bounds

(f) contacting a runner out of bounds. Defensive players must make an effort to avoid contact. Players on defense are responsible for knowing when a runner has crossed the boundary line, except in doubtful cases where he might step on a boundary line and continue parallel with it;

Spearing

(g) a tackler using his helmet to butt, spear, or ram an opponent; and

(h) any player who uses the crown or top of his helmet against a passer, a receiver in the act of catching a pass, or a runner who is in the grasp of a tackler;

(i) any player who hooks his fingers under the helmet of an opponent and forcibly twists his head.

Penalty: For unnecessary roughness: Loss of 15 yards. *The player may be disqualified if the action is judged by the official(s) to be flagrant.*

A.R. 12.17 Third-and-20 on A30. Runner A1 runs to the A33, where he is tackled by B1, who hooks his fingers under the front of the runner's helmet, but not his facemask, and forcibly twists his head.
Ruling: 15 yards for unnecessary roughness. It is an automatic first down. A's ball, first-and-10, on A48.

Clipping

Article 9 There shall be no clipping from behind below the waist (3-5, p. 6). This does not apply to offensive blocking in close line play or a runner.

Penalty: For clipping: Loss of 15 yards.

Close
Line
Play

SUPPLEMENTAL NOTES

(1) Close line play is that which occurs in an area extending laterally to the position originally occupied by the offensive tackles and longitudinally three yards on either side of each line of scrimmage.

Exception: An offensive lineman may not clip a defender who, at the snap, is aligned on the line of scrimmage opposite another offensive lineman who is more than one position away when the defender is responding to the flow of the ball away from the blocker.

Example: Tackle cannot clip nose tackle on sweep away.

(2) Doubtful cases involving a side block or the opponent turning his back as the block is being made are to be judged according to whether the opponent was able to see or ward off the blocker.

(3) The use of hands from behind above the waist on a non-runner is illegal use of hands (see 12-1-3, p. 75).

(4) The use of hands on the back is not clipping when it is by:

a) one of the kickers in warding off a receiver, while going downfield under a kick, or

b) any player in an actual personal legal attempt to recover a loose ball.

(5) It is not considered clipping if:

a) a blocker is moving in the same direction as the opponent, and while his head is in advance of the opponent he then contacts the opponent from behind with any part of his body, or

b) in any case if an official has not observed the blocker's initial contact.

A.R. 12.18 Second-and-10 on B30. B1 is hit from behind, below the waist at the B25 by A2 throwing his body across the back of B1's legs. Runner A1 is downed on B15.
Ruling: Clipping. A's ball second-and-20 on B40.

A.R. 12.19 Second-and-10 B30. A2 pushes B1 from behind above the waist at the B25. Runner A1 is down on B15.
Ruling: Illegal use of hands, A's ball second-and-15 on B35.

Crackback
(Illegal)

Article 10 At the snap, an offensive player who is aligned in a position more than two yards laterally outside an offensive tackle, or a player who is in a backfield position at the snap and then moves to a position two or more yards outside a tackle, may not clip an opponent anywhere, nor may he contact an opponent below the waist if the blocker is moving forward to the position where the ball was snapped from, and the contact occurs within an area five yards on either side of the line of scrimmage.

Note: A player aligned two or more yards outside a tackle at the snap is designated as being flexed.

Penalty: Illegal crackback block: Loss of 15 yards.

A.R. 12.20 Second-and-10 on A40. Flanker A1 sets up five yards outside of offensive tackle A2. At snap A1 comes back and crackback blocks B1. Contact is made at the A38 behind the offensive tackle's original position. Runner goes to 50.
Ruling: A's ball second-and-25 on A25. Illegal crackback block. Penalize from previous spot.

Roughing
Passer

Article 11 A player of the defensive team shall not run into a passer (legal forward pass) after the ball has left his hand.

Penalty: For running into the passer: Loss of 15 yards from the previous spot, and disqualification when flagrant (special attention of the referee).

SUPPLEMENTAL NOTES

Grasp and Control

(1) The NFL is committed to a policy of protecting the quarterback. Officials are to blow the play dead as soon as the quarterback is clearly in the grasp and control of any tackler behind the line and his safety is in jeopardy.

(2) A passer who is standing still or fading backwards is obviously out of the play after the ball has left his hands or hand and is to be protected until the pass ends or until he starts to move into a distinctly defensive position.

(3) The referee must determine whether an opponent had a reasonable chance to stop his momentum during an attempt to block or bat a pass or to tackle the passer while he was still in possession. See 12-2-11, p. 80.

(4) A passer may use his hands or arms to ward off an opponent prior to a pass from behind the line, but thereafter, and only while he is obviously out of the play, as a purely protective action to ward him off.

(5) The general philosophy of roughing-the-passer rules will be to construe as a violation any unwarranted or flagrant physical acts against passers which, in the judgment of the Referee, are not called for in the circumstances of the play. For example, this would prohibit a rusher from committing such intimidating and punishing acts as "stuffing" the quarterback into the ground or unnecessarily wrestling or driving him down after he has thrown the ball, and would prohibit a rusher who has an unrestricted path to the passer from flagrantly hitting him while going after his knees or below.

Note: Current rules prohibiting use of crown of the helmet as a weapon and hitting the passer in the head and neck area continue to apply.

A.R. 12.21 Passer A1 is run into or tackled by defensive B1 after a pass. B1 had started his action prior to the pass.
Ruling: A legal action, unless the official rules that B1 had a reasonable chance to avoid or minimize the contact and made no attempt to do so.

A.R. 12.22 Defensive B1 bats or punches the ball out of the potential passer's hand.
Ruling: Illegal bat or punch. Loss of 10 yards from the previous spot (12-1-6, p. 77).

Blocking Below Waist On Kicks and Change of Possession

Article 12 All players on the receiving team are prohibited from blocking below the waist during a down in which there is a kickoff, safety kick, or punt. All players on the kicking team are prohibited from blocking below the waist after a kickoff, safety kick, or punt. On all other plays, neither team may block below the waist after there is a change of possession.

Penalty: Loss of 15 yards

A.R. 12.23 Third-and-6 on B26. B1 intercepts a forward pass in the end zone and runs it out to the B31. During B1's run, A2 blocks B3 low from the side at the B28, so that A4 could tackle B1 at the B31.
Ruling: Illegal block. B's ball first-and-10 on B46 (12-2-12, p. 81).

Use of Helmet as a Weapon

Article 13 A player may not use a helmet (that is no longer worn by anyone) as a weapon to strike, swing at, or throw at an opponent.

Penalty: For illegal use of a helmet as a weapon: Loss of 15 yards and automatic disqualification.

Chop Block Pass

Article 14 During a forward pass or any play in which an offensive player indicates an apparent attempt to pass block, no offensive player may deliberately block (chop) a defensive player in the area of the thigh or lower while the defensive player is physically engaged by the blocking attempt of another offensive player.

Chop block would not apply to an offensive player who fires out aggressively at an opponent at the snap unless the offensive player blocks in the area of the thigh or lower and the defensive player is then double teamed by another offensive player.

Exception: If while a tackle is showing pass set, even though not engaged, a team-mate lined up outside the tackle may not deliberately block (chop) down in the area of the thigh or lower on an opponent who is in a position over the tackle.

Note: If the defensive end lines up over any part of the tight end, this rule does not apply.

Penalty: For Chop Block-Pass: loss of 15 yards.

Chop
Block
Run

Article 15 During a running play, if an offensive player who was on the line of scrimmage at the snap engages a defensive player above the waist, whether on or behind the line of scrimmage in an area extending laterally to the positions originally occupied by the tight end on either side, no offensive player who was lined up in the backfield at the snap may deliberately block (chop) the engaged defensive player in the area of the thigh or lower.

Penalty: For Chop Block-Run: loss of 15 yards.

Section 3 Unsportsmanlike Conduct

Article 1 There shall be no unsportsmanlike conduct. This applies to any act which is contrary to the generally understood principles of sportsmanship. Such acts specifically include, among others:

(a) The use of abusive or insulting language or gestures to opponents, teammates, or officials.

Taunting

(b) The use of baiting or taunting acts or words that engender ill will between teams.

Demonstrations

(c) Any prolonged, excessive, or premeditated celebration by individual players or groups of players will be construed as unsportsmanlike conduct.

Note: Spontaneous expressions of exuberance will be permitted.

Penalty: (a) and (b): Loss of 15 yards from succeeding spot.

Penalty: (c): Loss of five yards from succeeding spot and down is repeated. (If by the defense, there is no automatic first down and down repeated.) Exception: If score resulted from play, score counts and enforce from succeeding spot.

(d) The defensive use of acts or words designed to disconcert an offensive team at the snap. Sound your whistle to stop play.

(e) Concealing a ball underneath the clothing or using any article of equipment to simulate a ball.

Lingering

(f) Using entering substitutes, legally returning players, substitutes on sidelines, or withdrawn players to confuse opponents. The clarification is also to be interpreted as covering any lingering by players leaving the field when being substituted for. See 5-2-1, p. 25, 26.

Hide
Out

(g) An offensive player lines up or is in motion less than five yards from the sideline in front of his team's designated bench area. However, an offensive player can line up less than five yards from the sidelines on the same side as his team's player bench, as long as he is not in front of the designated bench area.

(h) Repeatedly abusing the substitution rule (time in) in attempts to conserve or consume time. See 5-2-2, p. 27.

(i) More than two successive 40/25 second penalties (after warning) during same down.

Leverage

(j) Jumping or standing on a teammate or opponent to block or attempt to block an opponent's kick.

(k) Placing a hand or hands on a teammate to get leverage for additional height in the block or attempt to block an opponent's kick.

(l) Being picked up by a teammate in a block or an attempt to block an opponent's kick.

(m) Throwing a punch, or a forearm, or kicking at an opponent even though no contact is made.

Leaping

(n) Clearly running forward and leaping in an obvious attempt to block a field goal or point after touchdown and landing on players within one yard of the line of scrimmage unless the leaping player was originally lined up within one yard of the line of scrimmage when the ball was snapped.

Goal
Tending

Note: Goal-tending by any player leaping up to deflect a kick as it passes above the crossbar of a goalpost is prohibited.

(o) A punter, placekicker, or holder who simulates being roughed or run into by a defensive player.

Penalty: For unsportsmanlike player conduct (d) through (o): Loss of 15 yards from:

a) the succeeding spot if the ball is dead.

b) the previous spot if the ball was in play.

If the infraction is flagrant, the player is also disqualified.

Note: Under no condition is an official to allow a player to shove, push, strike, or lay a hand on him in an offensive or unsportsmanlike manner. Any such action must be reported to the Commissioner.

Fouls to
Prevent Score

Article 2 The defense, when near its goal line, shall not commit successive or continued fouls (half distance penalties) to prevent a score.

Penalty: For continuous fouls to prevent a score: if the violation is repeated after a warning, the score involved is awarded to the offensive team.

Palpably
Unfair Act
(Player)

Article 3 A player or substitute shall not interfere with play by any act which is palpably unfair.

Penalty: For a palpably unfair act: Offender may be disqualified. The Referee, after consulting his crew, enforces any such distance penalty as they consider equitable and irrespective of any other specified code penalty. The Referee could award a score. 15-1-6, p. 99.

Rule 13　Non-Player Conduct

Section 1　Non-Player Conduct

Non-Player Fouls

Article 1　There shall be no unsportsmanlike conduct by a substitute, coach, attendant, or any other non-player (entitled to sit on a team's bench) during any period or time out (including between halves).

SUPPLEMENTAL NOTES

(1) "Loud speaker" coaching from the sidelines is not permissible.

(2) A player may communicate with a coach provided the coach is in his prescribed area during dead ball periods.

Attendants on Field Only on Team Time Outs

Article 2　Either or both team attendants and their helpers may enter the field to attend their team during a team time out by either team. No other non-player may come on the field without the referee's permission, unless he is an incoming substitute (5-2-1, p. 25).

Bench Credentials

Article 3　With the exception of uniformed players eligible to participate in the game, all persons in a team's bench area must wear a visible credential clearly marked "BENCH." For all NFL games — preseason, regular-season, and postseason — the home club will be issued a maximum of 27 credentials and the visiting club will be issued a maximum of 25 credentials for use in its bench area. Such credentials must be worn by coaches, players under contract to the applicable club but ineligible to participate in the game, and team support personnel (trainers, doctors, equipment men). From time to time, persons with game-services credentials (e.g., oxygen technicians, ball boys) and authorized club personnel not regularly assigned to the bench area may be in a team's bench area for a brief period without bench credentials. Clubs are prohibited from allowing into their bench areas any persons who are not officially affiliated with the club or otherwise serving a necessary game day function.

Restricted Areas

Article 4　All team personnel must observe the zone restrictions applicable to the bench area and the border rimming the playing field. The only persons permitted within the solid six-foot white border (1-1, p. 1) while play is in progress on the field are game officials. For reasons involving the safety of participating players whose actions may carry them out of bounds, officials' unobstructed coverage of the game, and spectators' sightlines to the field, the border rules must be observed by all coaches and players in the bench area. Violators are subject to penalty by the officials.

Movement On Sidelines

Article 5　Coaches and other non-participating team personnel (including uniformed players not in the game at the time) are prohibited from moving laterally along the sidelines any further than the points that are 18 yards from the middle of the bench area (i.e., 32-yard lines to left and right of bench areas when benches are placed on opposite sides of the field). Lateral movement within the bench area must be behind the solid six-foot white border (see Article 4 above).

Non-Bench Areas

Article 6　Clubs are prohibited from allowing into the non-bench areas of field level any persons who have not been accredited to those locations by the home club's public-relations office for purposes related to news-media coverage, stadium operations, or pregame and halftime entertainment. The home club is responsible for keeping the field level cleared of all unauthorized persons. Photographers and other personnel accredited for field-level work must not be permitted in the end zones or any other part of the official playing field while play is in progress.

Penalty: For illegal acts under Articles 1 through 6 above: Loss of 15 yards from team for whose supposed benefit foul was made.

Enforcement is from:

a)　Succeeding spot if the ball is dead.

b)　Previous spot if the ball was in play.

For a flagrant violation, the referee may exclude offender or offenders from the playing field enclosure for the remainder of the game.

Note: See 4-1-4, Note, p. 15, for a foul by non-players between halves.

Palpably
Unfair Act
(Non-Player)

Article 7 A non-player shall not commit any act which is palpably unfair.

Penalty: For a palpably unfair act, see 12-3-3, p. 83. The referee, after consulting the crew, shall make such ruling as they consider equitable (15-1-6 and Note, p. 99).

Note: Various actions involving a palpably unfair act may arise during a game. In such cases, the officials may award a distance penalty in accordance with 12-3-3, p. 83, even when it does not involve disqualification of a player or substitute. See 17-1, p. 107.

Rule 14 Penalty Enforcement

(Governing all cases not otherwise specifically provided for)

Section 1 Spot From Which Penalty in Foul is Enforced

Spots of
Enforcement

Article 1 The general provisions of Rule 14 govern all spots of enforcement.

Note: The spot of enforcement for fouls by players or the actual distance penalty or both, when not specific, are subordinate to the specific rules governing a foul during a fumble, pass or kick. These in turn are both subordinate to Rule 14.

> **A.R. 14.1** Second-and-15 on A4. QB A1 throws a legal pass which is incomplete. A2 held in end zone.
> **Ruling:** Safety or A's ball third-and-15 on A4.

Fouls
Between
Downs

Article 2 When a foul by a player occurs between downs, enforcement is from the succeeding spot (14-5-S.N. 3, p. 95).

Fouls
by
Non-Players

Article 3 Penalties for fouls committed by non-players shall be enforced as specifically provided under Rule 13, p. 85.

Enforcement
Spot Not
Governed

Article 4 When the spot of enforcement is not governed by a general or specific rule, it is the spot of the foul.

Basic Spots
of
Enforcement

Article 5 The basic spots of enforcement (3-11-1, p. 7) are:

(a) The previous spot for a forward pass (8-3-2, p. 53); a scrimmage kick (9-1-17, p. 63); or a free kick (6-2-5, p. 32).

(b) The succeeding spot on a running play (14-1-12, p. 90).

(c) The spot of snap, backward pass, or fumble (8-4-4, p. 56).

(d) The spot of the foul (14-1-4, p. 87; 14-1-13, p. 90).

Note: If a foul is committed during a run, a fumble, or a backward pass, the penalty is assessed from the basic spot if:

i)   Defense fouls in advance of the basic spot

ii) Defense fouls behind the basic spot

iii) Offense fouls in advance of the basic spot

If the offense fouls behind the basic spot, enforcement is from the spot of the foul (3 and 1).

Exceptions:

1) All fouls committed by the offensive team behind the line of scrimmage (except in the end zone) shall be penalized from the previous spot. If the foul is in the end zone, it is a safety (14-1-11-b, p. 89).

2) If a runner (3-27-1, p. 12) is downed behind the line of scrimmage (except in the end zone) and the foul by an offensive player is beyond the line of scrimmage, enforcement shall be from the previous spot. If the runner is down in the end zone, it is a safety (11-4-1-a, p. 70).

> **A.R. 14.2** Second-and-10 on A30. Runner A1 is downed on the A35. Defensive B1 illegally uses his hands on the A45 during run.
> **Ruling:** The defensive foul is in advance of the basic spot (A35 where downed). Penalize from the basic spot (A35). A's ball first-and-10 on A40.

> **A.R. 14.3** Second-and-10 on A30. Runner A1 is downed on the A35. Offensive player A2 uses his hands illegally on the A45.
> **Ruling:** The offensive foul is in advance of the basic spot (A35 where downed). Penalize from the basic spot (A35). A's ball second-and-15 on A25.

> **A.R. 14.4** Second-and-10 on A30. Runner A1 is downed on the A40. An offensive player illegally uses his hands on the A35.
> **Ruling:** The offensive foul is behind the basic spot (spot where downed). Penalize from the spot of the foul (A35). A's ball second-and-15 on A25.

A.R. 14.5   Second-and-10 on A30. Quarterback A1 is downed on the A40. Offensive player A2 held on the A25.
Ruling: Penalize 10 yards from the previous spot as the offensive foul was behind the line of scrimmage. A's ball second-and-20 on A20.

A.R. 14.6   Second-and-10 on A30. Runner A1 is downed on the A25. An offensive player held on the A32.
Ruling: A's ball second-and-20 on the A20. The offensive runner was downed behind the line of scrimmage. Enforcement is from the previous spot. Team B has option of refusing the penalty and taking the play which would then be A's ball third-and-15 on the A25 (14-6, p. 96).

Fouls Out of Bounds

Article 6   When the spot of a player foul is out of bounds between the end lines, it is assumed to be at an inbounds line on a yard line (extended) through the spot where the foul was committed. If this spot is behind an end line, it is assumed to be in the end zone. See 7-3-7, p. 41, and 14-1-11, p. 89.

Continuing Action Fouls When Game Clock is Stopped

Article 7   The penalty is enforced from the succeeding spot as a foul between downs (14-5, p. 95) if there is a continuing action foul (subsequent foul) (3-11-2-a, p. 8) after:

(a) a ball is dead in touch;

(b) an out of bounds;

(c) a kick is (legally or illegally) recovered by the kickers;

(d) an incompletion; *or*

(e) a ball is dead when caught after a fair catch signal or interference with one

See 6-2-4, p. 32 and 9-1-4, p. 59, Note for Exceptions to (a) and (c) respectively.

A.R. 14.7   Second-and-10 on A30. Runner A1 goes out of bounds on the A35. Offensive player A2 then clips B1 either on the A40 or A30.
Ruling: Enforce from the succeeding spot (out of bounds) as a foul between downs. Continuing action foul. The down is counted as the foul occurred after the ball was dead from runner A1 going out of bounds. A's ball third-and-20 on A20.

A.R. 14.8   Fourth-and-10 on A30. A punt goes to the B30 where kicking team player A1 illegally touches the ball and then falls on it there, after which:

a) kicking team player A2 clips any place on the field.
Ruling: B's ball first-and-10 on B45.

b) receiver B1 commits a personal foul any place on the field.
Ruling: B's ball first-and-10 on B15.

A.R. 14.9   Fourth-and-8 on B12. A legal forward pass is incomplete behind the goal line. During continuing action:

a) B1 roughs passer.
Ruling: Enforce from the succeeding spot (B12) as the pass was incomplete in the end zone on fourth down (8-1-5 Penalty a, p. 47) (14-1-7, p. 88). B's ball first-and-10 on B6.

b) A1 clips.
Ruling: Enforce from the succeeding spot (B12). B's ball first-and-10 on B27.

Continuing Action by Both Teams

Article 8   Continuing action fouls by both teams, after the ball is dead anywhere, are offset except when one or both are disqualifying or as provided in 4-1-9, p. 89. See 14-3-2, p. 93.

A.R. 14.10   Fourth-and-5 on B14. A legal forward pass is incomplete behind the goal line, after which:

a) A1 clips B1 and B2 roughs A2.
Ruling: Fouls are offset. They occurred during continuing action and the succeeding spot is B14. B's ball first-and-10 on B14.

b) A1 punches B1 and B1 punches A1.
Ruling: Disqualify both A1 and B1. Continuing action fouls. Offsetting fouls; in addition, A1 and B1 are disqualified. B's ball first-and-10 on B14.

A.R. 14.11   Second-and-10 on A30. A legal forward pass is incomplete, after which (during continuing action):

a) B1 clips A1 and A1 punches B1.
   Ruling: Disqualify A1. Penalties offset. The down counts as the foul occurred after the down had ended. A's ball third-and-10 on A30. See 14-1-8, p. 88.

b) A1 clips B1 and B1 punches A1.
   Ruling: Disqualify B1. Penalties offset. A's ball third-and-10 on A30.

A.R. 14.12 Receiver B1 is offside on the kickoff. The kickoff is legally out of bounds on the B30 (last touching a receiving team player) after which:

a) A1 is penalized for roughness.
   Ruling: Rekick. Double foul (14-3-1, p. 92; 14-1-9, p. 89).

b) B1 is penalized for roughness.
   Ruling: Choice for Team A. Rekick from the A40 (offside penalty) or B's ball first-and-10 on B15. A continuing action foul is penalized from the succeeding spot (B30). If the kick is illegally out of bounds, it is a rekick in either case (14-3-1, p. 92).

Foul and Continuing Action Foul

Article 9 If there has been a foul by either team during a down not including:

(a) an incompletion, or

(b) an illegal recovery of a kick (other than a free kick). Then a continuing action foul by the opponents after the down ends. Articles 7 and 8, p. 88, are not in force, and it is a double foul (14-3-1, p. 92).

A.R. 14.13 Second-and-10 on A30. Runner A1 is out of bounds on the A40, after which A2 clips any place. Team B was offside.
Ruling: A's ball second-and-25 on A15. See 14-3-1, Exception 1, p. 92.

Legal Acts After Continuing Action

Article 10 There is no penalty unless the contact was avoidable and it is deemed unnecessary roughness, if a player:

(a) uses his hands, arms, or body in a manner ordinarily illegal (other than striking) during continuing action after a down ends, or

(b) completes a legal action (blocking or tackling) started during the down.

A.R. 14.14 Second-and-10 on A30. Runner A1 goes out of bounds on the A35 after which:

a) offensive A2 holds on the A30.
   Ruling: Ignore the foul as it was illegal use of hands and not a personal foul. A's ball third-and-five on A35.

b) offensive A2 clips on the A30.
   Ruling: A personal foul on continuing action penalized as stated in Article 7, p. 88.
   A's ball third-and-20 on A20.

c) offensive A2 strikes B1 on the A30.
   Ruling: Disqualify A2. Penalize from the succeeding spot as in 14-1-7, p. 88. A's ball third-and-20 on A20.

Spot of Enforcement Behind Offensive Goal Line

Article 11 When a spot of enforcement is behind the offensive goal line, and the foul is:

(a) by the defense, a distance penalty is measured from the goal line (unless a touchback, one during a backward pass, or fumble, or 12-1-4 Penalty Exception, p. 76), or

(b) by the offense, it is a safety. See 8-4-4, p. 56, for Exception.

Note: During a loose ball there is always an offensive and defensive team, and enforcement is provided for in the specific section governing passes, fumbles, and kicks. See 3-2-3, p. 4; 3-16, p. 9; 3-35-1, p. 13; and 14-1-5, p. 87.

A.R. 14.15 Receiver B1 fumbles a punt on his one-yard line. The ball enters the end zone where B1 recovers. During a run in the end zone, he fumbles. A1 clips anywhere during the last fumble. B1 is downed in the end zone.
Ruling: Enforce from the goal line. B's ball first-and-10 on B15.

A.R. 14.16 Second-and-15 on A4. Runner A1 is downed in the end zone. During the run A2 held on the A10.
Ruling: Safety.

A.R. 14.17 Second-and-goal on B2. Runner A1 fumbles into B's end zone. B1 recovers in his end zone (downed) or goes out of bounds from there. While B1 is a runner, B2 fouls in the end zone.
Ruling: Safety.

Foul on
Running Play
With No
Change
of Possession

Article 12   When a foul occurs during a running play (3-27-2, p. 12) and the run in which the foul occurs is not followed by a change of team possession during the down, the spot of enforcement is the spot where the ball is dead.

Exceptions:

1) When the spot of a foul by the offense is behind the spot where dead, enforcement is from the spot of the foul.

Offensive
Foul Behind
Goal

2) When the spot of a foul by the offense is behind the line of scrimmage, enforcement is from the previous spot unless in offensive's end zone. Then it is a safety (14-1-11-b, p. 89).

3) When the spot of a foul by the offense is beyond the line of scrimmage and a runner (3-27-1, p. 12) is downed behind the line, enforcement is from the previous spot unless he is downed in the end zone. Then it is a safety (11-4-1, p. 70).

Illegal
Forward
Pass

4) When the spot of foul is that of an illegal forward pass, enforcement is from the spot of the foul. This does not apply to a second forward pass from behind the line, or a pass after the ball had gone beyond the line, which is enforced from the previous spot.

5) If the spot of a defensive foul occurs on or beyond the line of scrimmage and the ball becomes dead behind the line, penalty is enforced from the previous spot.

6) When the spot of enforcement for the defense is behind the offensive goal line, enforcement is from the goal line. See 14-1-11-a, p. 89; 14-1-12-5, p. 90; and 14-1-14, p. 91.

Defensive
Foul
Behind Line

7) When the spot of a foul by the defense is behind the line of scrimmage and the ball becomes dead behind the line, enforcement is from the spot of the foul or the spot where the ball is dead. If such foul incurs a penalty that results in the offended team being short of the line, the ball will be advanced to the previous spot and no additional yardage assessed.

A.R. 14.18   While B1 is returning a kickoff, B2 holds on the B30. B1 is downed on the B20.
Ruling: The offensive foul is in advance of the dead ball; enforce from the dead ball spot (B20). First-and-10 on B10.

Foul
Enforcement
on Running
Play With
Possession
Change

Article 13   When a defensive foul occurs during a running play (3-27-2, p. 12) and the run in which the foul occurs is followed by a change of possession, the spot of enforcement is the spot of the foul and ball reverts to offensive team. See 14-1-12-Exception, 5, p. 90.

Exceptions:

(1) When the spot of a foul is in advance of the spot where the offensive player lost possession, the spot of enforcement is the spot where player possession was lost and the ball reverts to offensive team.

(2) When the spot of a foul by the defense is behind the line of scrimmage, and such foul incurs a penalty that results in the offensive team being short of the line, the ball will be advanced to the previous spot.

A.R. 14.19   Second-and-10 on A30. Runner A1 goes to the A40 where he fumbles and B1 recovers. During A1's run, B2 held on the line of scrimmage (A30).
Ruling: Penalize from the spot of the foul on change of possession. A's ball first-and-10 on A35.

A.R. 14.20   Second-and-10 on A30. Runner A1 goes to the A40 where he fumbles and B1 recovers. During A1's run, B2 held on the A45.
Ruling: Enforce from the spot where the offensive player A1 lost possession as the foul was in advance of where player A1 lost possession. If Team A had been the only one to foul, Team B would refuse the penalty and keep the ball. A's ball first-and-10 on A45.

A.R. 14.21   Second-and-10 on A30. QB A1 scrambles to A20, fumbles and B1 recovers. During A1's scramble, B2 holds at A22.
Ruling: A's ball first-and-10 on A30. See 14-1-13. Exc. 2, p. 90

SUPPLEMENTAL NOTES

(1) A foul during a run prior to a kick or pass from behind the line, is enforced as if it had occurred during a pass or kick which follows. See 8-4-4, p. 56, 8-3-2,3,4, p. 53, 9-1-17, p. 63 and 14-1-5, p. 87.

(2) If an offensive player fouls behind the defensive goal line during a running play in which the runner crosses that line, the penalty is enforced from the spot where the runner crossed the goal line. See 7-3-7, p. 41.

(3) After a penalty for a foul during a running play, the general provisions of 14-8-1, p. 97, relative to the number of the ensuing down, always apply.

(4) Any foul prior to possession by a runner is enforced as otherwise specified.

A.R. 14.22 Second-and-10 on A30. Runner A1 crosses the goal line. During A1's run:

    a) A2 clips on the B20.
    Ruling: Enforce from the spot of the foul. A's ball first-and-10 on B35.

    b) A2 clips in B's end zone before Runner A1 crosses the goal line.
    Ruling: Enforcement is from the goal line. A's ball first-and-10 on B15.

    c) A2 clips on the B10 after Runner A1 crosses the goal line.
    Ruling: Touchdown. Kick off on A20.

Score and Personal Foul or Unsportsmanlike Conduct Foul by Opponent

Article 14 If a team scores and the opponent commits a personal or unsportsmanlike conduct foul or a palpably unfair act during the down, the penalty is enforced on the succeeding free kick unless the enforcement resulted in the score.

A.R. 14.23 Second-and-10 on B30. A legal forward pass is caught by end A1 who then runs for a score. Prior to the pass B1 holds A2 on the line of scrimmage.
Ruling: Touchdown. Kick off on A35. No enforcement of penalty as it was not a personal foul but defensive holding.

A.R. 14.24 Second-and-15 on A2. Runner A1 is downed in the end zone. A2 clipped in the end zone during the run.
Ruling: Safety. Free kick from A10. The personal foul is penalized from the succeeding spot (A20) as the foul did not result in a score.

A.R. 14.25 B1 clips during a kickoff. B1 muffs the kick on the B5 and forces it into his end zone (new impetus) where he recovers and is downed or the kick is out of bounds from the end zone.
Ruling: Safety. B free kicks from its 10 as the penalty is also enforced for the clip from the succeeding spot (B20). Team A has the choice to rekick from the 50 if it refuses the other option.

A.R. 14.26 Second-and-12 on A4. Runner A1 fumbles in his end zone, where B1 recovers. During A's run:

    a) A2 fouls anywhere.
    Ruling: Touchdown. If the foul by A2 was personal, it is enforced on the kickoff (50).

    b) B2 holds anywhere.
    Ruling: Enforce from the goal line. A's ball first-and-10 on A5. (14-1-13, p. 90).

A.R. 14.27 During a successful try, B1:

    a) is offside.
    Ruling: Point awarded. Enforce five-yard penalty against B on kickoff. See 11-3-C, p. 70.

    b) piles on holder of a placekick or runs into the kicker.
    Ruling: Point awarded. Enforce the penalty on the succeeding kickoff (11-3-e, p. 70).

Section 2   Location of Foul

Half Distance Penalty

Article 1 If a distance penalty, enforced from a specific spot between the goal lines would place the ball more than half the distance to the offender's goal line, the penalty shall be half the distance from that spot to their goal line.

Note: This general rule supersedes any other general or specific rule other than for a palpably unfair act or the enforcement for intentional grounding, if appropriate.

A.R. 14.28 Second-and-20 on B24. A legal forward pass is caught by end A1 on the B12 and he runs to the B10. B1 roughed the passer.
Ruling: Half the distance from the end of the run. A's ball first-and-goal on B5.

Location
of Foul

Article 2

   (a) If a foul occurs behind a goal line during a down, the penalty shall be enforced as provided for under the specific running play, pass or fumble rule involved.

   (b) If a foul occurs between downs, enforcement is from the succeeding spot (14-5, p. 95).

   (c) If any enforcement leaves or places the ball behind a line, Rule 11, Section 3, 4, and 6, pp. 69-74, govern. See 14-1-11 and Note, p. 89.

Section 3   Fouls by Both Teams

Double Foul
Without
Change of
Possession

Article 1   If there is a double foul (3-11-2-c, p. 8) without a change of possession, the penalties are offset and the down is replayed at the previous spot. If it was a scrimmage down, the number of the next down and the necessary line is the same as for the down for which the new one is substituted.

Exceptions:

15 Yards
Versus
5 Yards

   1) If one of the fouls is of a nature that incurs a 15-yard penalty and the other foul of a double foul normally would result in a loss of 5 yards *only* (15 yards versus 5 yards), the major penalty yardage is to be assessed from the previous spot.

Note: If a score occurs on a play that would normally involve a 5 vs. 15 yard enforcement, enforce the major penalty from the previous spot.

   2) Any disqualified player is removed immediately, even when one or both fouls are disqualifying or are disregarded otherwise. See 14-1-8, p. 88.

Double Foul
Disqualification

   3) If both fouls involve disqualification, the down is replayed at the previous spot. If both fouls occur during the continuing action or are treated as such (14-1-8, p. 88), the fouls are disregarded and the ball is next put in play at the succeeding spot. See Exception 1 in either case.

Illegal
Touching
and Foul

   4) If the one foul by the kickers during a down is illegal touching of a scrimmage kick, the down is not replayed at the previous spot. The foul (illegal touching) by the kickers is disregarded provided the distance penalty for a foul by the receivers is enforced. If not enforced, the receivers next put the ball in play at any spot of illegal touching or at any other spot where they are entitled to possession at the end of the down.

Note: Any foul by either team after a kick ends is enforced as ordinary. See 9-1-17, p. 63.

A.R. 14.29   Second-and-20 on A30. Runner A1 goes to the A35. During the run A2 holds B1 who punches A2.
      Ruling: Disqualify B1. Penalties offset. A's ball second-and-20 on A30.

A.R. 14.30   Third-and-eight on B10. A2 is offside and B1 slugs on the B6 during the play. Runner A1 scored on the play.
      Ruling: Disqualify B1. A's ball first-and-goal on B5.

A.R. 14.31   Second-and-10 on A30. B1 is offside. Runner A1 goes to B30. During A's run A2 clips at the 50.
      Ruling: A's ball second-and-25 on A15. See 14-3-1, Exc. 1 p. 92.

A.R. 14.32   Second-and-10 on A30. After the ball is dead anywhere A1 and B2 strike each other with their fists during continuing action. Runner A1 was downed on the A35.
      Ruling: Fouls are disregarded except for disqualifying both players. A's ball third-and-five on A35.

A.R. 14.33   Fourth-and-10 on B18. A forward pass alights in the end zone, after which A1 clips. B2 then strikes A1.
      Ruling: Disqualify B2. B's ball first-and-10 on B18.

A.R. 14.34   A kickoff is illegally out of bounds on the B30. During continuing action:

      a) A1 clips and B blocks below the waist.
        Ruling: Replay. A kickoff out of bounds is an offensive foul.

      b) A1 clips and B1 punches A1.
        Ruling: Team A rekicks from the 35. B1 disqualified.

Double Foul With Change of Possession (Clean Hands)

Article 2 If there is a double foul (3-11-2-c, p. 8) during a down (including kickoffs, punts, field goals, and safety kicks) in which there is a change of possession, the team gaining possession must keep the ball after enforcement for its foul, provided its foul occurred after the change of possession (clean hands).

If a score would result from a foul by a team gaining possession, the down is replayed at the previous spot.

If the team gaining possession fouls and loses possession, the penalties offset and the down is replayed at the previous spot.

Double Foul Prior to Change of Possession (Not Clean Hands)

If the team gaining possession fouls prior to the change of possession (not clean hands), the penalties offset and the down is replayed at the previous spot.

Double Foul After Change of Possession

Article 3 If a double foul occurs after a change in possession, the team in possession retains the ball at the spot where the team in possession's foul occurred so long as that spot is not in advance of the dead ball spot. In that event, ball is spotted at dead ball spot.

(a) If this spot is normally a touchback, the ball is placed on the 20 yard line.

(b) If normally a safety, place the ball on 1 yard line.

SUPPLEMENTAL NOTES

Double Foul Disregarded

(1) When enforcement for a double foul is disregarded, the number of the next down, if a scrimmage down, is the same as if no foul had occurred. See 14-3-2, p. 93.

(2) If there is a foul by the defensive team from the start of a snap until a legal forward pass ends, it is not treated as a double foul except as provided in 8-3-3,4, p. 53.

(3) Change of possession refers to the physical change of possession from one team to the other except for kicks from scrimmage (9-1-17, p. 63), and free kick (4-3-1 — Note (4), p. 16).

(4) If a team fouls before it gains possession on a double foul, it cannot score.

(5) Illegal touching, while technically a foul (page 92), does not offset a foul committed by its opponent. It is *not* considered part of a double foul. See 14-3-1-Exc. 4, p. 92.

(6) If there is a continuing action foul by the defensive team after a legal forward pass becomes incomplete, both penalties are enforced. See 14-1-7, p. 88.

A.R. 14.35 Second-and-10 on B40. Offensive Team A is offside. B1 intercepts a forward pass and runs it back to the A30. On the runback, B2 clips on the B45.
Ruling: Team B keeps the ball as its foul was not prior to change of possession and foul enforced. B's ball first-and-10 on B30.

A.R. 14.36 On the kickoff to start the game, kicking team player A1 is offside. Receiver B1 catches the ball in the end zone and runs it back to the A20. On the runback B2 clips on the A26.
Ruling: B's ball first-and-10 on A41 (14-3-2, p. 93).

A.R. 14.37 Fourth-and-10 on A40. Kicking team player A1 is offside. A punt hits on the B20 where receiver B1 picks it up and runs to the 50. On B's runback, B2 clips on the B40.
Ruling: B's ball first-and-10 on B25 (14-3-2, p. 93).

A.R. 14.38 Fourth-and-10 on A40. Kicking team player A1 is offside. A punt hits on the B20 where receiver B1 picks it up and runs for a touchdown. After B1 scores, B2 clips on the A10.
Ruling: Touchdown B. Kickoff B20 (14-3-2, p. 93).

A.R. 14.39 Second-and-five on B45. Team A is offside. B1 intercepts a pass on the B10 and runs it back to the B30 and is tackled and fumbles on the B30 where A1 recovers. On B1's run, B2 clipped on the B25.
Ruling: A's ball second-and-5 on B45 (14-3-2, p. 93).

A.R. 14.40 Second-and-10 on A30. Team A is offside. B1 intercepts and runs for a touchdown, then clips.
Ruling: Touchdown. Penalize Team B on the kickoff. Kickoff from its 20 yard line as the foul did not result in a score.

A.R. 14.41 Second-and-10 on B45. B1 intercepts a pass on the B10 and runs it back to the A30. On the runback, B2 clips on the A35 and A1 piles on runner B1 just as he is tackled on the A30.
Ruling: Team B retains ball at spot of its foul. B's ball first-and-10 on A35.

A.R. 14.42 B1 receives a kick at the B10, advances to the B40 and fumbles when he is tackled. A2 recovers. During B1's run, B2 clips at the B30, after which A1 trips B3.
Ruling: Double foul following change of possession. B's ball at spot of its foul, first-and-10 on B30.

A.R. 14.43 Defensive B1 intercepts on the B10. During B1's run, B2 clips at the B30 and is downed at the B40. B1 is flagrantly roughed by A1 who piles on.
Ruling: A1 disqualified. B's ball first-and-10 on B30.

A.R. 14.44 Second-and-10 on B45. B1 holds tight end A1 on the line of scrimmage. B2 intercepts the ball on the B10 and runs it back to the B30 where he is tackled, fumbles, and A2 recovers the ball. A2 runs to the B20. On A2's run, A3 holds on the B25.
Ruling: Team A keeps the ball as it gained possession prior to its foul. A's ball first-and-10 on B35.

A.R. 14.45 B1 receives a kickoff in the end zone and clips there. The runner advances to the B25 and is piled on by A1.
Ruling: B's ball first-and-10 on B1. See 14-3-3-b, p. 93.

A.R. 14.46 B1 legally bats a kickoff back into his own end zone, thereby creating a new impetus. After B3 picks up the ball in the end zone, B2 clips in the end zone and A1 piles on.
Ruling: Both fouls occurred after B gained possession. Normally, if this spot was in the end zone, the succeeding spot would be the B20. In this case, B1 created the impetus which would have resulted in a safety if the fouls had not been committed. The ball is transferred to the one-yard line. B's ball first-and-10 on B1. See 14-3-3-B, p. 93.

A.R. 14.47 Second-and-10 on B30. Offensive A1 offside. B1 intercepts in the end zone and clips there. Runner B1 is downed on the B10.
Ruling: Replay. A score cannot result from one of the fouls of a double foul. A's ball second-and-10 on B30. See 14-3-2-Exc., p. 93.

Section 4   Choice of Penalties

Only One Penalty Enforced

If there is a multiple foul (3-11-2-b, p. 8) or a foul and a forward pass violation by the same team during the same down, only one penalty may be enforced after the referee has explained the alternatives. The captain of the offended team shall make the choice.

Exceptions: A continuing action foul by:

1) passers after an incompletion or the team whose foul results in a touchback or safety, enforcement is from the succeeding spot.

2) kickers after a fair catch or interference with one, enforcement is from the succeeding spot.

3) kickers after a free kick is illegally out of bounds between the goal lines or is illegally recovered, enforcement is from the succeeding spot (6-3-1, Pen., p. 33).

Disqualified Player Removed

Note: A disqualified player is always removed, regardless of any captain's choice. See 5-1-3, p. 25 and 5-1-5(a), p. 25.

A.R. 14.48 Second-and-10 on A30. Runner A1 goes to the A35. During the run, A2 clipped on the A30. Team A was offside.
Ruling: A multiple foul and only one penalty can be enforced. Option for defensive Team B. A's ball second-and-15 on A25 or A's ball second-and-25 on A15. If both declined, it is third-and-five on A35.

A.R. 14.49 After a fair catch signal, B1 who did or did not signal, catches. After the catch he (a) comes to a reasonable stop or (b) unduly advances. In either case there is a foul after the catch.
Ruling: Enforcement is from the succeeding spot in either case. In (b) it is either a double or multiple foul.

A.R. 14.50 B1 intercepts a pass in the end zone. He runs and is downed in the end zone. B2 holds in the end zone during B1's run. B3 clips after the ball is dead.
Ruling: If the penalty for holding is declined, it is B on its 10 (touchback minus 10). If the penalty for holding is enforced (which it would be), it is a safety and B free kicks from its 10 (14-1-14, p. 91).

A.R. 14.51 B1 fumbles a punt on his 2 yard line. In attempting to recover in the end zone, he deliberately kicks the ball out of bounds behind the goal line.

a) B2 clips on his 4 during the fumble.
Ruling: If A accepts the penalty for clipping, it is B on its one-yard line. Otherwise, it is a safety. Safety kick from B10.

b) B2 clips on his 4 after the ball is out of bounds.
Ruling: Safety. B free kicks from its 10 (14-1-14, p. 91) (continuous action foul).

Section 5 Time of Foul

Time of Foul

If a foul occurs between downs (3-11-2-d, p. 8), a distance penalty is enforced from the succeeding spot. If it is a continuing action foul (3-11-2-a, p. 8) at the end of a play from scrimmage, a down is charged provided the ball is not dead in touch. See 14-1-7 to 10, pp. 88-89.

A.R. 14.52 Second-and-10 on A30. Runner A1 goes out of bounds on the A35, after which offensive player A2 clips on the A30.
Ruling: The down counts and enforce from the succeeding spot (A35)(14-1-7-a, p. 88). A's ball third-and-20 on A20.

A.R. 14.53 Third-and-five on A30. Offensive team is offside and runner A1 fails to gain. A2 clips just as the ball is declared dead.
Ruling: If defensive team B declines both penalties, it is fourth-and-five on the A30. If the penalty for clipping is enforced, it is third-and-20 on A15.

A.R. 14.54 Fourth-and-10 on A40. Kicking team player A1 first touches and recovers a scrimmage kick on the B10:

a) after an illegal recovery by A1, A2 roughs an opponent.
Ruling: B's ball first-and-10 on B25.

b) after an illegal recovery by A1, B2 roughs an opponent.
Ruling: B's ball first-and-10 on B5.

SUPPLEMENTAL NOTES

Continuing Action Foul

(1) When a foul occurs simultaneously with an out of bounds or after a loose ball crosses the plane of the boundary line in the air and then first touches anything out of bounds, it is considered to be a continuing action foul.

Foul After Touchdown

(2) The succeeding spot for a foul after a touchdown and before a whistle for a Try-kick is the next kickoff (3-11-2-d, p. 8).

Foul Between Downs

(3) The time between downs is the interval during all time outs (including intermissions) and from the time the ball is dead until it is next put in play (time in). See 3-36-1, 2, p. 14.

Defensive Foul Continuing Action

(4) For a continuing action foul by the defensive team or by either team at the end of a play not from scrimmage, see 14-8-5 and 6, pp. 97-98.

Special Enforcement Between Downs

(5) See 5-1-5-S.N. 2, p. 25 for a special enforcement between downs.

A.R. 14.55 Third-and-20 on B40. Runner A1 is out of bounds on the B15, after which offensive player A2 clips on the B20.
Ruling: Team A had made its first down, and as it was a continuing action foul, enforce from the succeeding spot (14-1-7-b, p. 88). A's ball first-and-25 on B30.

A.R. 14.56 Third-and-10 on B30. A forward pass is out of bounds on the B10 after which A1 clips on B15.
Ruling: A's ball fourth-and-25 on B45.

A.R. 14.57 Offensive Team A has made a first down and its captain calls time out for the fourth time in the half without making a substitution for an injured player.
Ruling: A's ball first-and-15.

A.R. 14.58 Receiver B1 catches a punt on the B30 and goes out of bounds on the B40, after which B2 clips on the B35.
Ruling: Continuing action foul (14-1-7-b, p. 88). B's ball first-and-10 on B25.

A.R. 14.59   Second-and-15 on A30. Runner A1 steps out of bounds on A40, after which A2 clips on 50.
Ruling: Enforce from the dead ball spot (A40)(14-1-7, p. 88). A's ball third-and-20 on A25.

A.R. 14.60   Second-and-15 on A30. Runner A1 steps out of bounds on the 50, after which A2 clips on A40.
Ruling: Enforce from dead ball spot (50)(14-1-7, p. 88). First-and-25 on A35.

Section 6   Refusal of Penalties

Refusal of
Penalties

Penalties for all fouls, unless otherwise expressly provided for, may be declined by the Captain of the offended team, in which case play proceeds as though no foul had been committed.

Note: The yardage distance for any penalty may be declined, even though the penalty is accepted.

A.R. 14.61   Second-and-10 on A30. A legal forward pass is completed to end A1 on the A45 where he is downed. Defensive B1 held flanker A2 on the A35 prior to the pass.
Ruling: Declines holding penalty which would have been five yards from the previous spot and a first down. A's ball first-and-10 on A45.

Exceptions:

Disqualifi-
cation Foul
Removes
Player

1)   A disqualified or suspended player is always removed, even when an accompanying distance penalty is declined, or when a penalty for another foul is chosen (multiple foul).

2)   During a down a foul occurs (includes an incomplete forward pass) for which the ball is dead immediately.

3)   The penalty for certain illegal actions prior to or pertaining to a snap or to a free kick may not be declined, i.e., the ball remains dead.

   a) 40/25-second violations (4-3-9, p. 21-22).

   b) Snap made before the referee can assume his normal stance (7-3-3-c-2, p. 39).

Distance
Penalty
Declined

4)   When a 40/25-second penalty occurs prior to the snap, the defensive team may decline a distance penalty, in which case the down is replayed from the previous spot.

5)   If fouls are committed by both teams during the same down (double foul), no penalty may be declined, except as provided for kickers when their only foul is illegal touching of a scrimmage or return kick. See 14-3-1-Exception 4, p. 92.

6)   If the defensive team commits a foul during an unsuccessful try, the offensive team may decline the distance penalty and the down is replayed from the previous spot.

A.R. 14.62   Second-and-10 on A30. On a legal forward pass B1 interferes with eligible A1 on the B40 where the ball falls incomplete. B2 strikes A2 on the line of scrimmage.
Ruling: Disqualify B2 although the penalty for interference is taken. A's ball first-and-10 on B40.

A.R. 14.63   During time in, A1 illegally recovers a kick, unduly advances, and fumbles. B2 recovers and advances beyond the spot where the penalty for delay by A1 would place the ball.
Ruling: B may not decline the penalty as ball is dead when A1 recovers.

Section 7   On Incomplete Forward Pass

Illegal
Forward
Pass and
Incomplete
Forward
Pass

An illegal forward pass is a foul, but an incomplete forward pass is not classed as a foul and the penalties provided therefore may not be declined.

Exception: If a team commits a foul during the same play in which it makes an incomplete forward pass, the captain of the offended team may elect which of the penalties is to be enforced (14-4, p. 94).

Note: If there is a continuing action foul by either team after an incompletion, enforcement is from the succeeding spot. See 14-5, p. 95.

Section 8   Number of Down After Penalty

Number of Down After Penalty

Article 1   After a distance penalty (not combined with a loss of down penalty) for a foul by the offensive team prior to (between downs) or during a play from scrimmage which results in the ball being in its possession behind the necessary line, the number of the ensuing down is the same as that of the down before which or during which the foul occurred.

Combination Penalty

Article 2   A combination penalty involving both distance and loss of down is enforced for certain forward pass fouls by the offensive team.

Examples:

Loss of Distance and Down

(a) from beyond the line (8-1-1, Penalty, c, p. 45); or

(b) intentionally grounded (8-3-1, p. 52).

Note: After a loss of down penalty (prior to fourth down), the number of the ensuing down is one greater than that of the previous down. If it occurs on fourth down, it is loss of the ball to the defensive team unless it is a combination penalty, in which case the distance penalty is enforced in addition to the loss of the ball. See 8-1-1 and S.N. 4, p. 45.

Foul and Change of Possession

Article 3   When a foul occurs during a play from scrimmage, the necessary line remains the same regardless of any change of team possession thereafter.

A.R. 14.64   Second-and-10 on A30. Team A is offside. A legal forward pass is intercepted by defensive B1 on the 50. B1 runs to the A40, fumbles, and A2 recovers there.
Ruling: A's ball second-and-15 on A25. (If Team B refused the penalty, it would have been A's ball first-and-10 on A40).

Advance of Necessary Line First-and-10

Article 4   After a distance penalty for a foul by the offensive team during a play from scrimmage which results in the ball being in advance of the necessary line, it is a first-and-10 for the offensive team.

Articles 4 and 6 also apply to a continuing action foul of the offensive team at the end of a play from scrimmage during which it has been constantly in possession. For exceptions, see 14-1-7, p. 88.

A.R. 14.65   Second-and-4 on A30. Runner A1 goes to the B45. During the run, A2 clipped on the 50.
Ruling: After the penalty, the ball is still in advance of the necessary line for the first down. A's ball first-and-10 on A35.

Defensive Foul First-and-10 for Offense

Article 5   After a penalty for a foul by the defense prior to (between downs) or during a play from scrimmage, the ensuing down is first-and-10 for the offense.

Defensive Foul and No First Down

Exceptions are:

1) delay of the game;

2) offside;

3) incidental grasp of face mask;

4) illegal substitution;

5) encroaching on the neutral zone;

6) excess time out; and

7) prolonged, excessive, or premeditated celebrations by individual players or groups of players.

8) running into the kicker

In the above eight exceptions the number of the down and the necessary line remain the same unless a distance penalty places the ball on or in advance of that line, in which case it is first-and-10 for A. See 4-3-9, p. 21-22.

A.R. 14.66   Second-and-15 on A30. Runner A1 is downed on the A35. During the run defensive B1 held on the line of scrimmage.
Ruling: A's ball first-and-10 on A40.

A.R. 14.67 Third-and-goal on B4. The forward rod of the chains is one yard past the goal line. The defensive team is offside and A1 gains one yard.
Ruling: A's ball third-and-two on the B2 (14-2-1, p. 91).

Foul After
Change of
Possession

Article 6 After a distance penalty for a foul which occurs during a play after team possession has changed following a snap or free kick, it is first-and-10 for the team that was in possession at the time of the foul or at the time of the continuing action foul.

A.R. 14.68 On a kickoff B1 runs to the B45 where he steps out of bounds, after which B2 clips on the 50.
Ruling: B's ball first-and-10 on B30.

Enforcement
and First-
and-10

Article 7 After a loss of ball penalty, it is first-and-10 for the offended team after enforcement, unless the offended team free kicks following the fair catch interference.

Note: Loss of ball results only from illegal touching of kick (other than a free kick) or a fair catch interference. See 6-2-4, p. 32 and 10-1-4, p. 66.

A.R. 14.69 Second-and-10 on A30. B1 intercepts a legal forward pass on the A40. He fumbles and A1 recovers on the A25. A1 runs to the A45. During A1's run A2 clipped on the 50.
Ruling: A's ball first-and-10 on A30 (change of possession).

Rule 15   Officials: Jurisdiction, Duties

Section 1   Officials

Officials'
Manual

Article 1   By League action, the officials' manual is an integral part of the Official rules, especially in regard to the specific duties, mechanics and procedures for each official during any play situations. For that reason, many such specific items are omitted in Sections 1 to 7 to avoid needless repetition, and only the primary duties of each official are stated. Some of the technical terms used hereafter are defined only in the manual.

Note: The terms "On Ball" or "Cover" imply that an official is nearest or in close proximity to a loose ball or runner and is in position to declare the ball dead when the down ends by rule. See 15-1-11-S.N., p. 100.

Game
Officials

Article 2   The game Officials are: referee, umpire, head linesman, line judge, back judge, side judge, and field judge.

Note: In the absence of seven officials, the crew is to be rearranged, on the most feasible basis, according to the other members of crew.

Article 3   All officials are to wear uniforms prescribed by the League (including a black cap with visor and piping for all except the Referee, who will wear a white cap). All officials will carry a whistle and a weighted bright gold flag.

Sound
Whistle

Article 4   An official is to sound his whistle:

(a) for any foul for which ball remains dead or is dead immediately;

(b) to signal time out at end of a down, during which he has indicated a foul, by means of dropping his flag and provided no other official signalled time out at end of down;

(c) to indicate dead ball when he is covering a runner. See 7-4-1, 2, 3, 4, 5, p. 41.

(d) at any other time, when he is nearest to ball, when a down ends. See 15-8-3, p. 104.

Note: The flag is to be used to indicate a foul. See 7-4-5-Note, p. 43.

Crew
Meeting

Article 5   Members of the crew are required to meet in their dressing quarters at least two hours-fifteen minutes before game time.

Officials'
Dressing
Room

Note: By order of the Commissioner, from the time any official first enters the dressing room and until all officials have left it, at the end of the game, no person other than clubhouse attendants or those possessing a working pass (League) shall be allowed to enter it. This prohibition includes coaches and owners.

Officials'
Responsibility
and Crew
Conference

Article 6   All officials are responsible for any decision involving the application of a rule, its interpretation or an enforcement. If an official errs in his interpretation of a rule, the other officials must check him before play is resumed, otherwise they are equally responsible. In the event of a disagreement, the crew should draw aside for a conference.

Note: If because of injury, the officials' vote is tied, referee's decision will be the deciding factor. Any dissenting opinion is to be reported to the supervisor.

Article 7   All officials have concurrent jurisdiction over any foul, and there is no fixed territorial division in this respect. When an official signals a foul, he must report it to referee, informing him of its nature, position of ball at time of foul, the offender (when known), the penalty and spot of enforcement.

Recording
Fouls

Article 8   Each official is to record every foul he signals and the total number of officials signalling the same foul. During the game, these are to be recorded on white game cards provided by league. They are to be preserved after each game in case they should be needed to revise an official's final game card.

League
Game
Reports

Article 9 At the end of the game the officials are to record their own fouls on the yellow game cards provided by the league, and are to check them with other officials, for duplications, before leaving the dressing room.

Note: Both white and yellow game cards are to be made out in accordance with the yearly bulletin issued for that purpose.

Crew
Errors

Article 10 All members of a crew are equally responsible for any errors in Officiating Mechanics as prescribed by the Manual, and are required to call the attention of this fact to an official who had been remiss.

Note: This applies to such errors, in mechanics or applications of rules, as tend to increase the length of the game (elapsed time) and particularly so to those which result in undue loss of playing time (Crew Time). In the latter case, if the referee has clearly failed to signal a referee's time out as specified by rule, any official should do so. See 4-3-7, p. 19 and 4-3-9, p. 21.

Coin Toss

Article 11 Ten minutes before the opening kickoff, the entire crew is to appear on the field. Three minutes prior to the kickoff the referee is to make the toss of the coin. He is to indicate which team is to receive and is to do the same when teams first appear on the field prior to the start of the second half. See 4-2-1 and S.N., p. 15-16.

Note: All officials record results of coin toss and options chosen.

SUPPLEMENTAL NOTES

(1) During any running play (includes runbacks), or a loose ball, the nearest official is to cover and remain with the ball or runner, unless outdistanced until end of down. In such case any nearer official is to cover. See 15-2-9-Note, p. 101, for referee entering a side zone and 15-3-4, p. 101 for umpire.

(2) When a ball is dead inbounds near a sideline, during time in, the official covering is to use the clock signal to indicate this fact.

(3) Any officials not involved in an enforcement are to see that all players other than captains remain aside during any conference between referee and captains. See 15-2-5, p. 100.

Recording
Time Outs

Article 12 All officials must record charged team time outs.

Section 2   Referee

Referee
Authority

Article 1 The referee is to have general oversight and control of game. He is the final authority for the score, and the number of a down in case of a disagreement. His decisions upon all matters not specifically placed under the jurisdiction of other officials, either by rule or the officials' manual, are to be final. See 15-1-6, p. 99, Note, and 15-1-10, p. 100.

Article 2 Prior to the kickoff to start each half and after every time out, the referee shall sound his whistle for play to start without asking captains if they are ready. In such cases where time is in with his whistle, he is to indicate it by use of clock signal.

Ball Put
in Play

Article 3 He is to see that the ball is properly put in play and shall decide on all matters pertaining to its position and disposition at end of down. If any official sounds his whistle, the ball is dead (7-4-1, p. 41). In case the referee is informed or believes that ball was dead before such signal or down ends, he has the authority to make a retroactive ruling after consulting the crew or the official involved.

Article 4 The referee must notify the coach and field captain when his team has used its three charged time outs, signal both coaches when two minutes remain in a half, and positively inform the coach of any disqualified player. He may not delegate any such notifications to any other person. See 4-3-8, Exception, p. 21.

Foul
Options

Article 5 After a foul, the referee (in the presence of both captains) must announce the penalty and explain to the offended captain the decision and choice (if any) as well as number of next down and distance (usually approximate) to necessary line for any possible positions of ball. See 7-1-2, p. 35. The referee is to designate the offending player, when known. After an enforcement (7-3-2, p. 39) he shall signal to spectators the nature of penalty by means of the visual signals specifically provided for herein.

Note: It is not necessary for the referee to explain to both captains the decision and distance to the necessary line in such cases when: the enforcement is entirely automatic and/or when there is obviously no choice.

Field captains only may appeal to referee, and then solely on questions of interpretation of the rules. They shall not be allowed to question the judgment of jurisdiction of any particular official in regard to a foul or in signalling dead ball.

Referee's Position

Article 6 Prior to the snap, the referee shall assume such a stance that he is in the clear of and behind any backfield player. This is also to be construed as including the normal path of any player in motion behind the line as well as the line of vision between such a player and the maker of a pass (forward or backward). He shall also favor the right side (if the passer is right-handed). He will count offensive players.

Measurement

Article 7 At the end of any down, the referee may (when in doubt or at the request of a captain unless obviously unnecessary) request the linesman and his assistants to bring the yardage chains on field to determine whether the ball has reached the necessary line. See 4-3-10-S.N. 3, p. 23.

Article 8 Prior to each snap, the referee is to positively check the number of the ensuing down and distance to be gained with the linesman, signal the field judge when to start his watch for the timing of 25 seconds (when appropriate), and know the eligible pass receivers.

Spotting Ball

Article 9 He is primarily responsible for spotting the ball at the inbounds spot on plays from scrimmage, and should not enter a side zone to cover a runner (other than the quarterback) when the linesman, back judge or line judge is in position to do so. See 15-1-11-S.N. 1, p. 100.

Note: When the ball is dead near the sideline during time in, he is not to assist in a relay to the inbounds spot, unless the umpire has been remiss or delayed in doing so (15-1-10 Note, p. 100, and 15-3-4, p. 101). In such a case, the umpire is to spot. See Rule 2, Note, p. 3, in regard to using a new ball at start of second and fourth periods in case of a wet ball.

Section 3 Umpire

Article 1 The umpire has primary jurisdiction over the equipment and the conduct and actions of players on the scrimmage line.

Equipment Inspection

Article 2 Before the game, the umpire with assistance of other officials shall inspect the equipment of players. He may order any changes he deems necessary to any proposed equipment which is considered dangerous or confusing (5-3, p. 27). This authority extends throughout the game.

Article 3 He shall assist in relaying the ball:

(a) to the inbounds spot when it is dead near a sideline during time in when feasible (15-2-9-Note, p. 101);

(b) to the previous spot after an incompletion; and

(c) to the spot of a free kick when indicated. See 15-1-11-S.N., p. 100.

Duties of Umpire

Article 4 The umpire shall record:

(a) all charged team time outs during the game;

(b) the winner of the toss; and

(c) the score.

He is to assist the referee on decisions involving possession of the ball in close proximity to the line, after a loose ball or runner has crossed it. He and the linesman are to determine whether ineligible linesmen illegally cross the line prior to a pass, and he must wipe a wet ball in accordance with the proper timing. He should count the offensive players on the field at the snap.

Section 4 Linesman

Linesman Position

Article 1 The linesman operates on the side of field designated by the referee during the first half and on opposite side during the second half unless ordered otherwise. See 1-4, Note, p. 2 for exception.

Article 2   He is responsible for illegal motion, offside, encroaching, and any actions pertaining to scrimmage line prior to or at snap; and for covering in his side zone. See 15-1-11-S.N. 1, p. 100, 15-2-9 and 15-3-4, p. 101. He will count offensive players.

Article 3   Prior to the game, he shall see that his chain crew is properly instructed as to their specific duties and mechanics.

Note: Each home team appoints the official chain crew (boxman, two rodmen and alternate, drive start and forward stake indicator) subject to approval by the league office. Each member carries a working pass to that effect and it is prohibited for anyone else to work as such. The standardized yardage chains and downs box must be used and if any others are furnished this fact is to be reported to the Commissioner.

Article 4   The linesman shall use a clamp on the chain when measuring for first down.

Marking and Chains

Article 5   The linesman is to mark with his foot (when up with ball) the yard line touched by forward point of ball at end of each scrimmage down. At the start of each new series of downs, he and the rodmen set the yardage chains when the referee so signals. He positively must check with the referee as to the number of each down that is about to start.

Note: It is mandatory for linesman to personally see that rear rod is accurately set and also to see that the forward rodman and boxman have set the safety markers for the forward rod and the previous spot, during any series of downs, as prescribed by the officials' manual.

Linesman Duties

Article 6   On his own side, he is to assist the line judge as to illegal motion or a shift and umpire in regard to holding or illegal use of hands on end of line (especially during kicks or passes), and know eligible pass receivers.

Article 7   He and the umpire are to determine whether ineligible linesmen illegally cross the line prior to a pass. He is to mark out of bounds spot on his side of field when within his range and is to supervise substitutions made by team seated on his side of field during either half.

Note: See 15-1-11-S.N. 1, p. 100, 15-2-9 and 15-3-4, p. 101.

Section 5   Line Judge

Line Judge Duties

Article 1   The line judge is to operate on side of field opposite the linesman.

Article 2   He is responsible for the timing of game. He also is responsible for illegal motion, illegal shift, and for covering in his side zone. See 15-1-11-S.N. 1, p. 100, 15-2-9, p. 101. He will count offensive players.

Article 3   He is responsible for supervision of the timing and in case the game clock becomes inoperative, or for any other reason is not being operated correctly, he shall take over the official timing on the field.

Article 4   He is to time each period and intermission between halves (4-1-3, 4, p. 15), signal the referee when two minutes remain in a half and leave in ample time with the back judge to notify their respective teams of five minutes before the start of the second half.

Article 5   He shall signal the referee by firing a pistol when time has expired at end of a period. However, if ball is in play it must not be fired until down ends.

Article 6   He must notify both captains, through the referee, of the time remaining for play not more than 10 or less than five minutes before the end of each half and must signal referee when two minutes remain in each half.

Note: Upon inquiry of a field captain, he may state the approximate time remaining for play at any time during the game, provided he does not comply with such request more than three times during the last five minutes of either half, and provided it will not affect playing time near the end of a half (4-3-10, p. 22).

Article 7   On his own side, he is to:

(a) assist the linesman as to offside or encroaching;

(b) assist the umpire as to holding or illegal use of hands on the end of the line (especially during kicks or passes);

(c) assist the referee as to forward laterals behind the line and false starts; and

(d) be responsible for knowing the eligible pass receivers.

Article 8   He is to:

(a) mark the out of bounds spot of all plays on his side, when within his range (see 15-1-11-S.N., p. 100 and 15-2-9, p. 101),

(b) supervise substitutions made by the team seated on his side of the field during either half (see 5-2-1, p. 25 and 26);

Notify Home Team Coach

(c) notify the home team head coach with the back judge five minutes before the start of the second half.

Section 6   Back Judge

Back Judge's Position and Duties

Article 1   The back judge will operate on the same side of the field as line judge, 20 yards deep.

Article 2   The back judge shall count the number of defensive players on the field at the snap.

Article 3   He shall be responsible for all eligible receivers on his side of the field.

Article 4   After receivers have cleared line of scrimmage, the back judge will concentrate on action in the area between the umpire and field judge. Be aware of "trapped balls" in this vital area.

Article 5   In addition to the specified use of the whistle by all officials (15-1-4, p. 99), the back judge is also to use his whistle when upon his positive knowledge he knows:

(a) that ball is dead;

(b) that time is out;

(c) that time is out at the end of a down, during which a foul was signaled by a marker, no whistle has sounded in such cases; and

(d) that even in the presence of a whistle up or down field, he is to sound his whistle when players are some distance from such signal. This will help prevent continuing action fouls.

Article 6   The back judge will assist referee in decisions involving any catching, recovery, out of bounds spot, or illegal touching, of a loose ball, after it has crossed scrimmage line and particularly so for such actions that are out of the range of the line judge and umpire. See 15-1-11, S.N. 1, p. 100.

Position on Field Goal Attempt and Try

Article 7   On field goal attempts, the back judge will station himself on the end line and cover the upright opposite the field judge. He, along with the field judge, is responsible for indication to the referee whether the kick is high enough and through the uprights.

Section 7   Side Judge

Side Judge's Position and Duties

Article 1   The side judge will operate on the same side of the field as the head linesman, 20 yards deep.

Article 2   The side judge shall count the number of defensive players on the field at the snap.

Article 3   He shall be responsible for all eligible receivers on his side of the field.

Article 4   After receivers have cleared line of scrimmage, the side judge will concentrate on action in the area between the umpire and field judge. Be aware of "trapped balls" in this vital area.

Article 5   In addition to the specified use of the whistle by all officials (15-1-4, p. 99), the side judge is also to use his whistle when upon his positive knowledge he knows:

(a) that ball is dead;

(b) that time is out;

(c) that time is out at the end of a down, during which a foul was signaled by a marker, no whistle has sounded in such cases; and

(d) that even in the presence of a whistle up or down field, he is to sound his whistle when players are some distance from such signal. This will help prevent continuing action fouls.

Article 6   The side judge will assist referee in decisions involving any catching, recovery, out of bounds spot, or illegal touching, of a loose ball, after it has crossed scrimmage line and particularly so for such actions that are out of the range of the head linesman and umpire.

Article 7   The side judge will line up in a position laterally from the umpire on punts, field goals, and extra points.

Section 8   Field Judge

Duties of Field Judge

Article 1   The field judge is primarily responsible in regard to: covering kicks from scrimmage (unless a try-kick) or forward passes crossing the defensive goal line and all such loose balls, out of the range of umpire, back judge and linesman, noting an illegal substitution or withdrawal during dead ball with time in (see 5-2-1-Notes, p. 26), and a foul signalled by a flag or cap during down. He will count defensive team.

Article 2   He is to time the intermission between the two periods of each half (4-1-2, p. 15), the length of all team time outs (4-3-4-S.N. 1 and 2, p. 18), and the 40/25 seconds permitted Team A to put ball in play (4-3-10-S.N. 1, p. 22). He is to utilize the 40/25 second clock provided for by the home team. If this clock is inoperative he should take over the official timing of the 40/25 seconds on the field.

Article 3   In addition to the specified use of the whistle by all officials (15-1-4, p. 99), the Field Judge is also to use his whistle, when upon his own positive knowledge he knows:

(a) that ball is dead,

(b) time is out or

(c) is out at end of down, during which a foul was signalled by a flag or cap, and no whistle has sounded in such cases.

Even in the presence of a whistle upfield, he is to sound his when downfield players are some distance away from such signal, and in order to prevent continuing action fouls. He should be particularly alert for item (c).

Article 4   He shall assist the referee in decisions involving any catching, recovery, out of bounds spot, or illegal touching, of a loose ball, after it has crossed scrimmage line and particularly so for such actions as are out of the range of the back judge, linesman and umpire. See 15-1-11-S.N. 1, p. 100. He should count the defensive players on the field at the snap.

Article 5   The field judge has the absolute responsibility:

(a) to instruct kicker and/or placekicker that "kickoff" *must* be made by placekick or dropkick.

(b) that the height of the tee (artificial or natural) used for the kickoff conforms to the governing rules.

Notify Visiting Team Coach

Note: He is to notify the visiting team at least five minutes before the start of the second half.

Rule 16 Sudden Death Procedures

Section 1 Sudden Death Procedures

Sudden
Death
Procedure

Article 1 The sudden death system of determining the winner shall prevail when the score is tied at the end of the regulation playing time of *all NFL games.* Under this system, the team scoring first during overtime play herein provided for, shall be the winner of the game and the game is automatically ended upon any score (including a safety) or when a score is awarded by the referee for a palpably unfair act.

Article 2 At the end of regulation playing time, the referee shall immediately toss a coin at the center of the field, in accordance with rules pertaining to a usual pregame toss (4-2-1, p. 15). The visiting team captain is to again call the toss.

Article 3 Following a three-minute intermission after the end of regular game, play shall continue by 15-minute periods with a two-minute intermission between each such overtime period with no halftime intermission.

Exception: Preseason and regular season league games shall have a maximum of one fifteen (15) minute period with the rule for 2 time outs instead of 3 as in a regular game and include the general provisions for the fourth quarter of a regular game.

At the end of each extra 15-minute period, starting with the end of the first one, teams must change goals in accordance with rule 4-2-2, p. 16. Disqualified player(s) may not re-enter during overtime period(s).

Article 4 During any intermission or team time out a player may leave the field.

Sudden
Death
Timing

Article 5 If there is an excess time out during the first and second, third and fourth, etc., extra periods, the usual rules shall apply (4-3-3 to 7, pp. 17-19).

Article 6 Near the end of any period or during the last two (2) minutes of the second, fourth, etc., extra periods, the usual rules in regard to attempts to conserve or consume time shall apply (4-3-10, p. 22-23 and 5-2-1, p. 25).

The rules for time outs shall be the same as in a regular game, including the last two (2) minutes of the second and fourth quarters.

Article 7 The clock operator shall time all extra fifteen (15) minute periods (4-3-1, p. 16). The field judge shall time the three (3) and two (2) minute intermissions, and is to sound his whistle 30 seconds before the expiration of each intermission. The referee shall sound his whistle for play to start, immediately upon the field judge's signal. See 4-3-9, p. 21, 4-3-10-S.N., p. 22.

Article 8 Except as specifically provided for above, all other general and specific rules shall apply during any extra period.

Rule 17　Emergencies, Unfair Acts

Section 1　Emergencies

**Non-Player
On
Field**

Article 1　If any non-player, including photographers, reporters, employees, police or spectators, enters the field of play or end zones, and in the judgment of an official said party or parties interfere with the play, the referee, after consulting his crew (12-3-3, p. 83 and 15-1-6, p. 99), shall enforce any such penalty or score as the interference warrants.

**Field
Control**

Article 2　If spectators enter the field and/or interfere with the progress of the game in such a manner that in the opinion of the referee the game cannot continue, he shall declare time out. In such a case he shall record the number of the down, distance to be gained, and position of ball on field. He shall also secure from the line judge the playing time remaining and record it. He shall then order the home club through its management to have the field cleared, and when it is cleared and order restored and the safety of the spectators, players and officials is assured to the satisfaction of the referee, the game must continue even if it is necessary to use lights.

**Game
Called**

Article 3　If the game must be called due to a state or municipal law, or by darkness if no lights are available, an immediate report shall be made to the Commissioner by the home club, visiting club and officials. On receipt of all reports the Commissioner shall make a decision which will be final.

**Emergency
Situations**

Article 4　The NFL affirms the position that in most circumstances all regular-season and postseason games should be played to their conclusion. If, in the opinion of appropriate League authorities, it is impossible to begin or continue a game due to an emergency, or a game is deemed to be imminently threatened by any such emergency (e.g., severely inclement weather, lightning, flooding, power failure), the following procedures (Articles 5 through 11) will serve as guidelines for the Commissioner and/or his duly appointed representatives. The Commissioner has the authority to review the circumstances of each emergency and to adjust the following procedures in whatever manner he deems appropriate. If, in the Commissioner's opinion, it is reasonable to project that the resumption of an interrupted game would not change its ultimate result or adversely affect any other inter-team competitive issue, he is empowered to terminate the game.

**League
Authority**

Article 5　The League employees vested with the authority to define emergencies under these procedures are the Commissioner, designated representatives from his League office staff, and the game referee. In those instances where neither the Commissioner nor his designated representative is in attendance at a game, the referee will have sole authority; provided, however, that if a referee delays the beginning of or interrupts a game for a significant period of time due to an emergency, he must make every effort to contact the Commissioner or the Commissioner's designated representative for consultation. In all cases of significant delay, the League authorities will consult with the management of the participating clubs and will attempt to obtain appropriate information from outside sources, if applicable (e.g., weather bureau, police).

Later Date

Article 6　If, due to an emergency, a regular-season or postseason game is not started at its scheduled time and cannot be played at any later time that same day, the game nevertheless must be played on a subsequent date to be determined by the Commissioner.

**Pregame
Threat**

Article 7　If there is deemed to be a threat of an emergency that may occur during the playing of a game (e.g., an incoming tropical storm), the starting time of such game will not be moved to an earlier time unless there is clearly sufficient time to make an orderly change.

**Interrupted
Game**

Article 8　If, under emergency circumstances, an interrupted regular-season or postseason game cannot be completed on the same day, such game will be rescheduled by the Commissioner and resumed at that point.

Alternate
Dates, Sites

Article 9 In instances under these emergency procedures which require the Commissioner to reschedule a regular-season game, he will make every effort to set the game for no later than two days after its originally scheduled date, and he will attempt to schedule the game at its original site. If unable to do so, he will schedule it at the nearest available facility. If it is impossible to schedule the game within two days after its original date, the Commissioner will attempt to schedule it on the Tuesday of the next calendar week in which the two involved clubs play other clubs (or each other). Further, the Commissioner will keep in mind the potential for competitive inequities if one or both of the involved clubs has already been scheduled for a game following the Tuesday of that week (e.g., Thanksgiving).

Postseason
Interruption

Article 10 If an emergency interrupts a postseason game and such game cannot be resumed on that same date, the Commissioner will make every effort to arrange for its completion as soon as possible. If unable to schedule the game at the same site, he will select an appropriate alternate site. He will terminate the game short of completion only if in his judgment the continuation of the game would not be normally expected to alter the ultimate result.

Game
Resumption

Article 11 In all instances where a game is resumed after interruption, either on the same date or a subsequent date, the resumption will begin at the point at which the game was interrupted. At the time of interruption, the referee will call time out and he will make a record of the following: the team possessing the ball, the direction in which its offense was headed, position of the ball on the field, down, distance, period, time remaining in the period, and any other pertinent information required for an efficient and equitable resumption of play.

Section 2 Extraordinarily Unfair Acts

Commissioner
Authority

Article 1 The Commissioner has the sole authority to investigate and take appropriate disciplinary and/or corrective measures if any club action, non-participant interference, or calamity occurs in an NFL game which he deems so extraordinarily unfair or outside the accepted tactics encountered in professional football that such action has a major effect on the result of the game.

No Club
Protests

Article 2 The authority and measures provided for in this entire Section 2 do not constitute a protest machinery for NFL clubs to avail themselves of in the event a dispute arises over the result of a game. The investigation called for in this Section 2 will be conducted solely on the Commissioner's initiative to review an act or occurrence that he deems so extraordinary or unfair that the result of the game in question would be inequitable to one of the participating teams. The Commissioner will not apply his authority in cases of complaints by clubs concerning judgmental errors or routine errors of omission by game officials. Games involving such complaints will continue to stand as completed.

Penalties for
Unfair Acts

Article 3 The Commissioner's powers under this Section 2 include the imposition of monetary fines and draft-choice forfeitures, suspension of persons involved in unfair acts, and, if appropriate, the reversal of a game's result or the rescheduling of a game, either from the beginning or from the point at which the extraordinary act occurred. In the event of rescheduling a game, the Commissioner will be guided by the procedures specified in Rule 17, Section 1, Articles 5 through 11, above. In all cases, the Commissioner will conduct a full investigation, including the opportunity for hearings, use of game videotape, and any other procedure he deems appropriate.

Rule 18 Guidelines for Captains

Section 1 Guidelines for Captains

Article 1 One hour prior to kickoff:
Respective coaches designate the captain(s) — a maximum of six per team.

Coin
Toss
Option

Article 2 Coin toss:

(a) Up to six captains per team can participate in the coin toss ceremony; only one captain from the visiting team (or captain designated by Referee if there is no home team) can declare the choice of coin toss.

(b) The team that won the toss may then have only one captain declare its option.

(c) The team that lost the coin toss may then have only one captain declare its option.

Penalty
Option

Article 3 Choice on Penalty Option:
Only one captain is permitted to indicate the team's penalty option.

Change of
Captains

Article 4 Change of Captains:

(a) The coach has prerogative of informing Referee when he wishes to make a change in team captains; or

(b) A captain who is leaving can inform the Referee which player will act as captain in his place when he is substituted for; or

(c) When a captain leaves the game, the incoming substitute is permitted to inform the Referee which player the respective coach has designated as captain.

Note: A captain on the field has no authority to request a change of fellow team captain when that captain remains on the field.

Penalty Summary

Distance Penalties

Loss of Five Yards

Each time out in each half being in excess of three unless not notified or unless a fourth time out for injured player as specified (see charged time out penalties) . . . . .4-3-5 and 6, p. 18

Delay of game, i.e.,
exceeding 40/25 seconds in putting ball in play . . . . .4-3-9, p. 21

failing to play immediately when ordered . . . . .4-3-9, p. 22

player exercising privileges of captain . . .4-3-9, p. 22

repeatedly snapping ball before referee can assume normal position . . . . .4-3-9, p. 22, and 7-3-3-(c)-(2), p. 39

runner repeatedly attempting to advance when securely held .4-3-9, p. 22

runner remaining on ball or opponent remaining on runner to consume time . . . . .4-3-9, p. 22

undue delay in assembling after a time out . . . . .4-3-9, p. 22

repeatedly entering neutral zone when not otherwise encroaching . . . . .4-3-9, p. 22

unduly delaying establishment of neutral zone especially during time in . . . . .4-3-9, p. 22

illegal return . . . . .5-1-5, p. 25

kickers advancing recovered kick (not behind line) causes delay . . . . .4-3-9, p. 22, and 9-1-4, p. 59

substituting while ball is in play unless interference . . . . .4-3-9, p. 22, and 12-3-1, p. 82

contacting snapper or ball . . . . .7-3-5, p. 40

catcher unduly advancing after fair catch signal . . . . .4-3-9, p. 22, and 10-1-2, p. 65

attempting to conserve or consume time near end of period, especially during last two minutes of half (also stop or not to stop watch to nullify) . . . . .4-3-10, p. 23

more than eleven players on field during play . . . . .5-1-1, p. 25

Illegal substitution, i.e.,
substitute entering during play, withdrawn player on field at snap or free kick (unless interference) or withdrawing on opponents' side or across end line .5-2-1, p. 26

Illegal kick at free kick (ball remains dead and replay) . . . . .6-1-3, p. 30

Violation of free kick formation (includes kickoff), i.e. kickers failing to be behind ball or inbounds (except place kick holder) . . . . .6-1-3, p. 30, and 6-1-5, p. 31

receivers failing to be in bounds or behind their free kick line . . . . .6-1-5, p. 31

Prolonged, excessive, or premeditated celebrations by individual players or groups of players . . . . .12-3-1, p. 82

making short free kick . . . . .6-2-1, p. 31

illegally touching free kick (a) before it goes 10 yards or (b) after being out of bounds 6-2-4, p. 32

kicking free kick out of bounds between goal lines unless B last touches . . . . .6-3-1, p. 33

Illegal position of A players at snap, i.e., having fewer than seven players on line . . . . .7-2-1, p. 36

Having player neither on nor one yard behind his line unless man under center . . . . .7-2-1, p. 36

Player entering neutral zone contacts opponent, causes him to charge or be offside (encroaching) or repeatedly entering it after warning (when not otherwise encroaching) . . . . .7-2-2, p. 36

Player not reporting change in eligibility . . . . .7-2-3, p. 37

Being offside at snap . . . . .7-2-2, p. 36

Illegal motion by A at snap, i.e.,
player not being stationary (except) one only in motion clearly backward . . . . .7-2-5, p. 38

Single player not moving clearly backward at snap . . . . .7-2-5, p. 38

Moving backward from on scrimmage line and not being one yard back at snap . . . . . .7-2-4, p. 37

Pausing less than one second after a shift . . . . .7-2-6, p. 38

Being out of bounds at snap . . . . .7-2-7, p. 39

Not snapping ball when prescribed . . . . . . .7-3-1, p. 39

Illegally snapping ball, i.e.,
failing to make backward pass . . . . .7-3-3, p. 39

Failing to place ball on ground as specified . . . . .7-3-3, p. 39

Failing to give impulse by continuous motion or sliding hands along ball before snap . . . .7-3-3, p. 39

Snapper moving his feet before ball leaves his hands during the snap . . . . .7-3-3, p. 39

False start . . . . .7-3-4, p. 40

Player under center not receiving snap 7-3-4, p.40

Snap going to receiver on line . . . . .7-3-6, p. 41

Making forward pass in field of play not from scrimmage . . . . .8-1-1, p. 45.

Making forward pass beyond line of scrimmage (also loss of down) . . . . 8-1-1, p. 45

Ineligible player downfield on kick . . . . 9-1-3, p. 59

Ineligible player downfield on pass . . . . 8-2-2, p. 49

Making invalid fair catch signal . . . . .10-1-1, p. 65

Catcher unduly advancing after fair catch signal, unless touched by kickers in flight or after ball strikes ground . . . . .10-1-2, 3, p. 65

Illegal use of hands or arms by defense, i.e.,
to hold an opponent who is not the
runner . . . . 12-1-4, pp. 75, 76
other than to ward off an opponent, to push or
pull him, to get a runner or ball or to
block . . . . 12-1-4, p. 76
Defensive player during pass behind
line pushes potential receiver behind
line . . . . 12-1-4-A.R. 7, p. 77
Running into kicker behind his line (not
roughing) . . . . 12-2-6, p. 78
Incidental grasp of face mask . . . . 12-2-5, p. 78

Loss of 10 Yards

Pass touched or caught by an ineligible offensive
player beyond line (or loss of down) . . . . . . 8-1-5, p. 47
Pass interference by team A . . . . 8-2-7, p. 51
Tripping, holding, illegal use of hands,
arms or body on offense . . . . 12-1-3, p. 75
Assisting runner . . . . 12-1-1, p. 75
Batting or punching ball, when loose (unless a
pass), towards opponents' goal line or in any
direction if an end zone, or from possession
of a runner . . . . 12-1-6, p. 77
Illegally kicking ball . . . . 12-1-7, p. 77

Loss of 15 Yards

Not being ready to start each half on
scheduled time . . . . 4-1-5, p. 15
Interfering with fair catch (and catch
awarded) . . . . 10-1-4, p. 66
Tackling or blocking maker of a fair catch or
avoidable running into . . . . 10-1-5, p. 67
Head slap . . . . 12-2-2, p. 78
Striking, kneeing and kicking
(also disqualification) . . . . 12-2-1, p. 77
Striking an opponent on head, neck, or face
with palm of hands . . . . 12-2-2, p. 78
Striking opponent below shoulders with forearm
or elbow by turning or pivoting . . . . 12-2-4, p. 78
Twisting, turning, or pulling of opponent's
face mask . . . . 12-2-5, p. 78
Blocking below waist on kicks and
change of possession . . . . 12-2-13, p. 81
Roughing the kicker . . . . 12-2-6, p. 78
Falling on or piling on a prostrate player . . 12-2-7, p. 79
Unnecessary roughness (also disqualification
when flagrant), i.e.,
striking an opponent above knee with
foot or shin . . . . 12-2-8, p. 79
tackling runner who is out of bounds . . . 12-2-8, p. 79
running into, throwing body against a player
obviously out of the play or after the ball is
dead . . . . 12-2-8, p. 79
running into from behind or dropping body
across back of legs of opponent who is
not the runner (clipping) . . . . 12-2-9, p. 80
illegal crackback . . . . 12-2-10, p. 80
running into passer after ball leaves
his hand . . . . 12-2-11, p. 80
Chop block—passing play . . . . 12-2-14, p. 82
Chop block—running play . . . . 12-2-15, p. 82
Illegal block after fair catch signal . . . . . . 10-1-3, p. 65

Unsportsmanlike conduct by players (also
disqualification when flagrant), i.e.
using abusive or insulting language or gestures
to players or officials or continuing acts
engendering ill will . . . . 12-3-10, p. 82
attempting to disconcert A at snap by words
or signals . . . . 12-3-1-d, p. 82
concealing the ball under clothing or substi-
tuting article for it . . . . 12-3-1-e, p. 82
leaping to attempt to block a field goal or
point after touchdown unless the player
was lined up on the line of scrimmage
when the ball was snapped . . . . 12-3-1-n, p. 83
a punter, placekicker, or holder who
simulates being roughed or run into by
a defensive player . . . . 12-3-1-o, p. 83
taunting . . . . 12-3-1-b, p. 82
lingering . . . . 12-3-1-f, p. 83
player pushing, shoving, or laying hand on
official (Note) . . . . 12-3-1-Pen. (Note), p. 83
using substitutes or withdrawn players to
confuse opponents (5-2-1-1) p. 26 . . . . . 12-3-1, p. 82
repeatedly violating substitution rule in
attempts to conserve time . . . . 5-2-2, p. 27, and
12-3-1-h, p. 83
violating 25-second rule more than twice
(same down) after a warning . . . . 12-3-1-i, p. 83
Illegal conduct by non-players (also exclusion
for flagrant violations), i.e.,
player on field communicating other than to
coach in prescribed area . . . . 13-1-1, p. 85
team representatives using unsportsmanlike
conduct during game or between halves or
sitting on bench when not qualified . . . . . 13-1-1, p. 85
non-players going on field without permission
(other than team attendants during a team
time out) . . . . 13-1-2, p. 85
non-players moving along boundary lines
(unless substitute warming up or coach in
prescribed area) . . . . 13-1-5, p. 85

Loss of Half Distance to Goal Line

Pass interfering by B in its end zone and previous
spot is inside their 2 yard line . . . . 8-2-5, p. 51
Distance penalty enforced from a spot between
goal lines carrying ball more than half the distance
to either goal line . . . . 14-2-1, p. 91

Ball Placed on 1 Yard Line

Pass interfering by B in its end zone and previous
spot is outside its 2 yard line . . . . 8-2-5, p. 51

Loss of Down Penalty

(Unless Touchback)

Making second forward pass from behind line
(same scrimmage) . . . . 8-1-1, p. 45
Pass after ball crossed line and returned . . 8-1-1, p. 45
Pass touching ineligible A
behind line . . . . 8-1-4, p. 46, and 8-1-5, p. 47

Withdrawal Penalties

Requesting fourth or more time out for
injury during last two minutes of either
half . . . . 4-3-4 and 4-3-5, p. 18

Player being disqualified, suspended
(illegal equipment), or
replaced . . . . 5-1-5, p. 25

Injured player taking more than two
minutes or repair of legal equipment
taking more than three
minutes . . . . 4-3-4, p. 18; and 5-1-5, p. 25

Player leaving field during
time out . . . . 4-3-3, p. 17, and 5-2-1, p. 25

Illegal return (loss of five also) . . . . 5-1-5, p. 25

Disqualification Penalties

Disqualification always occurs in combination
with a 15-yard penalty. Exceptions to distance
penalties:

    Both teams committing disqualifying fouls
    (double foul) . . . . 14-3-1, p. 92

Distance being declined . . . . 14-6, p. 96

Loss of 15 Yards

Flagrant striking, kicking, or kneeing an opponent or
striking him on head or neck with heel, back or
side of hand, wrist, elbow, or forearm . . . . 12-2-1, p. 77

Flagrant roughing of kicker . . . . 12-2-6, p. 78

Flagrant roughing of passer . . . . 12-2-11, p. 80

Flagrant unsportsmanlike conduct by
players . . . . 12-3-1, p. 83

Player using a helmet as a weapon . . . . . 12-2-13, p. 81

Disqualified player returning (exclusion
from field enclosure) . . . . 5-1-5, p. 25, and
13-1-4 penalty, p. 85

Suspended player illegally
returning . . . . 5-1-5, p. 25 and 13-1-4, p. 85

Loss of Ball Penalties

Ball being behind necessary line
at end of fourth down . . . . 7-1-1, p. 35

Kickers first touching kick (not a free kick)
in field of play . . . . 9-1-4, p. 59

Interfering with fair catch (also fair
catch allowed) . . . . 10-1-4, p. 66

Disqualification for Entire Game

Repeat violation by player wearing
or displaying illegal equipment . . . . . 5-3-8-Pen., p. 29A

Charged Time Out Penalties

Player requesting time out (includes for injured
player when one of first three time outs in
each half) . . . . 4-3-3, p. 17

Taking time out for injured player during last
two minutes of either half (withdrawal only
when fourth time out — also loss of five when
fifth or more) . . . . 4-3-6, p. 18

Taking time out for repair of legal equipment (also
withdrawal if more than three minutes) . . . . 4-3-4, p. 18

Time Penalty

Illegal conserving or consuming time near end of
period (stop or not stop watch) or start watch with
whistle when intent is in doubt . . . . 4-3-10, p. 22

Fouling by defense, illegal touching or fair catch
interfering by offense or fouling by both teams at
end of half during play in which time expires
(extend quarter) . . . . 4-3-11, p. 23

Replay Penalties

B fouling on try which fails . . . . 11-3-3, p. 70

Committing double foul unless continuing action
fouls by both teams after ball is dead, the one only
disqualifying foul is by B . . . . . 14-1-8 and 9, pp. 88, 89;
14-3-1, p. 92; and
14-3-2, p. 93

Score Penalties

Try-for-Point Awarded

Team B committing a foul during a try which would
ordinarily result in a safety . . . . 11-3-3, p. 70

Score Awarded

Repeated fouling by defense (near own goal line)
to prevent score by halving distance . . . . . 12-3-2, p. 83

Touchdown Awarded

Committing palpably unfair act which deprives
opponent of a touchdown . . . . 12-3-3, p. 83 and
13-1-7, p. 86

Safety

Offense fouling anywhere, and spot of enforcement
is behind its own goal line . . . . 11-4-2, p. 71, and
14-1-11, p. 89

Intentional grounding in own
end zone . . . . 8-3-1, p. 53

Making a forward pass (not from scrimmage)
from within passer's end zone . . . . 8-1-1, p. 45, and
14-1-11, p. 89

Score Not Allowed

Offending team scores after foul during
down in which time expires for half (also
no extension of time) . . . . 4-3-11, p. 23

Unsuccessful Try

Attempted kick ceasing to be in play . . . . 11-3-1, p. 69
Team A committing foul during a try which
would ordinarily result:

    in loss of down or in a touchback . . . . . . 11-3-3, p. 70

    in loss of ball in field of play (not during
    a kick) . . . . 11-3-3, p. 70

    B recovering ball . . . . 11-3-5, p. 70

New Series Penalties

B committing a foul during play from scrimmage
giving A first down irrespective of distance
penalty . . . . 14-8-5, p. 97

B committing a foul not giving A first down unless
enforcement places ball in advance of necessary
line, i.e.,

    excess time out . . . . 4-3-6, p. 19

Combination Penalties

Loss of Down and Five

Loss of Down and 10

Loss of Ball and 15

Touchback

Score, Distance or Disqualification

Miscellaneous Situations

Safety

Ball in possession of team behind or out of
bounds behind own goal line and impetus
which sent it in touch came from:

Kickoff Out of Bounds Between Goal Lines

Ball Remains Dead

Ball Dead Immediately

Penalty Enforced From Goal Line

Penalty Enforced on Next Free Kick

Index

Official Signals

1

**TOUCHDOWN, FIELD GOAL,
or SUCCESSFUL TRY**
Both arms extended above head.

2

SAFETY
Palms together above head.

3

FIRST DOWN
Arms pointed toward defensive
team's goal.

4

**CROWD NOISE,
DEAD BALL, or NEUTRAL
ZONE ESTABLISHED**
One arm above head
with an open hand.
With fist closed: **Fourth Down.**

5

**BALL ILLEGALLY
TOUCHED, KICKED,
OR BATTED**
Fingertips tap both shoulders.

6

TIME OUT
Hands crisscrossed above head.
Same signal followed by placing one
hand on top of cap: **Referee's Time Out.**
Same signal followed by arm swung at
side: **Touchback.**

7

**NO TIME OUT or
TIME IN WITH WHISTLE**
Full arm circled to
simulate moving clock.

8

**DELAY OF GAME,
ILLEGAL SUBSTITUTION,
OR EXCESS TIME OUT**
Folded arms.

9

**FALSE START, ILLEGAL
SHIFT, ILLEGAL
FORMATION, or KICKOFF OR
SAFETY KICK OUT OF
BOUNDS**
Forearms rotated over and over
in front of body.

10

PERSONAL FOUL
One wrist striking the other above head.
Same signal followed by swinging leg:
Roughing Kicker.
Same signal followed by raised arm
swinging forward:
Roughing Passer.
Same signal followed by hand striking
back of calf: **Clipping.**

11

HOLDING
Grasping one wrist,
the fist clenched,
in front of chest.

12

**ILLEGAL USE OF HANDS,
ARMS, OR BODY**
Grasping one wrist,
the hand open and facing
forward, in front of chest.

13

**PENALTY REFUSED,
INCOMPLETE
PASS, PLAY OVER, or
MISSED GOAL**
Hands shifted in horizontal plane.

14

**PASS JUGGLED INBOUNDS AND
CAUGHT OUT OF BOUNDS**
Hands up and down in front of chest
(following incomplete pass signal).

15

ILLEGAL FORWARD PASS
One hand waved behind back
followed by loss of down
signal (23).

16

**INTENTIONAL
GROUNDING OF PASS**
Parallel arms waved in a diagonal
plane across body. Followed by loss
of down signal (23).

17

**INTERFERENCE WITH FORWARD
PASS or FAIR CATCH**
Hands open
and extended forward from
shoulders with hands vertical.

18

INVALID FAIR CATCH SIGNAL
One hand waved above head.

19

**INELIGIBLE RECEIVER
or INELIGIBLE
MEMBER OF KICKING
TEAM DOWNFIELD**
Right hand touching top of cap.

20

ILLEGAL CONTACT
One open hand extended forward.

21

OFFSIDE or ENCROACHING
Hands on hips.

22

ILLEGAL MOTION AT SNAP
Horizontal arc with one hand.

23

LOSS OF DOWN
Both hands held behind head.

24

**CRAWLING, INTERLOCKING
INTERFERENCE, PUSHING, or
HELPING RUNNER**
Pushing movement of hands
to front with arms downward.

25

**TOUCHING A FORWARD
PASS OR SCRIMMAGE KICK**
Diagonal motion of
one hand across another.

26

**UNSPORTSMANLIKE
CONDUCT**
Arms outstretched, palms down.
(Same signal means continuous
action fouls are disregarded.)
Chop block.

27

ILLEGAL CUT
Hands striking front of thigh.
**ILLEGAL BLOCK BELOW
THE WAIST**
Hand striking front of thigh
preceded by personal foul
signal (10).

28

ILLEGAL CRACKBACK
Strike of an open right hand
against the right mid thigh
preceded by personal foul
signal (10).

29

**PLAYER
DISQUALIFIED**
Ejection signal.

30

TRIPPING
Repeated action
of right foot in
back of left heel.

31

**UNCATCHABLE
FORWARD PASS**
Palm of right hand
held parallel to ground
above head and moved
back and forth.

1993 NFL Roster of Officials

Jerry Seeman, Director of Officiating
Jack Reader, Assistant Director of Officiating
Leo Miles, Supervisor of Officials
Ron DeSouza, Supervisor of Officials

No.	Name	Position	College
25	Alderton, John	Line Judge	Portland State
115	Ancich, Hendi	Umpire	Harbor College
81	Anderson, Dave	Line Judge	Salem College
34	Austin, Gerald	Referee	Western Carolina
22	Baetz, Paul	Back Judge	Heidelberg
91	Baker, Ken	Back Judge	Eastern Illinois
26	Baltz, Mark	Head Linesman	Ohio University
55	Barnes, Tom	Line Judge	Minnesota
56	Baynes, Ron	Line Judge	Auburn
32	Bergman, Jeff	Line Judge	Robert Morris
17	Bergman, Jerry	Head Linesman	Duquesne
7	Blum, Ron	Referee	Marin College
90	Borgard, Mike	Side Judge	St. Louis
110	Botchan, Ron	Umpire	Occidental
101	Boylston, Bob	Umpire	Alabama
31	Brown, Chad	Umpire	East Texas State
94	Carey, Mike	Side Judge	Santa Clara
39	Carlsen, Don	Side Judge	Cal State-Chico
63	Carollo, Bill	Side Judge	Wisconsin
43	Cashion, Red	Referee	Texas A&M
24	Clymer, Roy	Back Judge	New Mexico State
45	Coleman, George	Back Judge	Bishop College
65	Coleman, Walt	Line Judge	Arkansas
27	Conway, Al	Umpire	Army
71	Coukart, Ed	Umpire	Northwestern
61	Creed, Dick	Side Judge	Louisville
75	Daopoulos, Jim	Back Judge	Kentucky
78	Demmas, Art	Umpire	Vanderbilt
113	Dorkowski, Don	Field Judge	Cal State-Los Angeles
74	Duke, James	Line Judge	Howard
57	Fiffick, Ed	Umpire	Marquette
47	Fincken, Tom	Side Judge	Kansas State
111	Frantz, Earnie	Head Linesman	No College
50	Gereb, Neil	Umpire	California
72	Gierke, Terry	Head Linesman	Portland State
15	Glass, Bama	Line Judge	Colorado
3	Golmont, Van	Side Judge	Miami
19	Green, Scott	Field Judge	Delaware
23	Grier, Johnny	Referee	University of D.C.
96	Hakes, Don	Field Judge	Bradley
104	Hamer, Dale	Referee	California, Pa.
42	Hamilton, Dave	Umpire	Utah
44	Hampton, Donnie	Field Judge	Georgia
105	Hantak, Dick	Referee	Southeastern Missouri
54	Hayward, George	Head Linesman	Missouri
85	Hochuli, Ed	Referee	Texas-El Paso
114	Johnson, Tom	Head Linesman	Miami, Ohio
97	Jones, Nathan	Side Judge	Lewis & Clark
106	Jury, Al	Back Judge	San Bernardino Valley
107	Kearney, Jim	Back Judge	Pennsylvania
67	Keck, John	Umpire	Cornell College
86	Kukar, Bernie	Referee	St. John's
120	Lane, Gary	Referee	Missouri
18	Lewis, Bob	Field Judge	No College
49	Look, Dean	Side Judge	Michigan State
98	Lovett, Bill	Back Judge	Maryland
59	Luckett, Phil	Field Judge	Texas-El Paso
82	Mallette, Pat	Field Judge	Nebraska
9	Markbreit, Jerry	Referee	Illinois
38	Maurer, Bruce	Line Judge	Ohio State
48	McCarter, Gordon	Referee	Western Reserve
95	McElwee, Bobby	Referee	Navy
35	McGrath, Bob	Head Linesman	Western Kentucky
41	McKenzie, Dick	Line Judge	Ashland
64	McPeters, Lloyd	Line Judge	Oklahoma State
76	Merrifield, Ed	Field Judge	Missouri
80	Millis, Tim	Back Judge	Millsaps
117	Montgomery, Ben	Line Judge	Morehouse
36	Moore, Bob	Back Judge	Dayton
60	Moore, Tommy	Side Judge	Stephen F. Austin
20	Nemmers, Larry	Referee	Upper Iowa
51	Orem, Dale	Line Judge	Louisville
77	Orr, Don	Field Judge	Vanderbilt
10	Phares, Ron	Head Linesman	Virginia Tech
79	Pointer, Aaron	Head Linesman	Pacific Lutheran
92	Poole, Jim	Back Judge	San Diego State
58	Quinby, Bill	Side Judge	Iowa
5	Quirk, Jim	Line Judge	Delaware
83	Reels, Richard	Field Judge	No college
53	Reynolds, Bill	Line Judge	West Chester State
68	Richard, Louis	Back Judge	S.W. Louisiana
30	Riggs, Dennis	Umpire	Bellarmine
121	Rivers, Sanford	Head Linesman	Youngstown State
46	Robison, John	Field Judge	Utah
33	Roe, Howard	Referee	Wichita State
21	Schleyer, John	Head Linesman	Millersville
122	Schmitz, Bill	Field Judge	Colorado State
109	Semon, Sid	Head Linesman	Southern California
118	Sifferman, Tom	Back Judge	Seattle
73	Skelton, Bobby	Field Judge	Alabama
29	Slavin, Howard	Side Judge	Southern California
119	Spitler, Ron	Side Judge	Panhandle State
62	Stewart, Charles	Line Judge	No College
88	Steenson, Scott	Back Judge	North Texas State
103	Stuart, Rex	Umpire	Appalachian State
4	Toole, Doug	Back Judge	Utah State
37	Upson, Larry	Field Judge	Prince George C.C.
93	Vaughan, Jack	Field Judge	Mississippi State
52	Veteri, Tony	Head Linesman	Manhattan College
100	Wagner, Bob	Umpire	Penn State
28	Wedge, Don	Side Judge	Ohio Wesleyan
87	Weidner, Paul	Head Linesman	Cincinnati
89	Wells, Gordon	Umpire	Occidental
123	White, Tom	Referee	Temple
99	Williams, Banks	Back Judge	Houston
8	Williams, Dale	Head Linesman	Cal St.-Northridge
16	Wyant, David	Side Judge	Virginia

Numerical Roster

No.	Name	Position
3	Van Golmont	SJ
4	Doug Toole	BJ
5	Jim Quirk	LJ
7	Ron Blum	R
8	Dale Williams	HL
9	Jerry Markbreit	R
10	Ron Phares	HL
15	Bama Glass	LJ
16	David Wyant	SJ
17	Jerry Bergman	HL
18	Bob Lewis	FJ
19	Scott Green	FJ
20	Larry Nemmers	R
21	John Schleyer	HL
22	Paul Baetz	BJ
23	Johnny Grier	R
24	Roy Clymer	BJ
25	John Alderton	LJ
26	Mark Baltz	HL
27	Al Conway	U
28	Don Wedge	SJ
29	Howard Slavin	SJ
30	Dennis Riggs	U
31	Chad Brown	U
32	Jeff Bergman	LJ
33	Howard Roe	R
34	Gerald Austin	R
35	Bob McGrath	HL
36	Bob Moore	BJ
37	Larry Upson	FJ
38	Bruce Maurer	LJ
39	Don Carlsen	SJ
41	Dick McKenzie	LJ
42	Dave Hamilton	U
43	Red Cashion	R
44	Donnie Hampton	FJ
45	George Coleman	BJ
46	John Robison	FJ
47	Tom Fincken	SJ
48	Gordon McCarter	R
49	Dean Look	SJ
50	Neil Gereb	U
51	Dale Orem	LJ
52	Tony Veteri	HL
53	Bill Reynolds	LJ
54	George Hayward	HL
55	Tom Barnes	LJ
56	Ron Baynes	LJ
57	Ed Fiffick	U
58	Bill Quinby	SJ
59	Phil Luckett	FJ
60	Tommy Moore	SJ
61	Dick Creed	SJ
62	Charles Stewart	LJ
63	Bill Carollo	SJ
64	Lloyd McPeters	LJ
65	Walt Coleman	LJ
67	John Keck	U
68	Louis Richard	BJ
71	Ed Coukart	U
72	Terry Gierke	HL
73	Bobby Skelton	FJ
74	James Duke	LJ
75	Jim Daopoulos	BJ
76	Ed Merrifield	FJ
77	Don Orr	FJ
78	Art Demmas	U
79	Aaron Pointer	HL
80	Tim Millis	BJ
81	Dave Anderson	LJ
82	Pat Mallette	FJ
83	Richard Reels	FJ
85	Ed Hochuli	R
86	Bernie Kukar	R
87	Paul Weidner	HL
88	Scott Steenson	BJ
89	Gordon Wells	U
90	Mike Borgard	SJ
91	Ken Baker	BJ
92	Jim Poole	BJ
93	Jack Vaughan	FJ
94	Mike Carey	SJ
95	Bob McElwee	R
96	Don Hakes	FJ
97	Nathan Jones	SJ
98	Bill Lovett	BJ
99	Banks Williams	BJ
100	Bob Wagner	U
101	Bob Boylston	U
103	Rex Stuart	U
104	Dale Hamer	R
105	Dick Hantak	R
106	Al Jury	BJ
107	Jim Kearney	BJ
109	Sid Semon	HL
110	Ron Botchan	U
111	Earnie Frantz	HL
113	Don Dorkowski	FJ
114	Tom Johnson	HL
115	Hendi Ancich	U
117	Ben Montgomery	LJ
118	Tom Sifferman	BJ
119	Ron Spitler	SJ
120	Gary Lane	R
121	Sanford Rivers	HL
122	Bill Schmitz	FJ
123	Tom White	R

1993 NFL SCHEDULE

(All times local. CBS and NBC television doubleheader games to be determined.)

FIRST WEEK

Sunday, September 5 (CBS-TV national weekend)

1. Atlanta at Detroit 1:00
2. Cincinnati at Cleveland 1:00
3. Denver at New York Jets 1:00
4. Kansas City at Tampa Bay 1:00
5. Los Angeles Rams vs. Green Bay at Milw. 12:00
6. Miami at Indianapolis 12:00
7. Minnesota at Los Angeles Raiders 1:00
8. New England at Buffalo 1:00
9. New York Giants at Chicago 3:00
10. Phoenix at Philadelphia 1:00
11. San Francisco at Pittsburgh 1:00
12. Seattle at San Diego 1:00

Sunday Night, September 5

13. Houston at New Orleans 7:00

Monday, September 6

14. Dallas at Washington 9:00

SECOND WEEK

Sunday, September 12 (NBC-TV national weekend)

15. Buffalo at Dallas 3:00
16. Chicago at Minnesota 12:00
17. Detroit at New England 1:00
18. Indianapolis at Cincinnati 1:00
19. Kansas City at Houston 12:00
20. New Orleans at Atlanta 1:00
21. New York Jets at Miami 4:00
22. Philadelphia at Green Bay 12:00
23. Phoenix at Washington 1:00
24. Pittsburgh at Los Angeles Rams 1:00
25. San Diego at Denver 2:00
26. Tampa Bay at New York Giants 1:00

Sunday Night, September 12

27. Los Angeles Raiders at Seattle 5:00

Monday, September 13

28. San Francisco at Cleveland 9:00

THIRD WEEK

Sunday, September 19 (NBC-TV national weekend)

29. Atlanta at San Francisco 1:00
30. Cincinnati at Pittsburgh 1:00
31. Cleveland at Los Angeles Raiders 1:00
32. Detroit at New Orleans 12:00
33. Houston at San Diego 1:00
34. Los Angeles Rams at New York Giants 1:00
35. Seattle at New England 1:00
36. Washington at Philadelphia 1:00

Sunday Night, September 19

37. Dallas at Phoenix 5:00

Monday, September 20

38. Denver at Kansas City 8:00

FOURTH WEEK

Sunday, September 26 (CBS-TV national weekend)

39. Cleveland at Indianapolis 12:00
40. Green Bay at Minnesota 12:00
41. Los Angeles Rams at Houston 12:00
42. Miami at Buffalo 1:00
43. Phoenix at Detroit 1:00
44. San Francisco at New Orleans 3:00
45. Seattle at Cincinnati 4:00
46. Tampa Bay at Chicago 12:00

Sunday Night, September 26

47. New England at New York Jets 8:00

Monday, September 27

48. Pittsburgh at Atlanta 9:00

FIFTH WEEK

Sunday, October 3 (CBS-TV national weekend)

49. Atlanta at Chicago 12:00
50. Detroit at Tampa Bay 1:00
51. Green Bay at Dallas 12:00
52. Indianapolis at Denver 2:00
53. Los Angeles Raiders at Kansas City 12:00
54. Minnesota at San Francisco 1:00
55. New Orleans at Los Angeles Rams 1:00
56. Philadelphia at New York Jets 4:00
57. San Diego at Seattle 1:00

Sunday Night, October 3

58. New York Giants at Buffalo 8:00

Monday, October 4

59. Washington at Miami 9:00

SIXTH WEEK

Sunday, October 10 (NBC-TV national weekend)

60. Chicago at Philadelphia 1:00
61. Cincinnati at Kansas City 12:00
62. Dallas at Indianapolis 12:00
63. Miami at Cleveland 1:00
64. New England at Phoenix 1:00
65. New York Giants at Washington 1:00
66. New York Jets at Los Angeles Raiders 1:00
67. San Diego at Pittsburgh 1:00
68. Tampa Bay at Minnesota 12:00

Sunday Night, October 10

69. Denver at Green Bay 6:30

Monday, October 11

70. Houston at Buffalo 9:00

SEVENTH WEEK

Thursday, October 14 (CBS-TV national weekend)

71. Los Angeles Rams at Atlanta 7:30

Sunday, October 17

72. Cleveland at Cincinnati 1:00
73. Houston at New England 1:00
74. Kansas City at San Diego 1:00
75. New Orleans at Pittsburgh 1:00
76. Philadelphia at New York Giants 1:00
77. San Francisco at Dallas 3:00
78. Seattle at Detroit 1:00
79. Washington at Phoenix 1:00

Monday, October 18

80. Los Angeles Raiders at Denver 7:00

EIGHTH WEEK

Sunday, October 24 (NBC-TV national weekend)

81. Atlanta at New Orleans 12:00
82. Buffalo at New York Jets 1:00
83. Cincinnati at Houston 12:00
84. Detroit at Los Angeles Rams 1:00
85. Green Bay at Tampa Bay 1:00
86. New England at Seattle 1:00
87. Phoenix at San Francisco 1:00
88. Pittsburgh at Cleveland 1:00

Sunday Night, October 24

89. Indianapolis at Miami 7:30

Monday, October 25

90. Minnesota at Chicago 8:00

NINTH WEEK

Sunday, October 31 (CBS-TV national weekend)

91. Chicago at Green Bay 12:00
92. Dallas at Philadelphia 1:00
93. Kansas City at Miami 1:00
94. Los Angeles Rams at San Francisco 1:00
95. New England at Indianapolis 1:00
96. New Orleans at Phoenix 2:00
97. New York Jets at New York Giants 1:00
98. San Diego at Los Angeles Raiders 1:00
99. Seattle at Denver 2:00
100. Tampa Bay at Atlanta 1:00

Sunday Night, October 31

101. Detroit at Minnesota 7:00

Monday, November 1

102. Washington at Buffalo 9:00

TENTH WEEK

Sunday, November 7 (NBC-TV national weekend)

103. Buffalo at New England 1:00
104. Denver at Cleveland 1:00
105. Los Angeles Raiders at Chicago 3:00
106. Miami at New York Jets 4:00
107. New York Giants at Dallas 12:00
108. Philadelphia at Phoenix 2:00
109. Pittsburgh at Cincinnati 1:00
110. San Diego at Minnesota 12:00
111. Seattle at Houston 12:00
112. Tampa Bay at Detroit 1:00

Sunday Night, November 7

113. Indianapolis at Washington 8:00

Monday, November 8

114. Green Bay at Kansas City 8:00

ELEVENTH WEEK

Sunday, November 14 (CBS-TV national weekend)

115. Atlanta at Los Angeles Rams 1:00
116. Cleveland at Seattle 1:00
117. Green Bay at New Orleans 12:00
118. Houston at Cincinnati 1:00
119. Kansas City at Los Angeles Raiders 1:00
120. Miami at Philadelphia 1:00
121. Minnesota at Denver 2:00
122. New York Jets at Indianapolis 4:00
123. Phoenix at Dallas 12:00
124. San Francisco at Tampa Bay 1:00
125. Washington at New York Giants 1:00

Sunday Night, November 14

126. Chicago at San Diego 5:00

Monday, November 15

127. Buffalo at Pittsburgh 9:00

TWELFTH WEEK

Sunday, November 21 (NBC-TV national weekend)

128. Chicago at Kansas City 12:00
129. Cincinnati at New York Jets 1:00
130. Dallas at Atlanta 1:00
131. Detroit vs. Green Bay at Milwaukee 12:00
132. Houston at Cleveland 1:00
133. Indianapolis at Buffalo 1:00
134. Los Angeles Raiders at San Diego 1:00
135. New England at Miami 1:00
136. New York Giants at Philadelphia 4:00
137. Pittsburgh at Denver 2:00
138. Washington at Los Angeles Rams 1:00

Sunday Night, November 21

139. Minnesota at Tampa Bay 8:00

Monday, November 22

140. New Orleans at San Francisco 6:00

THIRTEENTH WEEK

Thursday, November 25 (CBS-TV national weekend)

141. Chicago at Detroit 12:30
142. Miami at Dallas 3:00

Sunday, November 28

143. Buffalo at Kansas City 3:00
144. Cleveland at Atlanta 1:00
145. Denver at Seattle 1:00
146. Los Angeles Raiders at Cincinnati 1:00
147. New Orleans at Minnesota 12:00
148. New York Jets at New England 1:00
149. Philadelphia at Washington 1:00
150. Phoenix at New York Giants 4:00
151. San Francisco at Los Angeles Rams 1:00
152. Tampa Bay at Green Bay 12:00

Sunday Night, November 28

153. Pittsburgh at Houston 7:00

Monday, November 29

154. San Diego at Indianapolis 9:00

FOURTEENTH WEEK

Sunday, December 5 (NBC-TV national weekend)

155. Atlanta at Houston 12:00
156. Denver at San Diego 1:00
157. Green Bay at Chicago 12:00
158. Indianapolis at New York Jets 1:00
159. Kansas City at Seattle 1:00
160. Los Angeles Raiders at Buffalo 1:00
161. Los Angeles Rams at Phoenix 2:00
162. Minnesota at Detroit 1:00
163. New England at Pittsburgh 1:00
164. New Orleans at Cleveland 1:00
165. New York Giants at Miami 4:00
166. Washington at Tampa Bay 1:00

Sunday Night, December 5

167. Cincinnati at San Francisco 5:00

Monday, December 6

168. Philadelphia at Dallas 8:00

FIFTEENTH WEEK

Saturday, December 11 (NBC-TV national weekend)

169. New York Jets at Washington 12:30
170. San Francisco at Atlanta 4:00

Sunday, December 12

171. Buffalo at Philadelphia 1:00
172. Chicago at Tampa Bay 1:00
173. Cincinnati at New England 1:00
174. Cleveland at Houston 12:00
175. Dallas at Minnesota 3:00
176. Detroit at Phoenix 2:00
177. Indianapolis at New York Giants 1:00
178. Kansas City at Denver 2:00
179. Los Angeles Rams at New Orleans 12:00
180. Seattle at Los Angeles Raiders 1:00

Sunday Night, December 12

181. Green Bay at San Diego 5:00

Monday, December 13

182. Pittsburgh at Miami 9:00

SIXTEENTH WEEK

Saturday, December 18 (CBS-TV national weekend)

183. Dallas at New York Jets 4:00
184. Denver at Chicago 11:30

Sunday, December 19

185. Atlanta at Washington 1:00
186. Buffalo at Miami 1:00
187. Houston at Pittsburgh 1:00
188. Los Angeles Rams at Cincinnati 1:00
189. Minnesota vs. Green Bay at Milwaukee 12:00
190. New England at Cleveland 1:00
191. Phoenix at Seattle 1:00
192. San Diego at Kansas City 3:00
193. San Francisco at Detroit 4:00
194. Tampa Bay at Los Angeles Raiders 1:00

Sunday Night, December 19

195. Philadelphia at Indianapolis 8:00

Monday, December 20

196. New York Giants at New Orleans 8:00

SEVENTEENTH WEEK

Saturday, December 25 (CBS-TV national weekend)

197. Houston at San Francisco 2:30

Sunday, December 26

198. Atlanta at Cincinnati 1:00
199. Cleveland at Los Angeles Rams 1:00
200. Detroit at Chicago 12:00
201. Indianapolis at New England 1:00
202. Los Angeles Raiders at Green Bay 12:00
203. New Orleans at Philadelphia 1:00
204. New York Giants at Phoenix 2:00
205. New York Jets at Buffalo 1:00
206. Pittsburgh at Seattle 1:00
207. Tampa Bay at Denver 2:00
208. Washington at Dallas 3:00

Sunday Night, December 26

209. Kansas City at Minnesota 7:00

Monday, December 27

210. Miami at San Diego 6:00

EIGHTEENTH WEEK

Friday, December 31 (NBC-TV national weekend)

211. Minnesota at Washington 3:00

Sunday, January 2

212. Buffalo at Indianapolis 1:00
213. Chicago at Los Angeles Rams 1:00
214. Cincinnati at New Orleans 3:00
215. Cleveland at Pittsburgh 1:00
216. Dallas at New York Giants 1:00
217. Denver at Los Angeles Raiders 1:00
218. Green Bay at Detroit 1:00
219. Miami at New England 1:00
220. Phoenix at Atlanta 1:00
221. San Diego at Tampa Bay 4:00
222. Seattle at Kansas City 12:00

Sunday Night, January 2

223. New York Jets at Houston 7:00

Monday, January 3

224. Philadelphia at San Francisco 6:00

POSTSEASON

Saturday, Jan. 8 — AFC and NFC Wild Card Playoffs (ABC-TV)
Sunday, Jan. 9 — AFC and NFC Wild Card Playoffs (NBC-TV and CBS-TV)
Saturday, Jan. 15 — AFC and NFC Divisional Playoffs (NBC-TV and CBS-TV)
Sunday, Jan. 16 — AFC and NFC Divisional Playoffs (NBC-TV and CBS-TV)
Sunday, Jan. 23 — AFC and NFC Conference Championships (NBC-TV and CBS-TV)
Sunday, Jan. 30 — Super Bowl XXVIII at Georgia Dome, Atlanta, Georgia (NBC-TV)
Sunday, Feb. 6 — AFC-NFC Pro Bowl at Honolulu, Hawaii (ESPN)

NOTES

NOTES

NOTES

NOTES

NOTES

NOTES

NOTES